Notes to Literature

Volume One

European Perspectives

European Perspectives
A Series in Social Philosophy and Cultural Criticism

Lawrence D. Kritzman and
Richard Wolin, Editors

European Perspectives seeks to make available works of
interdisciplinary interest by leading European thinkers. By
presenting classic texts and outstanding contemporary works, the
series hopes to shape the major intellectual controversies of our
day and thereby to facilitate the tasks of historical understanding.

Complete series list follows the index.

NOTES
TO
LITERATURE

Volume One

THEODOR W. ADORNO

EDITED BY ROLF TIEDEMANN
TRANSLATED FROM THE GERMAN
BY SHIERRY WEBER NICHOLSEN

COLUMBIA UNIVERSITY PRESS
New York

Noten zur Literatur copyright © 1958, 1961, 1965, 1974 by Suhrkamp Verlag, Frankfurt am Main

COLUMBIA UNIVERSITY PRESS
NEW YORK   CHICHESTER, WEST SUSSEX

Copyright © 1991 Columbia University Press

Library of Congress Cataloging-in-Publication Data
Adorno, Theodor W. 1903–1969.
[Note zur Literatur. English]
Notes to literature / Theodor W. Adorno ; edited by Rolf Tiedemann ; translated from the German by Shierry Weber Nicholsen.
p.   cm.—(European perspectives)
Translation of: Note zur Literatur.
Includes bibliographical references (p.   ) and index.
ISBN 978-0-231-06332-6
ISBN 978-0-231-06333-3 (pbk.)
1. Literature—History and criticism.   I. Tiedemann, Rolf.
II. Title.   III. Series.
PN514.A313   1991
809—dc20   90-27732
CIP

Casebound editions of Columbia University Press books
are printed on permanent and
durable acid-free paper.

Printed in the United States of America
c 10 9 8 7 6 5 4
p 10 9

The Press gratefully acknowledges a grant from Inter Nationes toward costs of translating this work. The Press also wishes to express its appreciation of assistance given by the Pushkin Fund in the preparation of this translation.

Excerpts from *Realism In Our Time: Literature and the Class Struggle* by Georg Lukács, translated by John and Necke Mander. Copyright © 1962 by Merlin Press. Copyright © 1964 by George Steiner. Reprinted by permission of HarperCollins Publishers.

Excerpts from Paul Valéry, *The Collected Works*, Bollingen Series 45, Volume 3: *Plays*, translated by David Paul. Copyright 1960, © renewed 1988 by Princeton University Press; Volume 7: *The Art of Poetry*, translated by Denise Folliot. Copyright 1958, © renewed 1986 by Princeton University Press; Volume 10: *History and Politics*, translated by Denise Folliot and Jackson Mathews. Copyright 1962, © renewed 1990 by Princeton University Press; Volume 12: *Degas, Manet, Morisot*, translated by David Paul. Copyright 1960, © renewed 1988 by Princeton University Press; Volume 13: *Aesthetics*, translated by Ralph Manheim. Copyright © 1964 by Princeton University Press; Volume 14: *Analects*, translated by Stuart Gilbert. Copyright © 1970 by Princeton University Press. Reprinted by permission of Princeton University Press.

Excerpts from *Endgame* by Samuel Beckett. Copyright © 1958 by Grove Press. Copyright © 1958 by Faber and Faber. Reprinted by permission of Grove Press and Faber and Faber.

For Jutta Burger

Contents

TRANSLATOR'S PREFACE

ix

EDITORIAL REMARKS FROM THE GERMAN EDITION

xiii

I

The Essay as Form

3

On Epic Naiveté

24

The Position of the Narrator
in the Contemporary Novel

30

On Lyric Poetry and Society

37

In Memory of Eichendorff

55

Heine the Wound

80

Looking Back on Surrealism

86

Punctuation Marks

91

The Artist as Deputy

98

II

On the Final Scene of *Faust*
111

Reading Balzac
121

Valéry's Deviations
137

Short Commentaries on Proust
174

Words from Abroad
185

Ernst Bloch's *Spuren*
200

Extorted Reconciliation:
On Georg Lukács' *Realism in Our Time*
216

Trying to Understand *Endgame*
241

NOTES
277

INDEX
281

◘▓◘▓◘

Translator's Preface

*M*atters of language and presentational form are central to Adorno's thought, as is especially clear when he writes on aesthetic issues. Those matters are discussed explicitly in all the essays included here, and in some—"The Essay as Form," "Punctuation Marks," and "Words from Abroad"—Adorno is virtually explicating his own mode of writing. Accordingly, I have tried to produce a translation that represents the essential features of this highly self-conscious mode of presentation, and thus to produce a text that will give the reader a sense of what it is like to read Adorno in the original German.

Many of the specific features of the translation follow from this intention. Because, for instance, Adorno's paragraphs are not paragraphs in the sense to which we are accustomed but rather segments or fragments analogous to short movements in music, I have left them intact. While, on the other hand, I have broken down many of Adorno's very long and complex sentences, I have retained his extensive use of the semi-colon, colon, and dash, and have tried to capture the complex rhythms of his sentence structures with their inversions and appositions. If the text sometimes has the ring of eighteenth-century English, this is why.

Adorno repeatedly draws attention to the double-edged nature of language. On the one hand, language contains a utopian, logic-transcending moment and has certain affinities with music (I have translated the German title *Noten zur Literatur* as *Notes to Literature* rather than *Notes on Literature* in order to preserve the allusion to music that Adorno intended). But language is also logical in form, historically shaped, and inescapably contaminated by its "communicative" use. Adorno's writing draws on both these aspects of language. It is full of idiomatic expressions and extended metaphors, often taken from the sphere of commerce and finance. It is also full of allusions, plays on words, and a largely Hegelian-derived vocabulary that Adorno uses at least as idiosyncratically as systematically. All of these features I have tried to represent in some way — "reproduce" would be too ambitious a word here.

Adorno, who emphasizes the mediated quality of everything that pretends to immediacy, certainly does not conceive language as a medium for immediate subjective expression. It is constructed, and the foreign words and foreign borrowings that figure so prominently in the texture of Adorno's writing emphasize this constructive character of language, as he explains in the essay "Words from Abroad." At the same time, Adorno's explicit sensitivity to the different tonal qualities of the word choices available to him in specific contexts make his language an almost musical medium. Of course he also conceived music as a constructive enterprise; see his essay on Valéry. I have tried to suggest an analogous texture in English. Where Adorno used French, Latin, or Greek I have done so as well, often, however, providing glosses. And I have usually tried to preserve something of what is involved in Adorno's use of "foreignisms," often using the cognate English word, which is often as conspicuous in the English text as its analog was in the German. I have also given the original German text of the poems Adorno discusses, usually providing a fairly literal English translation for reference.

Certainly the translation lacks the "snap" of Adorno's German. This is not due solely to my lack of verbal inventiveness. English pronouns, lacking gender in most cases, are more ambiguous than German ones, and I have often spelled out referents where Adorno does not. Adorno's writing verges in some sense on an artificial, constructed language, a *Kunstsprache*, which sounds "the same" throughout his writings. But at the same time, it constantly violates expectations, that is, disrupts established patterns of thought and their verbal equivalents, and it does so without explanation. Accordingly, much of what Adorno says seems ambiguous, especially for the reader who has not been "acculturated" into his mode of thought. In addition, the mere fact that he is reading a text in translation undercuts the reader's confidence in what he is reading, rendering ambiguity even more problematic. I have spelled out referents in an attempt to counteract this increased ambiguity, and as a result much of the compactness of the original has been lost. On the other hand, I have not succumbed to the temptation to rewrite what Adorno says in order to make its implications clear. And since the essays are not intended as scholarly works, I have also largely refrained from producing an "annotated Adorno" with explanations of his allusions and his terminology. Where I have provided translator's notes they are clearly identifiable as such.

Many of the essays in this volume were previously published in translation by others, and I have consulted those versions with profit on a number of difficult passages. But I have retranslated everything for this volume.

A project as demanding as this was helped immeasurably by the contributions of friends and colleagues. I would like to express my gratitude to Marllan Meyer, Sally, Ben, and Karl Hufbauer, Lane Kauffmann, Jeremy J. Shapiro, and Richard Wolin; and to my colleagues at Antioch University in Yellow Springs, Jackson Kytle, Jim Malarkey, Elliot Robins, and Jon and Peggy Saari, all of whom read portions of the final manuscript and offered valuable comments and suggestions; to Bob Hullot-Kentor, who was instrumental in introducing me to the project; to Tom McCarthy for terminological help; to the staff of the Antioch College library, and especially Kim Iconis and Jan Miller, who went out of their way to help with texts and references; to Jennifer Crewe of Columbia University Press, who was a delight to work with; and to Arden H. Nicholsen, who read many of the essays and helped me to hear Adorno's voice.

Shierry Weber Nicholsen

◘◙◘◙

Editorial Remarks from the German Edition

*T*he English translation of *Noten zur Literatur* is based on the text in volume 11 of Adorno's *Gesammelte Schriften,* edited by Rolf Tiedemann (Frankfurt am Main: Suhrkamp, 1974).

The three volumes of *Noten zur Literatur* which Adorno published himself came out—in the Bibliothek Suhrkamp series—with Suhrkamp Verlag, Berlin and Frankfurt am Main (later, Frankfurt am Main). *Noten zur Literatur I,* which bore no number in the first edition, appeared in 1958 as volume 47 of the Bibliothek Suhrkamp, *Noten zur Literatur II* appeared in 1961 as volume 71, and *Noten zur Literatur III* appeared in 1965 as volume 146. The German edition on which this English translation is based follows the last edition to appear during the author's lifetime: for the *Noten zur Literatur I,* the printing of 18,000–20,000 in 1968, for the *Noten zur Literatur II,* the printing of 9,000–12,000 in 1965, and for the *Noten zur Literatur III,* the printing of 6,000–9,000 in 1966. Adorno provided information on the genesis and previous publications of the individual essays in the list of previous publications at the end of each of the three volumes of the *Noten zur Literatur,* as follows:

Publication Information (Noten zur Literatur I)

"Der Essay als Form," written 1954–1958. Unpublished.

"Über epische Naivetät," written in 1943 as part of the work in conjunction with the *Dialektik der Aufklärung,* composed jointly with Max Horkheimer. Unpublished.

"Standort des Erzählers im zeitgenössischen Roman," originally a talk for RIAS Berlin, published in *Akzente*, 1954, 5.

"Rede über Lyrik und Gesellschaft," originally a talk for RIAS Berlin, revised several times, published in *Akzente*, 1957, 1.

"Zum Gedächtnis Eichendorffs," originally a talk on Westdeutscher Rundfunk for the centennial of Eichendorff's death in November 1957, published in *Akzente*, 1958, 1.

"Die Wunde Heine," originally a talk on Westdeutscher Rundfunk for the centennial of Heine's death in February 1956, published in *Texte und Zeichen*, 1956, 3.

"Rückblickend auf den Surrealismus," published in *Texte und Zeichen*, 1956, 6.

"Satzzeichen," published in *Akzente*, 1956, 6.

"Der Artist als Statthalter," originally a talk for the Bayerischer Rundfunk, published in *Merkur* VII, 1953, 11.

Publication Information (Noten zur Literatur II)

"Zur Schlussszene des Faust," in *Akzente*, 1959, 6, pp. 567ff. A note added by Adorno: "I once teased Walter Benjamin about his predilection for unusual and out-of-the-way material by asking him when he planned to write an interpretation of *Faust,* and he immediately parried by saying that he would do so if it could be serialized in the *Frankfurter Zeitung.* The memory of that conversation occasioned the writing of the fragments published here."

"Balzac-Lektüre," unpublished.

"Valérys Abweichungen," in *Die Neue Rundschau*, vol. 71, 1960, 1, pp. 1ff.

"Kleine Proust-Kommentare," originally a talk for the Hessischer Rundfunk and the Süddeutscher Rundfunk celebrating the completion of the German edition of Proust's *À la recherche du temps perdu*. Marianne Hoppe read the selected passages and the author read his commentaries on them. Published without revision in *Akzente*, 1958, 6, pp. 564ff.

EDITORIAL REMARKS FROM THE GERMAN EDITION

"Wörter aus der Fremde," originally a talk for the Hessischer Rund-funk, published in *Akzente*, 1959, 2, pp. 176ff.

"Blochs Spuren," in *Neue Deutsche Hefte*, April 1960, pp. 14ff.

"Erpresste Versöhnung," in *Der Monat*, vol. 11, November 1958, pp. 37ff.

"Versuch, das Endspiel zu verstehen," unpublished. Portions were read at the seventh Suhrkamp Verlag evening on February 27, 1961, in Frankfurt am Main.

For *Noten zur Literatur I-III*, the editor of the complete German edition limited himself to correcting typographical errors and errors in citations and to making the citations somewhat more consistent.

Rolf Tiedemann

NOTES
TO
LITERATURE

I

⊟⦂⊟⦂⊟

The Essay as Form

Destined to see what is illuminated, not the light.
Goethe, *Pandora*

*T*hat in Germany the essay is condemned as a hybrid, that the form
has no compelling tradition, that its emphatic demands are met only
intermittently—all this has been said, and censured, often enough. "The
essay form has not yet, today, travelled the road to independence which
its sister, poetry, covered long ago; the road of development from a
primitive, undifferentiated unity with science, ethics, and art."[1] But
neither discomfort with this situation nor discomfort with the mentality
that reacts to it by fencing off art as a preserve for irrationality, equating
knowledge with organized science, and excluding anything that does not
fit that antithesis as impure, has changed anything in the prejudice
customary here in Germany. Even today, to praise someone as an *écrivain*
is enough to keep him out of academia. Despite the telling insights that
Simmel and the young Lukács, Kassner and Benjamin entrusted to the
essay as speculation on specific, culturally pre-formed objects,[2] the academic guild accepts as philosophy only what is clothed in the dignity of
the universal and the enduring—and today perhaps the originary. It gets
involved with particular cultural artifacts only to the extent to which they
can be used to exemplify universal categories, or to the extent to which
the particular becomes transparent when seen in terms of them. The
stubbornness with which this schema survives would be as puzzling as
the emotions attached to it if it were not fed by motives stronger than the
painful memory of the lack of cultivation in a culture in which the *homme
de lettres* is practically unknown. In Germany the essay arouses resistance
because it evokes intellectual freedom. Since the failure of an Enlightenment that has been lukewarm since Leibniz, even under present-day

conditions of formal freedom, that intellectual freedom has never quite developed but has always been ready to proclaim its subordination to external authorities as its real concern. The essay, however, does not let its domain be prescribed for it. Instead of accomplishing something scientifically or creating something artistically, its efforts reflect the leisure of a childlike person who has no qualms about taking his inspiration from what others have done before him. The essay reflects what is loved and hated instead of presenting the mind as creation *ex nihilo* on the model of an unrestrained work ethic. Luck and play are essential to it. It starts not with Adam and Eve but with what it wants to talk about; it says what occurs to it in that context and stops when it feels finished rather than when there is nothing to say. Hence it is classified a trivial endeavor. Its concepts are not derived from a first principle, nor do they fill out to become ultimate principles. Its interpretations are not philologically definitive and conscientious; in principle they are over-interpretations— according to the mechanized verdict of the vigilant intellect that hires out to stupidity as a watchdog against the mind. Out of fear of negativity, the subject's efforts to penetrate what hides behind the facade under the name of objectivity are branded as irrelevant. It's much simpler than that, we are told. The person who interprets instead of accepting what is given and classifying it is marked with the yellow star of one who squanders his intelligence in impotent speculation, reading things in where there is nothing to interpret. A man with his feet on the ground or a man with his head in the clouds—those are the alternatives. But letting oneself be terrorized by the prohibition against saying more than was meant right then and there means complying with the false conceptions that people and things harbor concerning themselves. Interpretation then becomes nothing but removing an outer shell to find what the author wanted to say, or possibly the individual psychological impulses to which the phenomenon points. But since it is scarcely possible to determine what someone may have thought or felt at any particular point, nothing essential is to be gained through such insights. The author's impulses are extinguished in the objective substance they seize hold of. In order to be disclosed, however, the objective wealth of meanings encapsulated in every intellectual phenomenon demands of the recipient the same spontaneity of subjective fantasy that is castigated in the name of objective discipline. Nothing can be interpreted out of something that is not interpreted into it at the same time. The criteria for such interpretation are its compatibility with the text and with itself, and its power to give voice to the elements of the object in conjunction with one another. In this, the essay has something like an aesthetic autonomy that is easily accused of being simply derived from art, although it is distinguished from art by its medium, concepts, and by its claim to a truth devoid of aesthetic semblance. Lukács failed to recognize this when he called the essay an art form in the letter to Leo Popper that introduces *Soul and Form*.[3] But the positivist maxim according to which what is written about art may in no way lay claim to artistic presentation, that is, autonomy of form, is no better. Here as elsewhere, the general positivist tendency to set every possible object, as an object of research, in stark opposition to the subject, does not go beyond the mere separation of form and content —for one can hardly speak of aesthetic matters unaesthetically, devoid of resemblance to the subject matter, without falling into philistinism and losing touch with the object a priori. In positivist practice, the content, once fixed on the model of the protocol sentence, is supposed to be neutral with respect to its presentation, which is supposed to be conventional and not determined by the subject. To the instinct of scientific purism, every expressive impulse in the presentation jeopardizes an objectivity that supposedly leaps forth when the subject has been removed. It thereby jeopardizes the authenticity of the object, which is all the better established the less it relies on support from the form, despite the fact that the criterion of form is whether it delivers the object pure and without admixture. In its allergy to forms as mere accidental attributes, the spirit of science and scholarship [*Wissenschaft*] comes to resemble that of rigid dogmatism. Positivism's irresponsibly sloppy language fancies that it documents responsibility in its object, and reflection on intellectual matters becomes the privilege of the mindless.

None of these offspring of resentment are pure falsehood. If the essay declines to begin by deriving cultural works from something underlying them, it embroils itself all too eagerly in the cultural enterprise promoting the prominence, success, and prestige of marketable products. Fictionalized biographies and all the related commercial writing that depend on them are not mere products of degeneration; they are a permanent temptation for a form whose suspiciousness of false profundity does not protect it from turning into slick superficiality. This can be seen even in Sainte-Beuve, from whom the genre of the modern essay derives. In products like Herbert Eulenberg's biographical silhouettes, the German prototype of a flood of cultural trash, and down to films about Rembrandt, Toulouse-Lautrec and the Bible, this involvement has promoted the neutralization of cultural works to commodities, a process that in recent intellectual history has irresistibly taken hold of what the Eastern bloc ignominiously calls "the heritage." The process is perhaps most obvious in Stefan Zweig, who produced several sophisticated essays in his youth and ended up descending to the psychology of the creative individual in his book on Balzac. This kind of writing does not criticize abstract fundamental concepts, aconceptual data, or habituated clichés; instead, it presupposes them, implicitly but by the same token with all the more complicity. The refuse of interpretive psychology is fused with current categories from the *Weltanschauung* of the cultural philistine, categories like "personality" or "the irrational." Such essays confuse themselves with the same feuilleton with which the enemies of the essay form confuse it. Forcibly separated from the discipline of academic unfreedom, intellectual freedom itself becomes unfree and serves the socially preformed needs of its clientele. Irresponsibility, itself an aspect of all truth that does not exhaust itself in responsibility to the status quo, then justifies itself to the needs of established consciousness; bad essays are just as conformist as bad dissertations. Responsibility, however, respects not only authorities and committees, but also the object itself.

The essay form, however, bears some responsibility for the fact that the bad essay tells stories about people instead of elucidating the matter at hand. The separation of science and scholarship from art is irreversible. Only the naiveté of the manufacturer of literature takes no notice of it; he considers himself at least an organizational genius and grinds good works of art down into bad ones. With the objectification of the world in the course of progressive demythologization, art and science have separated. A consciousness for which intuition and concept, image and sign would be one and the same—if such a consciousness ever existed— cannot be magically restored, and its restitution would constitute a regression to chaos. Such a consciousness is conceivable only as the completion of the process of mediation, as utopia, conceived by the idealist philosophers since Kant under the name of *intellektuelle Anschauung*, intellectual intuition, something that broke down whenever actual knowledge appealed to it. Wherever philosophy imagines that by borrowing from literature it can abolish objectified thought and its history—what is commonly termed the antithesis of subject and object—and even hopes that Being itself will speak, in a *poésie* concocted of Parmenides and Jungnickel, it starts to turn into a washed-out cultural babble. With a peasant cunning that justifies itself as primordiality, it refuses to honor the obligations of conceptual thought, to which, however, it had subscribed when it used concepts in its propositions and judgments. At the same time, its aesthetic element consists merely of watered-down, secondhand reminiscences of Hölderlin or Expressionism, or perhaps *Jugendstil*, because no thought can entrust itself as absolutely and blindly to language as the notion of a primordial utterance would lead us to believe. From the violence that image and concept thereby do to one another springs the jargon of authenticity, in which words vibrate with emotion while keeping quiet about what has moved them. Language's ambitious transcendence of meaning ends up in a meaninglessness which can be easily seized upon by a positivism to which one feels superior; one plays into the hands of positivism through the very meaninglessness it criticizes, a meaninglessness which one shares by adopting its tokens. Under the spell of such developments, language comes, where it still dares to stir in scholarship and science, to resemble the handicrafts, and the researcher who resists language altogether and, instead of degrading language to a mere paraphrase of his numbers uses tables that unqualifiedly acknowledge the reification of consciousness, is the one who demonstrates, negatively, faithfulness to the aesthetic. In his charts he finds something like a form for that reification without apologetic borrowing from art. To be sure, art has always been so intertwined with the dominant tendencies of enlightenment that it has made use of scientific and scholarly findings in its techniques since classical antiquity. But quantity becomes quality. If technique is made absolute in the work of art; if construction becomes total and eradicates expression, its opposite and its motivating force; if art thus claims to be direct scientific knowledge and correct by scientific standards, it is sanctioning a preartistic manipulation of materials as devoid of meaning as only the "Seyn" [Being] of the philosophy departments can be. It is fraternizing with reification—against which it has been and still is the function of what is functionless, of art, to protest, however mute and reified that protest itself may be.

But although art and science became separate in the course of history, the opposition between them should not be hypostatized. Aversion to an anachronistic conflation of the two does not render a compartmentalized culture sacrosanct. For all their necessity, those compartments represent institutional confirmation of the renunciation of the whole truth. The ideals of purity and tidiness that are common to the enterprises of a veritable philosophy versed in eternal values, an airtight and thoroughly organized science, and an aconceptual intuitive art, bear the marks of a repressive order. A certificate of competency is required of the mind so that it will not transgress upon official culture by crossing culturally confirmed boundary lines. Presupposed in this is the notion that all knowledge can potentially be converted to science. The epistemologies that distinguish prescientific from scientific consciousness have one and all conceived the distinction solely as one of degree. The fact that it has gone no farther than the mere assurance of this convertibility, without living consciousness ever in actuality having been transformed into scientific consciousness, points up the precariousness of the transition, a qualitative difference. The simplest reflection on the life of consciousness would teach us to what a slight extent insights, which are by no means arbitrary hunches, can be fully captured within the net of science. The work of Marcel Proust, which is no more lacking in a scientific-positivist element than Bergson's, is an attempt to express necessary and compelling insights into human beings and social relations that are not readily accommodated within science and scholarship, despite the fact that their claim to objectivity is neither diminished nor abandoned to a vague plausibility. The measure of such objectivity is not the verification of assertions through repeated testing but rather individual human experience, maintained through hope and disillusionment. Such experience throws its observations into relief through confirmation or refutation in the process of recollection. But its individually synthesized unity, in which the whole nevertheless appears, cannot be distributed and recategorized under the separate persons and apparatuses of psychology and sociology. Under the pressure of the scientistic spirit and its desiderata, which are ubiquitous, in latent form, even in the artist, Proust tried, through a technique itself modeled on the sciences, a kind of experimental method, to salvage, or perhaps restore, what used to be thought of—in the days of bourgeois individualism, when individual consciousness still had confidence in itself and was not intimidated by organizational censorship—as the knowledge of a man of experience like the now extinct *homme de lettres*, whom Proust conjures up as the highest form of the dilettante. It would not have occurred to anyone to dismiss what such a man of experience had to say as insignificant, arbitrary, and irrational on the grounds that it was only his own and could not simply be generalized in scientific fashion. Those of his findings that slip through the meshes of science most certainly elude science itself. As *Geisteswissenschaft*, literally the science of mind, scientific scholarship fails to deliver what it promises the mind: to illuminate its works from the inside. The young writer who wants to learn what a work of art is, what linguistic form, aesthetic quality, and even aesthetic technique are at college will usually learn about them only haphazardly, or at best receive information taken readymade from whatever philosophy is in vogue and more or less arbitrarily applied to the content of the works in question. But if he turns to philosophical aesthetics he is besieged with abstract propositions that are not related to the works he wants to understand and do not in fact represent the content he is groping toward. The division of labor in the *kosmos noetikos*, the intellectual world, between art on the one hand and science and scholarship on the other, however, is not solely responsible for all that; its lines of demarcation cannot be set aside through good will and comprehensive planning. Rather, an intellect irrevocably modeled on the domination of nature and material production abandons the recollection of the stage it has overcome, a stage that promises a future one, the transcendence of rigidified relations of production; and this cripples its specialist's approach precisely when it comes to its specific objects.

In its relationship to scientific procedure and its philosophical grounding as method, the essay, in accordance with its idea, draws the fullest conclusions from the critique of system. Even empiricist theories, which give priority to experience that is open-ended and cannot be anticipated, as opposed to fixed conceptual ordering, remain systematic in that they deal with preconditions for knowledge that are conceived as more or less constant and develop them in as homogeneous a context as possible. Since Bacon—himself an essayist—empiricism has been as much a "method" as rationalism. In the realm of thought it is virtually the essay alone that has successfully raised doubts about the absolute privilege of method. The essay allows for the consciousness of nonidentity, without expressing it directly; it is radical in its non-radicalism, in refraining from any reduction to a principle, in its accentuation of the partial against the total, in its fragmentary character.

Perhaps the great Sieur de Montaigne felt something like this when he gave his writings the wonderfully elegant and apt title of "Essay." The simple modesty of this word is an arrogant courtesy. The essayist dismisses his own proud hopes which sometimes lead him to believe that he has come close to the ultimate: he has, after all, no more to offer than explanations of the poems of others, or at best of his own ideas. But he ironically adapts himself to this smallness—the eternal smallness of the most profound work of the intellect in face of life—and even emphasizes it with ironic modesty.[4]

The essay does not play by the rules of organized science and theory, according to which, in Spinoza's formulation, the order of things is the same as the order of ideas. Because the unbroken order of concepts is not equivalent to what exists, the essay does not aim at a closed deductive or inductive structure. In particular, it rebels against the doctrine, deeply rooted since Plato, that what is transient and ephemeral is unworthy of philosophy—that old injustice done to the transitory, whereby it is condemned again in the concept. The essay recoils from the violence in the dogma according to which the result of the process of abstraction, the concept, which, in contrast to the individual it grasps, is temporally invariant, should be granted ontological dignity. The fallacy that the *ordo idearum*, the order of ideas, is the *ordo rerum*, the order of things, is founded on the imputation of immediacy to something mediated. Just as something that is merely factual cannot be conceived without a concept, because to think it is always already to conceive it, so too the purest concept cannot be thought except in relation to facticity. Even the constructs of fantasy, presumably free of time and space, refer, if derivatively, to individual existence. This is why the essay refuses to be intimidated by the depraved profundity according to which truth and history are incompatible and opposed to one another. If truth has in fact a temporal core, then the full historical content becomes an integral moment in it; the a posteriori becomes the a priori concretely and not merely in general, as Fichte and his followers claimed. The relationship to experience—and the essay invests experience with as much substance as traditional theory does mere categories—is the relationship to all of history. Merely individual experience, which consciousness takes as its point of departure, since it is what is closest to it, is itself mediated by the overarching experience of historical humankind. The notion that the latter is mediated and one's own experience unmediated is mere self-deception on the part of an individualistic society and ideology. Hence the essay challenges the notion that what has been produced historically is not a fit object of theory. The distinction between a *prima philosophia*, a first philosophy, and a mere philosophy of culture that would presuppose that first philosophy and build upon it—the distinction used as a theoretical rationalization for the taboo on the essay—cannot be salvaged. An intellectual *modus operandi* that honors the division between the temporal and the atemporal as though it were canonical loses its authority. Higher levels of abstraction invest thought with neither greater sanctity nor metaphysical substance; on the contrary, the latter tends to evaporate with the advance of abstraction, and the essay tries to compensate for some of that. The customary objection that the essay is fragmentary and contingent itself postulates that totality is given, and with it the identity of subject and object, and acts as though one were in possession of the whole. The essay, however, does not try to seek the eternal in the transient and distill it out; it tries to render the transient eternal. Its weakness bears witness to the very nonidentity it had to express. It also testifies to an excess of intention over object and thereby to the utopia which is blocked by the partition of the world into the eternal and the transient. In the emphatic essay thought divests itself of the traditional idea of truth.

In doing so it also suspends the traditional concept of method. Thought's depth depends on how deeply it penetrates its object, not on the extent to which it reduces it to something else. The essay gives this a polemical turn by dealing with objects that would be considered derivative, without itself pursuing their ultimate derivation. It thinks conjointly and in freedom about things that meet in its freely chosen object. It does not insist on something beyond mediations—and those are the historical mediations in which the whole society is sedimented—but seeks the truth content in its objects, itself inherently historical, It does not seek any primordial given, thus spiting a societalized [*vergesellschaftete*] society that, because it does not tolerate anything that does not bear its stamp, tolerates least of all anything that reminds it of its own ubiquity, and inevitably cites as its ideological complement the very nature its praxis has completely eliminated. The essay quietly puts an end to the illusion that thought could break out of the sphere of *thesis*, culture, and move into that of *physis*, nature. Spellbound by what is fixed and acknowledged to be derivative, by artifacts, it honors nature by confirming that it no longer exists for human beings. Its alexandrinism is a response to the fact that by their very existence, lilacs and nightingales—where the universal net has permitted them to survive—make us believe that life is still alive. The essay abandons the royal road to the origins, which leads only to what is most derivative—Being, the ideology that duplicates what already exists, but the idea of immediacy, an idea posited in the meaning of mediation itself, does not disappear completely. For the essay all levels of mediation are immediate until it begins to reflect.

Just as the essay rejects primordial givens, so it rejects definition of its concepts. Philosophy has arrived at a thoroughgoing critique of definitions from the most divergent perspectives—in Kant, in Hegel, in Nietzsche. But science has never adopted this critique. Whereas the movement that begins with Kant, a movement against the scholastic residues in modern thought, replaces verbal definitions with an understanding of concepts in terms of the process through which they are produced, the individual sciences, in order to prevent the security of their operations from being disturbed, still insist on the pre-critical obligation to define. In this the neopositivists, who call the scientific method philosophy, are in agreement with scholasticism. The essay, on the other hand, incorporates the antisystematic impulse into its own way of proceeding and introduces concepts unceremoniously, "immediately," just as it receives them. They are made more precise only through their relationship to one another. In this, however, the essay finds support in the concepts themselves. For it is mere superstition on the part of a science that operates by processing raw materials to think that concepts as such are unspecified and become determinate only when defined. Science needs the notion of the concept as a *tabula rasa* to consolidate its claim to authority, its claim to be the sole power to occupy the head of the table. In actuality, all concepts are already implicitly concretized through the language in which they stand. The essay starts with these meanings, and, being essentially language itself, takes them farther; it wants to help language in its relation to concepts, to take them in reflection as they have been named unreflectingly in language. The phenomenological method of interpretive analysis embodies a sense of this, but it fetishizes the relationship of concepts to language. The essay is as skeptical about this as it is about the definition of concepts. Unapologetically it lays itself open to the objection that one does not know for sure how one is to understand its concepts. For it understands that the demand for strict definition has long served to eliminate—through stipulative manipulations of the meanings of concepts—the irritating and dangerous aspects of the things that live in the concepts. But the essay does not make do without general concepts—even language that does not fetishize concepts cannot do without them—nor does it deal with them arbitrarily. Hence it takes presentation more seriously than do modes of proceeding that separate method and object and are indifferent to the presentation of their objectified contents. The manner of expression is to salvage the precision sacrificed when definition is omitted, without betraying the subject matter to the arbitrariness of conceptual meanings decreed once and for all. In this, Benjamin was the unsurpassed master. This kind of precision, however, cannot remain atomistic. Not less but more than a definitional procedure, the essay presses for the reciprocal interaction of its concepts in the process of intellectual experience. In such experience, concepts do not form a continuum of operations. Thought does not progress in a single direction; instead, the moments are interwoven as in a carpet. The fruitfulness of the thoughts depends on the density of the texture. The thinker does not actually think but rather makes himself into an arena for intellectual experience, without unraveling it. While even traditional thought is fed by impulses from such experience, it eliminates the memory of the process by virtue of its form. The essay, however, takes this experience as its model without, as reflected form, simply imitating it. The experience is mediated through the essay's own conceptual organization; the essay proceeds, so to speak, methodically unmethodically.

The way the essay appropriates concepts can best be compared to the behavior of someone in a foreign country who is forced to speak its language instead of piecing it together out of its elements according to rules learned in school. Such a person will read without a dictionary. If he sees the same word thirty times in continually changing contexts, he will have ascertained its meaning better than if he had looked up all the meanings listed, which are usually too narrow in relation to the changes that occur with changing contexts and too vague in relation to the unmistakable nuances that the context gives rise to in every individual case. This kind of learning remains vulnerable to error, as does the essay as form; it has to pay for its affinity with open intellectual experience with a lack of security that the norm of established thought fears like death. It is not so much that the essay neglects indubitable certainty as that it abrogates it as an ideal. The essay becomes true in its progress, which drives it beyond itself, not in a treasure-hunting obsession with foundations. Its concepts receive their light from a *terminus ad quem* hidden from the essay itself, not from any obvious *terminus a quo*, and in this the method itself expresses its utopian intention. All its concepts are to be presented in such a way that they support one another, that each becomes articulated through its configuration with the others. In the essay discrete elements set off against one another come together to form a readable context; the essay erects no scaffolding and no structure. But the elements crystallize as a configuration through their motion. The constellation is a force field, just as every intellectual structure is necessarily transformed into a force field under the essay's gaze.

The essay gently challenges the ideal of *clara et distincta perceptio* and indubitable certainty. Altogether, it might be interpreted as a protest against the four rules established by Descartes' *Discourse on Method* at the beginning of modern Western science and its theory. The second of those rules, the division of the object into "as many parts as possible, and as might be necessary for its adequate solution,"[5] outlines the analysis of elements under whose sign traditional theory equates conceptual schemata of classification with the structure of being. Artifacts, however, which are the subject matter of the essay, do not yield to an analysis of elements and can be constructed only from their specific idea. Kant had good reasons for treating works of art and organisms as analogous in this respect, although at the same time, in unerring opposition to Romantic obscurantism, he took pains to distinguish them. The totality can no more be hypostatized as something primary than can elements, the product of analysis. In contrast to both, the essay orients itself to the idea of a reciprocal interaction that is as rigorously intolerant of the quest for elements as of that for the elementary. The specific moments are not to be simply derived from the whole, nor vice versa. The whole is a monad, and yet it is not; its moments, which as moments are conceptual in nature, point beyond the specific object in which they are assembled. But the essay does not pursue them to the point where they would legitimate themselves outside the specific object; if it did so, it would end up in an infinity of the wrong kind. Instead, it moves in so close to the *hic et nunc* of the object that the object becomes dissociated into the moments in which it has its life instead of being a mere object.

The third Cartesian rule, "to conduct my thoughts in such an order that, by commencing with objects the simplest and easiest to know, I might ascend by little and little, and, as it were, step by step, to the knowledge of the more complex," is in glaring contradiction to the essay form, in that the latter starts from the most complex, not from what is simplest and already familiar. The essay form maintains the attitude of someone who is beginning to study philosophy and somehow already has its idea in his mind. He will hardly begin by reading the most simple-minded writers, whose common sense for the most part simply babbles on past the points where one should linger; instead, he reaches for those who are allegedly the most difficult and who then cast their light backwards onto the simple things and illuminate them as an "attitude of thought toward objectivity." The naiveté of the student who finds difficult and formidable things good enough for him has more wisdom in it than a grown-up pedantry that shakes its finger at thought, warning it that it should understand the simple things before it tackles the complex ones, which, however, are the only ones that tempt it. Postponing knowledge in this way only obstructs it. In opposition to the cliché of "comprehensibility," the notion of truth as a casual relationship, the essay requires that one's thought about the matter be from the outset as complex as the object itself; it serves as a corrective to the stubborn primitiveness that always accompanies the prevailing form of reason. If science and scholarship, falsifying as is their custom, reduce what is difficult and complex in a reality that is antagonistic and split into monads to simplified models and then differentiate the models in terms of their ostensible material, the essay, in contrast, shakes off the illusion of a simple and fundamentally logical world, an illusion well suited to the defense of the status quo. The essay's differentiatedness is not something added to it but its medium. Established thought is quick to ascribe that differentiatedness to the mere psychology of the cognitive subjects and thinks that by doing so it has eliminated what is compelling in it. In reality, science and scholarship's self-righteous denunciations of oversophistication are aimed not at a precocious and unreliable method but at the upsetting aspects of the object that method makes manifest.

The fourth Cartesian rule, that one "should in every case institute such exhaustive enumerations and such general surveys" that one "is sure of leaving nothing out," the true principle of systematic thought, recurs unchanged in Kant's polemic against Aristotle's "rhapsodic" thought. This rule corresponds to the charge that the essay is, as the schoolmaster would put it, not exhaustive, while in fact every object, and certainly an intellectual one, encompasses an infinite number of aspects, and only the intention of the cognitive subject decides among them. A "general overview" would be possible only if it were established in advance that the object to be dealt with was fully grasped by the concepts used to treat it, that nothing would be left over that could not be anticipated from the concepts. The rule about the exhaustive enumeration of the individual parts claims, as a consequence of that first assumption, that the object can be presented in a seamless deductive system, a supposition of the philosophies of identity. As in the requirement of definition, the Cartesian rule has survived the rationalist theorem it was based on, in the form of a guide to practical thought: the comprehensive overview and continuity of presentation are demanded even of empirically open science. What in Descartes was to be an intellectual conscience monitoring the necessity of knowledge is thereby transformed into arbitrariness, the arbitrariness of a "frame of reference," an axiomatics to be established at the outset to satisfy a methodological need and for the sake of the plausibility of the whole, but no longer able to demonstrate its own validity or self-evidence. In the German version, this is the arbitrariness of an *Entwurf*, a project, that merely hides its subjective determinants under a pathos-laden quest for Being. The demand for continuity in one's train of thought tends to prejudge the inner coherence of the object, its own harmony. A presentation characterized by continuity would contradict an antagonistic subject matter unless it defined continuity as discontinuity at the same time. In the essay as a form, the need makes itself felt, unconsciously and atheoretically, to annul theoretically outdated claims to completeness and continuity in the concrete *modus operandi* of the mind as well. If the essay opposes, aesthetically, the mean-spirited method whose sole concern is not to leave anything out, it is following an epistemological impulse. The romantic conception of the fragment as a construction that is not complete but rather progresses onward into the infinite through self-reflection champions this anti-idealist motive in the midst of Idealism. Even in the manner of its presentation, the essay may not act as though it had deduced its object and there was nothing left to say about it. Its self-relativization is inherent in its form: it has to be constructed as though it could always break off at any point. It thinks in fragments, just as reality is fragmentary, and finds its unity in and through the breaks and not by glossing them over. An unequivocal logical order deceives us about the antagonistic nature of what that order is imposed upon. Discontinuity is essential to the essay; its subject matter is always a conflict brought to a standstill. While the essay coordinates concepts with one another by means of their function in the parallelogram of forces in its objects, it shrinks from any overarching concept to which they could all be subordinated. What such concepts give the illusion of achieving, their method knows to be impossible and yet tries to accomplish. The word *Versuch*, attempt or essay, in which thought's utopian vision of hitting the bullseye is united with the consciousness of its own fallibility and provisional character, indicates, as do most historically surviving terminologies, something about the form, something to be taken all the more seriously in that it takes place not systematically but rather as a characteristic of an intention groping its way. The essay has to cause the totality to be illuminated in a partial feature, whether the feature be chosen or merely happened upon, without asserting the presence of the totality. It corrects what is contingent and isolated in its insights in that they multiply, confirm, and qualify themselves, whether in the further course of the essay itself or in a mosaiclike relationship to other essays, but not by a process of abstraction that ends in characteristic features derived from them. "This, then, is how the essay is distinguished from a treatise. The person who writes essayistically is the one who composes as he experiments, who turns his object around, questions it, feels it, tests it, reflects on it, who attacks it from different sides and assembles what he sees in his mind's eye and puts into words what the object allows one to see under the conditions created in the course of writing."[6] There is both truth and untruth in the discomfort this procedure arouses, the feeling that it could continue on arbitrarily. Truth, because the essay does not in fact come to a conclusion and displays its own inability to do so as a parody of its own a priori. The essay is then saddled with the blame for something for which forms that erase all trace of arbitrariness are actually responsible. That discomfort also has its untruth, however, because the essay's constellation is not arbitrary in the way a philosophical subjectivism that displaces the constraint emanating from the object onto the conceptual order imagines it to be. What determines the essay is the unity of its object along with that of the theory and experience that have migrated into the object. The essay's openness is not the vague openness of feeling and mood; it is given contour by its substance. It resists the idea of a masterpiece, an idea which itself reflects the idea of creation and totality. Its form complies with the critical idea that the human being is not a creator and that nothing human is a creation. The essay, which is always directed toward something already created, does not present itself as creation, nor does it covet something all-encompassing whose totality would resemble that of creation. Its totality, the unity of a form developed immanently, is that of something not total, a totality that does not maintain as form the thesis of the identity of thought and its object that it rejects as content. At times, emancipation from the compulsion of identity gives the essay something that eludes official thought—a moment of something inextinguishable, of indelible color. Certain foreign words in Georg Simmel's work—cachet, attitude—reveal this intention, although it is not discussed in theoretical terms.

The essay is both more open and more closed than traditional thought would like. It is more open in that its structure negates system, and it satisfies its inherent requirements better the more rigorously it holds to that negation; residues of system in essays, through which they hope to make themselves respectable, as for instance the infiltration of literary studies by ready-made popular philosophical ideas, are as worthless as psychological trivialities. But the essay is also more closed, because it works emphatically at the form of its presentation. Consciousness of the non-identity of presentation and subject matter forces presentation to unremitting efforts. In this alone the essay resembles art. In other respects it is necessarily related to theory by virtue of the concepts that appear in it, bringing with them not only their meanings but also their theoretical contexts. To be sure, the essay behaves as cautiously toward theory as it does toward concepts. It does not deduce itself rigorously from theory—the chief flaw in all Lukács' later essayistic works—nor is it a down payment on future syntheses. The more it strives to consolidate itself as theory and to act as though it held the philosopher's stone in its hands, the more intellectual experience courts disaster. At the same time, by its very nature intellectual experience strives for such objectification. This antinomy is reflected in the essay. Just as it absorbs concepts and experiences from the outside, so too it absorbs theories. Its relationship to them, however, is not that of a "perspective." If in the essay the lack of a standpoint is no longer naive and in bondage to the prominence of its objects, if instead the essay uses its relationship to its objects as an antidote to the spell cast by the notion of a beginning, then the essay carries out, in the form of parody, thought's otherwise impotent polemic against a philosophy of mere "perspectives." The essay devours the theories that are close to it; its tendency is always to liquidate opinion, including the opinion it takes as its point of departure. The essay is what it was from the beginning, the critical form par excellence; as immanent critique of intellectual constructions, as a confrontation of what they are with their concept, it is critique of ideology.

> The essay is the form of the critical category of the mind. For the person who criticizes must necessarily experiment, he must create conditions under which an object becomes visible anew, and do so still differently than an author does; above all, the object's frailties must be tried and tested, and this is the meaning of the slight variation the object experiences at the hands of its critic. [7]

When the essay is charged with having no point of view of its own and accused of relativism because it does not acknowledge any standpoint outside itself, the notion of truth as something "fixed," a hierarchy of concepts, has come into play, the very notion that Hegel, who did not like points of view, had destroyed. Here the essay is in accord with its polar opposite, the philosophy of absolute knowledge. It wants to heal thought of its arbitrary character by incorporating arbitrariness reflectively into its own approach rather than disguising it as immediacy.

Idealist philosophy, to be sure, suffered from the inconsistency of criticizing an abstract overarching concept, a mere "result," in the name of process, which is inherently discontinuous, while at the same time talking about dialectical method in the manner of idealism. For this reason the essay is more dialectical than the dialectic is when the latter discourses on itself. The essay takes Hegelian logic at its word: the truth of the totality cannot be played off against individual judgments. Nor can truth be made finite in the form of an individual judgment; instead, singularity's claim to truth is taken literally, up to the point where its untruth becomes evident. The daring, anticipatory, and not fully redeemed aspect of every essayistic detail attracts other such details as its negation; the untruth in which the essay knowingly entangles itself is the element in which its truth resides. Certainly there is untruth in its very form as well; it relates to something culturally preformed and derivative as though it were an autonomous entity. But the more vigorously the essay suspends the notion of something primary and refuses to concoct culture out of nature, the more fundamentally it acknowledges the quasi-natural character of culture itself. Even now, the blind context of nature, myth, perpetuates itself in culture, and this is precisely what the essay reflects on: the relationship of nature and culture is its true theme. Instead of "reducing" cultural phenomena, the essay immerses itself in them as though in a second nature, a second immediacy, in order to negate and transcend the illusion of immediacy through its perseverance. It has no more illusions about the difference between culture and what lies beneath it than does the philosophy of origin. But for it culture is not an epiphenomenon that covers Being and should be destroyed; instead, what lies beneath culture is itself *thesis*, something constructed, the false society. This is why the origin has no more value for the essay than the superstructure. It owes its freedom in the choice of its objects, its sovereignty in the face of all priorities of fact or theory, to the fact that for it all objects are in a certain sense equally close to the center—equally close to the principle that casts its spell over all of them. It does not glorify concern with the original as more primordial than concern with what is mediated, because for it primordiality is itself an object of reflection, something negative. This corresponds to a situation in which primordiality, as a standpoint of the spirit in the midst of a societalized world, becomes a lie. The lie extends from the elevation of historical concepts in historical languages to primal words, to academic instruction in "creative writing," and to primitiveness pursued as a handicraft, to recorders and finger painting, in which pedagogical necessity acts as though it were a metaphysical virtue. Baudelaire's revolt of literature against nature as a social preserve does not spare thought. The paradises of thought too are now only artificial ones, and the essay strolls in them. Since, in Hegel's dictum, there is nothing between heaven and earth that is not mediated, thought remains faithful to the idea of immediacy only in and through what is mediated; conversely, it falls prey to the mediated as soon as it tries to grasp the unmediated directly. The essay cunningly anchors itself in texts as though they were simply there and had authority. In this way, without the deception of a first principle, the essay gets a ground, however dubious, under its feet, comparable to theological exegeses of sacred texts in earlier times. Its tendency, however, is the opposite, a critical one: to shatter culture's claims by confronting texts with their own emphatic concept, with the truth that each one intends even if it does not want to intend it, and to move culture to become mindful of its own untruth, of the ideological illusion in which culture reveals its bondage to nature. Under the essay's gaze second nature recognizes itself as first nature.

If the essay's truth gains its force from its untruth, that truth should be sought not in mere opposition to the dishonorable and proscribed element in the essay but rather within that element itself, in the essay's mobility, its lack of the solidity the demand for which science transferred from property relations to the mind. Those who believe that they have to defend the mind against lack of solidity are its enemies: the mind itself, once emancipated, is mobile. Once it wants more than the mere administrative duplication and processing of what has always already existed, the mind seems to have an exposed quality; abandoned by play, truth would be nothing but tautology. For historically the essay too is related to rhetoric, which the scientific mentality has wanted to get rid of since Bacon and Descartes—until, appropriately, in a scientific age it degenerated to a science *sui generis,* that of communications. Rhetoric was probably never anything but thought in its adaptation to communicative language. Such thought aimed at something unmediated: the vicarious gratification of the listeners. The essay retains, precisely in the autonomy of its presentation, which distinguishes it from scientific and scholarly information, traces of the communicative element such information dispenses with. In the essay the satisfactions that rhetoric tries to provide for the listener are sublimated into the idea of a happiness in freedom vis à vis the object, a freedom that gives the object more of what belongs to it than if it were mercilessly incorporated into the order of ideas. Scientific consciousness, which opposes all anthropomorphic conceptions, was always allied with the reality principle and, like the latter, antagonistic to happiness. While happiness is always supposed to be the aim of all domination of nature, it is always envisioned as a regression to mere nature. This is evident all the way up to the highest philosophies, even those of Kant and Hegel. These philosophies have their pathos in the absolute idea of reason, but at the same time they always denigrate it as insolent and disrespectful when it relativizes accepted values. In opposition to this tendency, the essay salvages a moment of sophistry. The hostility to happiness in official critical thought is especially marked in Kant's transcendental dialectic, which wants to immortalize the line between understanding and speculation and prevent thought from "wandering off into intelligible worlds," as the characteristic metaphor expresses it. Whereas a self-critical reason should, according to Kant, have both feet firmly on the ground, should ground itself, it tends inherently to seal itself off from everything new and also from curiosity, the pleasure principle of thought, something existential ontology vilifies as well. What Kant saw, in terms of content, as the goal of reason, the creation of humankind, utopia, is hindered by the form of his thought, epistemology. It does not permit reason to go beyond the realm of experience, which, in the mechanism of mere material and invariant categories, shrinks to what has always already existed. The essay's object however, is the new in its newness, not as something that can be translated back into the old existing forms. By reflecting the object without violence, as it were, the essay mutely laments the fact that truth has betrayed happiness and itself along with it, and this lament provokes the rage directed against the essay. The persuasive element of communication is alienated from its original aim in the essay—just as the function of many musical features changes in autonomous music—and becomes a pure determinant of the presentation itself; it becomes the compelling element in its construction, whose aim is not to copy the object but to reconstitute it from its conceptual *membra disjecta*. The offensive transitions in rhetoric, in which association, verbal ambiguity, and a relaxation of logical synthesis made it easy for the listener and subjugated him, enfeebled, to the orator's will, are fused in the essay with the truth content. Its transitions repudiate conclusive deductions in favor of cross-connections between elements, something for which discursive logic has no place. The essay uses equivocations not out of sloppiness, nor in ignorance of the scientific ban on them, but to make it clear—something the critique of equivocation, which merely separates meanings, seldom succeeds in doing—that when a word covers different things they are not completely different; the unity of the word calls to mind a unity, however hidden, in the object itself. This unity, however, should not be mistaken for linguistic affinity, as is the practice of contemporary resto-rationist philosophies. Here too the essay approaches the logic of music, that stringent and yet aconceptual art of transition, in order to appro-priate for verbal language something it forfeited under the domination of discursive logic—although that logic cannot be set aside but only outwitted within its own forms by dint of incisive subjective expression. For the essay does not stand in simple opposition to discursive procedure. It is not unlogical; it obeys logical criteria insofar as the totality of its propositions must fit together coherently. No mere contradictions may remain unless they are established as belonging to the object itself. But the essay does not develop its ideas in accordance with discursive logic. It neither makes deductions from a principle nor draws conclusions from coherent individual observations. It coordinates elements instead of sub-ordinating them, and only the essence of its content, not the manner in which it is presented, is commensurable with logical criteria. In compar-ison with forms in which a preformed content is communicated indiffer-ently, the essay is more dynamic than traditional thought by virtue of the tension between the presentation and the matter presented. But at the same time, as a constructed juxtaposition of elements it is more static. Its affinity with the image lies solely in this, except that the staticness of the essay is one in which relationships of tension have been brought, as it were, to a standstill. The slight elasticity of the essayist's train of thought forces him to greater intensity than discursive thought, because the essay does not proceed blindly and automatically, as the latter does, but must reflect on itself at every moment. This reflection extends not only to its relationship to established thought but also to its relationship with rheto-ric and communication. Otherwise the essay, which fancies itself more than science, becomes fruitlessly prescientific.

The contemporary relevance of the essay is that of anachronism. The time is less favorable to it than ever. It is ground to pieces between an organized system of science and scholarship on the one side, in which everyone presumes to control everyone and everything and where everything not tailored to the current consensus is excluded while being praised hypocritically as "intuitive" or "stimulating," and on the other side a philosophy that has to make do with the empty and abstract remnants of what the scientific enterprise has not yet taken over and which thereby become the object of second-order operations on its part. The essay, however, is concerned with what is blind in its objects. It wants to use concepts to pry open the aspect of its objects that cannot be accommodated by concepts, the aspect that reveals, through the contradictions in which concepts become entangled, that the net of their objectivity is a merely subjective arrangement. It wants to polarize the opaque element and release the latent forces in it. Its efforts are directed toward concretizing a content defined in time and space; it constructs a complex of concepts interconnected in the same way it imagines them to be interconnected in the object. It eludes the dictates of the attributes that have been ascribed to ideas since Plato's definition in the *Symposium,* "existing eternally and neither coming into being nor passing away, neither changing nor diminishing," "a being in and for itself eternally uniform," and yet it remains idea in that it does not capitulate before the burden of what exists, does not submit to what merely is. The essay, however, judges what exists not against something eternal but by an enthusiastic fragment from Nietzsche's late period:

> If we affirm one single moment, we thus affirm not only ourselves but all existence. For nothing is self-sufficient, neither in us ourselves nor in things: and if our soul has trembled with happiness and sounded like a harp string just once, all eternity was needed to produce this one event— and in this single moment of affirmation all eternity was called good, redeemed, justified, and affirmed.[8]

Except that the essay distrusts even this kind of justification and affirmation. It has no name but a negative one for the happiness that was sacred to Nietzsche. Even the highest manifestations of the spirit, which express this happiness, are always also guilty of obstructing happiness as long as they remain mere spirit. Hence the essay's innermost formal law is heresy. Through violations of the orthodoxy of thought, something in the object becomes visible which it is orthodoxy's secret and objective aim to keep invisible.

⫸⫷ ⫸⫷

On Epic Naiveté

"And as when the land appears welcome to men who are swimming, / after Poseidon has smashed their strong-built ship on the open / water, pounding it with the weight of wind and the heavy / sea, . . . / . . . gladly they set foot on the shore, escaping the evil; / so welcome was her husband to her as she looked upon him, / and she could not let him go from the embrace of her white arms."[1] If we gauged the *Odyssey* by these lines, this simile for the happiness of reunited spouses, taking it not simply as a simile inserted into the narrative but as the substance appearing in naked form as the story nears its end, then the *Odyssey* would be none other than an attempt to attend to the endlessly renewed beating of the sea on the rocky coast, and to patiently reproduce the way the water floods over the rocks and then streams back from them with a roar, leaving the solid ground glowing with deeper color. This roaring is the sound of epic discourse, in which what is solid and unequivocal comes together with what is ambiguous and flowing, only to immediately part from it again. The amorphous flood of myth is the eternally invariant, but the *telos* of narrative is the differentiated, and the unrelentingly strict identity in which the epic subject matter is held serves to achieve its non-identity with what is simply identical, with unarticulated sameness: serves to create its differentness. The epic poem wants to report on something worth reporting on, something that is not the same as everything else, not exchangeable, something that deserves to be handed down for the sake of its name.

Because, however, the narrator turns to the world of myth for his material, his enterprise, now impossible, has always been contradictory.

For myth—and the narrator's rational, communicative discourse, with its subsumptive logic that equalizes everything it reports, is preoccupied with myth as the concrete, as something distinct from the leveling ordering of the conceptual system—this kind of myth itself partakes of the eternal sameness that awoke to self-consciousness in *ratio*. The storyteller has always been the one who resisted interchangeability, but historically and even today what he has to report has been the interchangeable. Hence there is an anachronistic element in all epic poetry: in Homer's archaistic practice of invoking the muse to help proclaim events of vast scope as well as in the desperate efforts of Stifter and the late Goethe to pass bourgeois conditions off as primordial reality, a reality as open to noninterchangeable language as to a name. But as long as great epic poetry has existed, this contradiction has informed the narrator's modus operandi; it is the element in epic poetry commonly referred to as objectivity or material concreteness *[Gegenständlichkeit]*. In comparison with the enlightened state of consciousness to which narrative discourse belongs, a state characterized by general concepts, this concrete or objective element always seems to be one of stupidity, lack of comprehension, ignorance, a stubborn clinging to the particular when it has already been dissolved into the universal. The epic poem imitates the spell of myth in order to soften it. Karl Theodor Preuss called this attitude *"Urdummheit,"* or "primal stupidity," and Gilbert Murray has characterized the first phase of Greek religion, the one preceding the Homeric-Olympian phase, in precisely these terms.[2] In the epic account's rigid fixation on its object, which is designed to break the intimidating power of the object of the identifying word's stare, the narrator gains control, as it were, of the gesture of fear. Naiveté is the price he pays for that, and the traditional view considers it something positive. The customary eulogizing of narrative stupidity, which emerges only with the dialectic of form, has made of that stupidity a restorationist ideology hostile to consciousness, an ideology whose last dregs are currently being sold off in the philosophical anthropologies of our day with their false concreteness.

But epic naiveté is not only a lie intended to keep general reflection at a distance from blind contemplation of the particular. As an anti-mythological enterprise, epic naiveté emerges from the enlightenment-oriented and positivist effort to adhere faithfully and without distortion to what once was as it was, and thereby break the spell cast by what has been, by myth in its true sense; hence in restricting itself to what occurred once and only once it retains an aspect that transcends limitation. For what occurred once and only once is not merely a defiant residue opposing the encompassing universality of thought; it is also thought's innermost yearning, the logical form of something real that would no longer be enclosed by social domination and the classificatory thought modeled upon it: the concept reconciled with its object. A critique of bourgeois reason dwells within epic naiveté. It holds fast to a possibility of experience that is destroyed by the bourgeois reason that ostensibly grounds it. Its restrictedness in the representation of its one subject is the corrective to the restrictedness that befalls all thought when it forgets its unique subject in its conceptual operations and covers the subject up instead of coming to know it. It is easy to either ridicule Homeric simplicity, which was the opposite of simplicity, or deploy it spitefully in opposition to the analytic spirit. Similarly, it would be easy to demonstrate the narrowmindedness of Gottfried Keller's last novel, *Martin Salander*, and to accuse that novel of ignoring what is essential and instead displaying a petit-bourgeois "things are terrible these days" ignorance of the economic bases of the crises and the social presuppositions of the *Gründerjahre*, the period of economic expansion in the late nineteenth century. But again, only this kind of naiveté permits one to tell the story of the fateful origins of the late capitalist era and appropriate them for anamnesis instead of merely reporting them and—through a protocol for which time is merely an index—casting them down in their deceptive actuality into a void where memory can find no purchase. Through this kind of remembrance of what cannot really be remembered any more, Keller expresses a truth in his description of the two shyster lawyers who are twin brothers, duplicates of one another: the truth about an interchangeability that is hostile to memory. Only a theory that went on to provide a transparent definition of the loss of experience in terms of the experience of society would be able to match his achievement. Through epic naiveté, narrative language, whose attitude toward the past always contains an apologetic element, justifying what has occurred as being worthy of attention, acts as its own corrective. The precision of descriptive language seeks to compensate for the falseness of all discourse. The impulse that drives Homer to describe a shield as though it were a landscape and to elaborate a metaphor until it becomes action, until it becomes autonomous and ultimately destroys the fabric of the narrative —that is the same impulse that repeatedly drove Goethe, Stifter, and Keller, the greatest storytellers of the nineteenth century, at least in Germany, to draw and paint instead of writing, and it may have inspired

Flaubert's archaeological studies as well. The attempt to emancipate representation from reflective reason is language's attempt, futile from the outset, to recover from the negativity of its intentionality, the conceptual manipulation of objects, by carrying its defining intention to the extreme and allowing what is real to emerge in pure form, undistorted by the violence of classificatory ordering. The narrator's stupidity and blindness—it is no accident that tradition has it that Homer was blind —expresses the impossibility and hopelessness of this enterprise. It is precisely the material element in the epic poem, the element that is the extreme opposite of all speculation and fantasy, that drives the narrative to the edge of madness through its a priori impossibility. Stifter's last novellas provide the clearest evidence of the transition from faithfulness to the object to manic obsession, and no narrative can partake of truth if it has not looked into the abyss into which language plunges when it tries to become name and image. Homeric prudence is no exception to this. In the last book of the *Odyssey,* in the second *nekyia,* or descent to the underworld, when the shade of the suitor Amphimedon tells that of Agamemnon in Hades about the revenge of Odysseus and his son, we read: "These two, / after compacting their plot of a foul death for the suitors, / made their way to the glorious town. In fact Odysseus / came afterwards; Telemachos led the way. . . ."[3] The German word "nämlich" [in Lattimore's translation, "in fact"][4] maintains the logical form, whether of explanation or of affirmation, for the sake of cohesion, while the content of the sentence, a purely descriptive statement, does not stand in any such connection to what precedes it. In the minimal meaninglessness of this coordinating particle the spirit of logical-intentional narrative language collides with the spirit of the wordless representation that the former is preoccupied with, and the logical form of coordination itself threatens to banish the idea, which is not coordinated with anything and is really not an idea any more, to the place where the relationship of syntax and material dissolves and the material affirms its superiority by belying the syntactic form that attempts to encompass it. This is the epic element, the element of genuine classical antiquity, in Hölderlin's madness. In his poem "An die Hoffnung" ["To Hope"] the following lines appear:

Im grünen Tale, dort, wo der frische Quell
Vom Berge täglich rauscht und die liebliche
Zeitlose mir am Herbsttag aufblüht,

Dort, in der Stille, du holde, will ich
Dich suchen, oder wenn in der Mitternacht
Das unsichtbare Leben im Haine wallt,
Und über mir die immerfrohen
Blumen, die blühenden Sterne glänzen.

[Below where daily down from the mountain purls
The limpid spring and where on an autumn day
The late and lovely saffron opens,
There in the stillness, beloved, will I
Look out for you, or when in the rustling copse
At midnight strange invisible creatures teem
And up above, the ever-joyful
Flowers, the blossoming stars, are glistening.]⁵

Hölderlin's "oder" [or], and often particles in Georg Trakl's poetry as well, resembles the Homeric "nämlich." While in these expressions language, in order to remain language at all, still claims to be a propositional synthesis of relations between things, it renounces judgment in the words whose use dissolves those relations. In the epic form of linkage, in which the train of thought finally goes slack, language shows a lenience toward judgment while at the same time unquestionably remaining judgment. The flight of ideas, discourse in its sacrificial form, is language's flight from its prison. If it is true, as J. A. K. Thomson has pointed out, that in Homer the similes acquire an autonomy vis-à-vis the content, the plot,⁶ then the same antagonism to the way language is constrained by the complex of intentions is expressed in them. Engrossed in its own meaning, the image developed in language becomes forgetful and pulls language itself into the image rather than making the image transparent and revealing the logical sense of the relationship. In great narrative the relationship between image and plot tends to reverse itself. Goethe's technique in the *Elective Affinities* and *Wilhelm Meister's Wander Years*, where interspersed miniature-like novellas reflect the nature of what is presented, testifies to this, and allegorical interpretations of Homer like Schelling's famous "odyssey of the spirit"⁷ are responses to the same thing. Not that the epic poems were dictated by an allegorical intention. But in those poems the force of the historical tendency at work in the language and the subject matter is so strong that in the course of the proceedings taking place between subjectivity and mythology human beings and things are transformed into mere arenas through the blindness with which the epic delivers itself over to their representation, arenas in which that historical tendency becomes visible precisely where the pragmatic linguistic context reveals its inadequacy. It is not individuals but ideas that are in combat, says Nietzsche in a fragment on "Homer's Contest."[8] It is the objective transformation of pure representation, detached from meaning, into the allegory of history that becomes visible in the logical disintegration of epic language, as in the detachment of metaphor from the course of the literal action. It is only by abandoning meaning that epic discourse comes to resemble the image, a figure of objective meaning emerging from the negation of subjectively rational meaning.

⚅

The Position of the Narrator in the Contemporary Novel

*T*he task of compressing some remarks on the current status of the
novel as form into the space of a few minutes forces me to select, albeit
by doing violence, one aspect of the problem. The aspect I have chosen
is the position of the narrator. Today that position is marked by a
paradox: it is no longer possible to tell a story, but the form of the novel
requires narration. The novel was the literary form specific to the bourgeois age. At its origins stands the experience of the disenchanted world
in *Don Quixote,* and the artistic treatment of mere existence has remained
the novel's sphere. Realism was inherent in the novel; even those that are
novels of fantasy as far as their subject matter is concerned attempt to
present their content in such a way that the suggestion of reality emanates
from them. Through a development that extends back into the nineteenth
century and has become accelerated in the extreme today, this mode of
proceeding has become questionable. Where the narrator is concerned,
this process has occurred through a subjectivism that leaves no material
untransformed and thereby undermines the epic precept of objectivity or
material concreteness [*Gegenständlichkeit*]. Nowadays, anyone who continued to dwell on concrete reality the way Stifter, for instance, did, and
wanted to derive his impact from the fullness and plasticity of a material
reality contemplated and humbly accepted, would be forced into an
imitative stance that would smack of arts and crafts. He would be guilty
of a lie: the lie of delivering himself over to the world with a love that
presupposes that the world is meaningful; and he would end up with
insufferable kitsch along the lines of a local-color commercialism. The
difficulties are just as great when considered from the point of view of

the subject matter. Just as painting lost many of its traditional tasks to photography, the novel has lost them to reportage and the media of the culture industry, especially film. This would imply that the novel should concentrate on what reportage will not handle. In contrast to painting, however, language imposes limits on the novel's emancipation from the object and forces the novel to present the semblance of a report: consistently, Joyce linked the novel's rebellion against realism with a rebellion against discursive language.

To oppose what Joyce was trying to do by calling it eccentric, individualistic, and arbitrary would be unconvincing. The identity of experience in the form of a life that is articulated and possesses internal continuity —and that life was the only thing that made the narrator's stance possible —has disintegrated. One need only note how impossible it would be for someone who participated in the war to tell stories about it the way people used to tell stories about their adventures. A narrative that presented itself as though the narrator had mastered this kind of experience would rightly meet with impatience and skepticism on the part of its audience. Notions like "sitting down with a good book" are archaic. The reason for this lies not merely in the reader's loss of concentration but also in the content and its form. For telling a story means having something *special* to say, and that is precisely what is prevented by the administered world, by standardization and eternal sameness. Apart from any message with ideological content, the narrator's implicit claim that the course of the world is still essentially one of individuation, that the individual with his impulses and his feelings is still the equal of fate, that the inner person is still directly capable of something, is ideological in itself; the cheap biographical literature one finds everywhere is a byproduct of the disintegration of the novel form itself.

The sphere of psychology, in which such projects take up residence, though with little success, is not exempt from the crisis of literary concreteness. Even the subject matter of the psychological novel is snapped up from under its nose: it has been rightly observed that at a time when journalists were constantly waxing enthusiastic about Dostoevski's psychological achievements, his discoveries had long since been surpassed by science, and especially by Freud's psychoanalysis. Moreover, this kind of overblown praise of Dostoevski probably missed the mark: to the extent to which there is any psychology in his work at all, it is a psychology of intelligible character, of essence, and not a psychology of empirical character, of human beings as we find them. It is precisely in this respect that Dostoevski is advanced. It is not only that communications and science have seized control of everything positive and tangible, including the facticity of inwardness, that forces the novel to break with the psychology of empirical character and give itself over to the presentation of essence [*Wesen*] and its antithesis [*Unwesen*]; it is also that the tighter and more seamless the surface of the social life process becomes the more it veils essence. *If the novel wants to remain true to its realistic heritage and tell how things really are, it must abandon a realism that only aids the facade in its work of camouflage by reproducing it.* The reification of all relationships between individuals, which transforms their human qualities into lubricating oil for the smooth running of the machinery, the universal alienation and self-alienation, needs to be called by name, and the novel is qualified to do so as few other art forms are. The novel has long since, and certainly since the eighteenth century and Fielding's *Tom Jones*, had as its true subject matter the conflict between living human beings and rigidified conditions. In this process, alienation itself becomes an aesthetic device for the novel. For the more human beings, individuals and collectivities, become alienated from one another, the more enigmatic they become to one another. The novel's true impulse, the attempt to decipher the riddle of external life, then becomes a striving for essence, which now for its part seems bewildering and doubly alien in the context of the everyday estrangement established by social conventions. The anti-realistic moment in the modern novel, its metaphysical dimension, is called forth by its true subject matter, a society in which human beings have been torn from one another and from themselves. What is reflected in aesthetic transcendence is the disenchantment of the world.

The novelist's conscious deliberations are hardly the place for all this, and there is reason to suppose that where such considerations do enter the novelist's reflections, as in Hermann Broch's very ambitious novels, it is not to the advantage of the work of art. Instead, historical changes in the form are converted to idiosyncratic sensitivities on the part of authors, and the extent to which they function as instruments for registering what is required and what is forbidden is a crucial determinant of their rank. No one surpasses Marcel Proust in aversion to the report form. His work belongs to the tradition of the realistic and psychological novel in the branch that leads to the novel's dissolution in extreme subjectivism, a line of development extending through works like Jacobsen's *Niels Lyhne* and Rilke's *Malte Laurids Brigge* but having no empirical historical connection with Proust. The more strictly the novel adheres to realism in external things, to the gesture that says "this is how it was," the more every word becomes a mere "as if," and the greater becomes the contradiction between this claim and the fact that it was not so. The immanent claim that the author cannot avoid making—that he knows precisely what went on—requires proof, and Proust's precision, which is taken to the point where it becomes chimerical, his micrological technique through which the unity of the living is ultimately split into its atoms, is an endeavor on the part of the aesthetic sensorium to provide that proof without transgressing the limits of form. He could not have brought himself to begin by reporting something unreal as though it had been real. For this reason, his cyclical work begins with the memory of what it was like to fall asleep, and the whole first book is nothing but an exposition of the difficulties one has in falling asleep when the beautiful mother has not given the boy his goodnight kiss. The narrator establishes an interior space, as it were, which spares him the false step into the alien world, a *faux pas* that would be revealed in the false tone of one who acted as though he were familiar with that world. The world is imperceptibly drawn into this interior space—the technique has been given the name "interior monologue"—and anything that takes place in the external world is presented the way the moment of falling asleep is presented on the first page: as a piece of the interior world, a moment in the stream of consciousness, protected against refutation by the objective order of time and space which Proust's work is committed to suspending. The novel of German Expressionism—Gustav Sack's *Ein verbummelter Student* [*A Student Vagabond*], for instance—aimed at something similar, although with completely different presuppositions and in a different spirit. The epic enterprise of depicting only those concrete things which can be given in their fullness ultimately cancels out the fundamental epic category of concreteness.

The traditional novel, whose idea is perhaps most authentically embodied in Flaubert, can be compared to the three-walled stage of bourgeois theater. This technique was one of illusion. The narrator raises a curtain: the reader is to take part in what occurs as though he were physically present. The narrator's subjectivity proves itself in the power to produce this illusion and—in Flaubert—in the purity of the language, which, by spiritualizing language, removes it from the empirical realm to which it is committed. There is a heavy taboo on reflection: it becomes the cardinal sin against objective purity. Today this taboo, along with the illusionary character of what is represented, is losing its strength. It has often been noted that in the modern novel, not only in Proust but also in the Gide of the *Faux-Monnayeurs*, in the late Thomas Mann, or in Musil's *The Man Without Qualities*, reflection breaks through the pure immanence of form. But this kind of reflection has scarcely anything but the name in common with pre-Flaubertian reflection. The latter was moral: taking a stand for or against characters in the novel. The new reflection takes a stand against the lie of representation, actually against the narrator himself, who tries, as an extra-alert commentator on events, to correct his unavoidable way of proceeding. This destruction of form is inherent in the very meaning of form. Only now can the form-constructing function of Thomas Mann's medium, the enigmatic irony that cannot be reduced to any mockery in the content, be fully understood: with an ironic gesture that undoes his own delivery, the author casts aside the claim that he is creating something real, a claim which, however, no word, not even his words, can escape. Mann does this most obviously, perhaps, in his late period, in the *Holy Sinner* and the *Black Swan*, where the writer, playing with a romantic motif, acknowledges the peep-show element in the narrative, the unreality of illusion, through his use of language. By doing so, he returns the work of art, as he says, to the status of a sublime joke, a status it had until, with the naiveté of lack of naiveté, it presented illusion as truth in an all too unreflected way.

When, in Proust, commentary is so thoroughly interwoven with action that the distinction between the two disappears, the narrator is attacking a fundamental component of his relationship to the reader: aesthetic distance. In the traditional novel, this distance was fixed. Now it varies, like the angle of the camera in film: sometimes the reader is left outside, and sometimes he is led by the commentary onto the stage, backstage, into the prop room. Among the extremes—and we can learn more about the contemporary novel from them than from any "typical" case—belongs Kafka's method of completely abolishing the distance. Through shocks, he destroys the reader's contemplative security in the face of what he reads. His novels, if indeed they even fall under that category, are an anticipatory response to a state of the world in which the contemplative attitude has become a mockery because the permanent threat of catastrophe no longer permits any human being to be an uninvolved spectator; nor does it permit the aesthetic imitation of that stance. The distance is collapsed even by lesser writers who do not dare to write a word that does not apologize for being born by claiming to report on the facts. Their work reveals the weakness of a state of consciousness that is too shortsighted to tolerate its own aesthetic representation and can scarcely produce human beings capable of that representation. In the most advanced production, however, to which such weakness is no stranger, the abolition of aesthetic distance is a requirement of form itself; it is one of the most effective means to break through foreground relationships and express what lies beneath them, the negativity of the positive. Not that the depiction of the imaginary necessarily replaces that of the real, as in Kafka. He is ill-suited to be a model. But the difference between the real and the *imago* is abolished in principle. A common feature of the great novelists of the age is that in their work the novelistic precept "this is how it is," thought through to its ultimate consequences, releases a series of historical archetypes; this occurs in Proust's involuntary memory as in Kafka's parables and Joyce's epic cryptograms. The literary subject who declares himself free of the conventions of concrete representation acknowledges his own impotence at the same time; he acknowledges the superior strength of the world of things that reappears in the midst of the monologue. Thus a second language is produced, distilled to a large extent from the residue of the first, a deteriorated associative language of things which permeates not only the novelist's monologue but also that of the innumerable people estranged from the first language who make up the masses. Forty years ago, in his *Theory of the Novel,* Lukács posed the question whether Dostoevski's novels were the foundation for future epics, or perhaps even themselves those epics. In fact, the contemporary novels that count, those in which an unleashed subjectivity turns into its opposite through its own momentum, are negative epics. They are testimonials to a state of affairs in which the individual liquidates himself, a state of affairs which converges with the pre-individual situation that once seemed to guarantee a world replete with meaning. These epics, along with all contemporary art, are ambiguous: it is not up to them to determine whether the goal of the historical tendency they register is a regression to barbarism or the realization of humanity, and many are all too comfortable with the barbaric. There is no modern work of art worth anything that does not delight in dissonance and release. But by uncompromisingly embodying the horror and putting all the pleasure of contemplation into the purity of this expression, such works of art serve freedom—something the average production betrays, simply because it does not bear witness to what has befallen the individual in the age of liberalism. These products fall outside the controversy over committed art and *l'art pour l'art*, outside the choice between the philistinism of art with a cause and the philistinism of art for enjoyment. Karl Kraus once formulated the idea that everything that spoke morally out of his works in the form of physical, non-aesthetic reality had been imparted to him solely under the law of language, thus in the name of *l'art pour l'art*. It is a tendency inherent in form that demands the abolition of aesthetic distance in the contemporary novel and its capitulation thereby to the superior power of reality—a reality that cannot be transfigured in an image but only altered concretely, in reality.

■:■:■

On Lyric Poetry and Society

*T*he announcement of a lecture on
lyric poetry and society will make
many of you uncomfortable. You will expect a sociological analysis of the
kind that can be made of any object, just as fifty years ago people came
up with psychologies, and thirty years ago with phenomenologies, of
everything conceivable. You will suspect that examination of the conditions under which works are created and their effect will try to usurp the
place of experience of the works as they are and that the process of
categorizing and relating will suppress insight into the truth or falsity of
the object itself. You will suspect that an intellectual will be guilty of
what Hegel accused the "formal understanding" of doing, namely that in
surveying the whole it stands above the individual existence it is talking
about, that is, it does not see it at all but only labels it. This approach
will seem especially distressing to you in the case of lyric poetry. The
most delicate, the most fragile thing that exists is to be encroached upon
and brought into conjunction with bustle and commotion, when part of
the ideal of lyric poetry, at least in its traditional sense, is to remain
unaffected by bustle and commotion. A sphere of expression whose very
essence lies in either not acknowledging the power of socialization or
overcoming it through the pathos of detachment, as in Baudelaire or
Nietzsche, is to be arrogantly turned into the opposite of what it conceives itself to be through the way it is examined. Can anyone, you will
ask, but a man who is insensitive to the Muse talk about lyric poetry and
society?

Clearly your suspicions will be allayed only if lyric works are not
abused by being made objects with which to demonstrate sociological

theses but if instead the social element in them is shown to reveal something essential about the basis of their quality. This relationship should lead not away from the work of art but deeper into it. But the most elementary reflection shows that this is to be expected. For the substance of a poem is not merely an expression of individual impulses and experiences. Those become a matter of art only when they come to participate in something universal by virtue of the specificity they acquire in being given aesthetic form. Not that what the lyric poem expresses must be immediately equivalent to what everyone experiences. Its universality is no *volonté de tous*, not the universality of simply communicating what others are unable to communicate. Rather, immersion in what has taken individual form elevates the lyric poem to the status of something universal by making manifest something not distorted, not grasped, not yet subsumed. It thereby anticipates, spiritually, a situation in which no false universality, that is, nothing profoundly particular, continues to fetter what is other than itself, the human. The lyric work hopes to attain universality through unrestrained individuation. The danger peculiar to the lyric, however, lies in the fact that its principle of individuation never guarantees that something binding and authentic will be produced. It has no say over whether the poem remains within the contingency of mere separate existence.

The universality of the lyric's substance, however, is social in nature. Only one who hears the voice of humankind in the poem's solitude can understand what the poem is saying; indeed, even the solitariness of lyrical language itself is prescribed by an individualistic and ultimately atomistic society, just as conversely its general cogency depends on the intensity of its individuation. For that reason, however, reflection on the work of art is justified in inquiring, and obligated to inquire concretely into its social content and not content itself with a vague feeling of something universal and inclusive. This kind of specification through thought is not some external reflection alien to art; on the contrary, all linguistic works of art demand it. The material proper to them, concepts, does not exhaust itself in mere contemplation. In order to be susceptible of aesthetic contemplation, works of art must always be thought through as well, and once thought has been called into play by the poem it does not let itself be stopped at the poem's behest.

Such thought, however—the social interpretation of lyric poetry as of all works of art—may not focus directly on the so-called social perspective or the social interests of the works or their authors. Instead, it must

discover how the entirety of a society, conceived as an internally contradictory unity, is manifested in the work of art, in what way the work of
art remains subject to society and in what way it transcends it. In
philosophical terms, the approach must be an immanent one. Social
concepts should not be applied to the works from without but rather
drawn from an exacting examination of the works themselves. Goethe's
statement in his *Maxims and Reflections* that what you do not understand
you do not possess holds not only for the aesthetic attitude to works of art
but for aesthetic theory as well; nothing that is not in the works, not part
of their own form, can legitimate a determination of what their substance, that which has entered into their poetry, represents in social
terms. To determine that, of course, requires both knowledge of the
interior of the works of art and knowledge of the society outside. But this
knowledge is binding only if it is rediscovered through complete submission to the matter at hand. Special vigilance is required when it comes to
the concept of ideology, which these days is belabored to the point of
intolerability. For ideology is untruth, false consciousness, deceit. It
manifests itself in the failure of works of art, in their inherent falseness,
and it is countered by criticism. To repeat mechanically, however, that
great works of art, whose essence consists in giving form to the crucial
contradictions in real existence, and only in that sense in a tendency to
reconcile them, are ideology, not only does an injustice to their truth
content but also misrepresents the concept of ideology. That concept does
not maintain that all spirit serves only for some human beings to falsely
present some particular values as general ones; rather, it is intended to
unmask spirit that is specifically false and at the same time to grasp it in
its necessity. The greatness of works of art, however, consists solely in
the fact that they give voice to what ideology hides. Their very success
moves beyond false consciousness, whether intentionally or not.

Let me take your own misgivings as a starting point. You experience
lyric poetry as something opposed to society, something wholly individual. Your feelings insist that it remain so, that lyric expression, having
escaped from the weight of material existence, evoke the image of a life
free from the coercion of reigning practices, of utility, of the relentless
pressures of self-preservation. This demand, however, the demand that
the lyric word be virginal, is itself social in nature. It implies a protest
against a social situation that every individual experiences as hostile,
alien, cold, oppressive, and this situation is imprinted in reverse on the
poetic work: the more heavily the situation weighs upon it, the more

firmly the work resists it by refusing to submit to anything heteronomous and constituting itself solely in accordance with its own laws. The work's distance from mere existence becomes the measure of what is false and bad in the latter. In its protest the poem expresses the dream of a world in which things would be different. The lyric spirit's idiosyncratic opposition to the superior power of material things is a form of reaction to the reification of the world, to the domination of human beings by commodities that has developed since the beginning of the modern area, since the industrial revolution became the dominant force in life. Rilke's cult of the thing [as in his *Dinggedichte* or "thing poems"] is part of this idiosyncratic opposition; it attempts to assimilate even alien objects to pure subjective expression and to dissolve them, to give them metaphysical credit for their alienness. The aesthetic weakness of this cult of the thing, its obscurantist demeanor and its blending of religion with arts and crafts, reveals the real power of reification, which can no longer be gilded with a lyrical halo and brought back within the sphere of meaning.

To say that the concept of lyric poetry that is in some sense second nature to us is a completely modern one is only to express this insight into the social nature of the lyric in different form. Analogously, landscape painting and its idea of "nature" have had an autonomous development only in the modern period. I know that I exaggerate in saying this, that you could adduce many counterexamples. The most compelling would be Sappho. I will not discuss the Chinese, Japanese, and Arabic lyric, since I cannot read them in the original and I suspect that translation involves them in an adaptive mechanism that makes adequate understanding completely impossible. But the manifestations in earlier periods of the specifically lyric spirit familiar to us are only isolated flashes, just as the backgrounds in older painting occasionally anticipate the idea of landscape painting. They do not establish it as a form. The great poets of the distant past—Pindar and Alcaeus, for instance, but the greater part of Walther von der Vogelweide's work as well—whom literary history classifies as lyric poets are uncommonly far from our primary conception of the lyric. They lack the quality of immediacy, of immateriality, which we are accustomed, rightly or not, to consider the criterion of the lyric and which we transcend only through rigorous education.

Until we have either broadened it historically or turned it critically against the sphere of individualism, however, our conception of lyric poetry has a moment of discontinuity in it—all the more so, the more pure it claims to be. The "I" whose voice is heard in the lyric is an "I" that defines and expresses itself as something opposed to the collective, to objectivity; it is not immediately at one with the nature to which its expression refers. It has lost it, as it were, and attempts to restore it through animation, through immersion in the "I" itself. It is only through humanization that nature is to be restored the rights that human domination took from it. Even lyric works in which no trace of conventional and concrete existence, no crude materiality remains, the greatest lyric works in our language, owe their quality to the force with which the "I" creates the illusion of nature emerging from alienation. Their pure subjectivity, the aspect of them that appears seamless and harmonious, bears witness to its opposite, to suffering in an existence alien to the subject and to love for it as well—indeed, their harmoniousness is actually nothing but the mutual accord of this suffering and this love. Even the line from Goethe's "Wanderers Nachtlied" ["Wanderer's Night-Song"], "Warte nur, balde / ruhest du auch" ["Only wait, soon / you too shall rest"] has an air of consolation: its unfathomable beauty cannot be separated from something it makes no reference to, the notion of a world that withholds peace. Only in resonating with sadness about that withholding does the poem maintain that there is peace nevertheless. One is tempted to use the line "Ach, ich bin des Treibens müde" ["I am weary of restless activity"] from the companion poem of the same title to interpret the "Wanderers Nachtlied." To be sure, the greatness of the latter poem derives from the fact that it does not speak about what is alienated and disturbing, from the fact that within the poem the restlessness of the object is not opposed to the subject; instead, the subject's own restlessness echoes it. A second immediacy is promised: what is human, language itself, seems to become creation again, while everything external dies away in the echo of the soul. This becomes more than an illusion, however; it becomes full truth, because through the expression in language of a good kind of tiredness, the shadow of yearning and even of death continues to fall across the reconciliation. In the line "Warte nur, balde" the whole of life, with an enigmatic smile of sorrow, turns into the brief moment before one falls asleep. The note of peacefulness attests to the fact that peace cannot be achieved without the dream disintegrating. The shadow has no power over the image of life come back into its own, but as a last reminder of life's deformation it gives the dream its profound depths beneath the surface of the song. In the face of nature at rest, a nature from which all traces of anything resembling the human have been eradicated, the subject becomes aware of its own insignificance. Imperceptibly, silently, irony tinges the poem's consolation: the seconds before the bliss of sleep are the same seconds that separate our brief life from death. After Goethe, this sublime irony became a debased and spiteful irony. But it was always bourgeois: the shadow-side of the elevation of the liberated subject is its degradation to something exchangeable, to something that exists merely for something else; the shadow-side of personality is the "So who are you?" The authenticity of the "Nachtlied," however, lies in its moment in time: the background of that destructive force removes it from the sphere of play, while the destructive force has no power over the peaceable power of consolation. It is commonly said that a perfect lyric poem must possess totality or universality, must provide the whole within the bounds of the poem and the infinite within the poem's finitude. If that is to be more than a platitude of an aesthetics that is always ready to use the concept of the symbolic as a panacea, it indicates that in every lyric poem the historical relationship of the subject to objectivity, of the individual to society, must have found its precipitate in the medium of a subjective spirit thrown back upon itself. The less the work thematizes the relationship of "I" and society, the more spontaneously it crystallizes of its own accord in the poem, the more complete this process of precipitation will be.

You may accuse me of so sublimating the relationship of lyric and society in this definition out of fear of a crude sociologism that there is really nothing left of it; it is precisely what is not social in the lyric poem that is now to become its social aspect. You could call my attention to Gustav Doré's caricature of the arch-reactionary deputy whose praise of the *ancien régime* culminated in the exclamation, "And to whom, gentlemen, do we owe the revolution of 1789 if not to Louis XVI!" You could apply that to my view of lyric poetry and society: in my view, you could say, society plays the role of the executed king and the lyric the role of his opponents; but lyric poetry, you say, can no more be explained on the basis of society than the revolution can be made the achievement of the monarch it deposed and without whose inanities it might not have occurred at that time. We will leave it an open question whether Doré's deputy was truly only the stupid, cynical propagandist the artist derided him for being or whether there might be more truth in his unintentional joke than common sense admits; Hegel's philosophy of history would have a lot to say in his defense. In any case, the comparison does not really work. I am not trying to deduce lyric poetry form society; its social substance is precisely what is spontaneous in it, what does not simply follow from the existing conditions at the time. But philosophy—Hegel's again—is familiar with the speculative proposition that the individual is mediated by the universal and vice versa. That means that even resistance to social pressure is not something absolutely individual; the artistic forces in that resistance, which operate in and through the individual and his spontaneity, are objective forces that impel a constricted and constricting social condition to transcend itself and become worthy of human beings; forces, that is, that are part of the constitution of the whole and not at all merely forces of a rigid individuality blindly opposing society. If, by virtue of its own subjectivity, the substance of the lyric can in fact be addressed as an objective substance—and otherwise one could not explain the very simple fact that grounds the possibility of the lyric as an artistic genre, its effect on people other than the poet speaking his monologue—then it is only because the lyric work of art's withdrawal into itself, its self-absorption, its detachment from the social surface, is socially motivated behind the author's back. But the medium of this is language. The paradox specific to the lyric work, a subjectivity that turns into objectivity, is tied to the priority of linguistic form in the lyric; it is that priority from which the primacy of language in literature in general (even in prose forms) is derived. For language is itself something double. Through its configurations it assimilates itself completely into subjective impulses; one would almost think it had produced them. But at the same time language remains the medium of concepts, remains that which establishes an inescapable relationship to the universal and to society. Hence the highest lyric works are those in which the subject, with no remaining trace of mere matter, sounds forth in language until language itself acquires a voice. The unself-consciousness of the subject submitting itself to language as to something objective, and the immediacy and spontaneity of that subject's expression are one and the same: thus language mediates lyric poetry and society in their innermost core. This is why the lyric reveals itself to be most deeply grounded in society when it does not chime in with society, when it communicates nothing, when, instead, the subject whose expression is successful reaches an accord with language itself, with the inherent tendency of language.

On the other hand, however, language should also not be absolutized as the voice of Being as opposed to the lyric subject, as many of the current ontological theories of language would have it. The subject, whose expression—as opposed to mere signification of objective contents—is necessary to attain to that level of linguistic objectivity, is not something added to the contents proper to that layer, not something external to it. The moment of unself-consciousness in which the subject submerges itself in language is not a sacrifice of the subject to Being. It is a moment not of violence, nor of violence against the subject, but reconciliation: language itself speaks only when it speaks not as something alien to the subject but as the subject's own voice. When the "I" becomes oblivious to itself in language it is fully present nevertheless; if it were not, language would become a consecrated abracadabra and succumb to reification, as it does in communicative discourse. But that brings us back to the actual relationship between the individual and society. It is not only that the individual is inherently socially mediated, not only that its contents are always social as well. Conversely, society is formed and continues to live only by virtue of the individuals whose quintessence it is. Classical philosophy once formulated a truth now disdained by scientific logic: subject and object are not rigid and isolated poles but can be defined only in the process in which they distinguish themselves from one another and change. The lyric is the aesthetic test of that dialectical philosophical proposition. In the lyric poem the subject, through its identification with language, negates both its opposition to society as something merely monadological and its mere functioning within a wholly socialized society [*vergesellschaftete Gesellschaft*]. But the more the latter's ascendancy over the subject increases, the more precarious the situation of the lyric becomes. Baudelaire's work was the first to record this; his work, the ultimate consequence of European *Weltschmerz,* did not stop with the sufferings of the individual but chose the modern itself, as the antilyrical pure and simple, for its theme and struck a poetic spark in it by dint of a heroically stylized language. In Baudelaire a note of despair already makes itself felt, a note that barely maintains its balance on the tip of its own paradoxicalness. As the contradiction between poetic and communicative language reached an extreme, lyric poetry became a game in which one goes for broke; not, as philistine opinion would have it, because it had become incomprehensible but because in acquiring self-consciousness as a literary language, in striving for an absolute objectivity unrestricted by any considerations of communication, language both distances itself from the objectivity of spirit, of living language, and substitutes a poetic event for a language that is no longer present. The elevated, poeticizing, subjectively violent moment in weak later lyric poetry is the price it has to pay for its attempt to keep itself undisfigured, immaculate, objective; its false glitter is the complement to the disenchanted world from which it extricates itself.

Everything I have said needs to be qualified if it is to avoid misinterpretation. My thesis is that the lyric work is always the subjective expression of a social antagonism. But since the objective world that produces the lyric is an inherently antagonistic world, the concept of the lyric is not simply that of the expression of a subjectivity to which language grants objectivity. Not only does the lyric subject embody the whole all the more cogently, the more it expresses itself; in addition, poetic subjectivity is itself indebted to privilege: the pressures of the struggle for survival allow only a few human beings to grasp the universal through immersion in the self or to develop as autonomous subjects capable of freely expressing themselves. The others, however, those who not only stand alienated, as though they were objects, facing the disconcerted poetic subject but who have also literally been degraded to objects of history, have the same right, or a greater right, to grope for the sounds in which sufferings and dreams are welded. This inalienable right has asserted itself again and again, in forms however impure, mutilated, fragmentary, and intermittent—the only forms possible for those who have to bear the burden.

A collective undercurrent provides the foundation for all individual lyric poetry. When that poetry actually bears the whole in mind and is not simply an expression of the privilege, refinement, and gentility of those who can afford to be gentle, participation in this undercurrent is an essential part of the substantiality of the individual lyric as well: it is this undercurrent that makes language the medium in which the subject becomes more than a mere subject. Romanticism's link to the folksong is only the most obvious, certainly not the most compelling example of this. For Romanticism practices a kind of programmatic transfusion of the collective into the individual through which the individual lyric poem indulged in a technical illusion of universal cogency without that cogency characterizing it inherently. Often, in contrast, poets who abjure any borrowing from the collective language participate in that collective undercurrent by virtue of their historical experience. Let me mention Baudelaire again, whose lyric poetry is a slap in the face not only to the *juste milieu* but also to all bourgeois social sentiment, and who nevertheless, in poems like the "Petites vieilles" or the poem about the servant woman with the generous heart in the *Tableaux Parisiens*, was truer to the masses toward whom he turned his tragic, arrogant mask than any "poor people's" poetry. Today, when individual expression, which is the precondition for the conception of lyric poetry that is my point of departure, seems shaken to its very core in the crisis of the individual, the collective undercurrent in the lyric surfaces in the most diverse places: first merely as the ferment of individual expression and then perhaps also as an anticipation of a situation that transcends mere individuality in a positive way. If the translations can be trusted, García Lorca, whom Franco's henchmen murdered and whom no totalitarian regime could have tolerated, was the bearer of a force of this kind; and Brecht's name comes to mind as a lyric poet who was granted linguistic integrity without having to pay the price of esotericism. I will forgo making a judgment about whether the poetic principle of individuation was in fact sublated to a higher level here, or whether its basis lies in regression, a weakening of the ego. The collective power of contemporary lyric poetry may be largely due to the linguistic and psychic residues of a condition that is not yet fully individuated, a state of affairs that is prebourgeois in the broadest sense—dialect. Until now, however, the traditional lyric, as the most rigorous aesthetic negation of bourgeois convention, has by that very token been tied to bourgeois society.

Because considerations of principle are not sufficient. I would like to use a few poems to concretize the relationship of the poetic subject, which always stands for a far more general collective subject, to the social reality that is its antithesis. In this process the thematic elements, which no linguistic work, even *poésie pure*, can completely divest itself of, will need interpretation just as the so-called formal elements will. The way the two interpenetrate will require special emphasis, for it is only by virtue of such interpenetration that the lyric poem actually captures the historical moment within its bounds. I want to choose not poems like Goethe's, aspects of which I commented on without analyzing, but later ones, poems which do not have the unqualified authenticity of the "Nachtlied." The two poems I will be talking about do indeed share in the collective undercurrent. But I would like to call your attention especially to the way in which in them different levels of a contradictory fundamental condition of society are represented in the medium of the poetic subject. Permit me to repeat that we are concerned not with the poet as a private person, not with his psychology or his so-called social perspective, but with the poem as a philosophical sundial telling the time of history.

Let me begin by reading you Eduard Mörike's "Auf einer Wanderung" ["On a Walking Tour"]:

In ein freundliches Städtchen tret' ich ein
In den Strassen liegt roter Abendschein,
Aus einem offenen Fenster eben,
Über den reichsten Blumenflor
Hinweg, hört man Goldglockentöne schweben,
Und *eine* Stimme scheint ein Nachtigallenchor,
Daß die Blüten beben,
Daß die Lüfte leben,
Daß in höherem Rot die Rosen leuchten vor.

Lang' hielt ich staunend, lustbeklommen.
Wie ich hinaus vors Tor gekommen,
Ich weiss es wahrlich selber nicht,
Ach hier, wie liegt die Welt so licht!
Der Himmel wogt in purpurnem Gewühle,
Rückwärts die Stadt in goldnem Rauch;
Wie rauscht der Erlenbach, wie rauscht im Grund die Mühle!
Ich bin wie trunken, irrgeführt—
O Muse, du hast mein Herz berührt
Mit einem Liebeshauch!

[I enter a friendly little town,
On the streets lies the red evening light,
From an open window,
Across the richest profusion of flowers
One hears golden bell-tones hover,
And *one* voice seems to be a choir of nightingales,
So that the blossoms quaver,
So that the breezes are lively,
So that the roses glow forth in a higher red.

I stood a long while marvelling, oppressed with pleasure.
How I got out beyond the city gate,
I really do not know myself,
Oh, how bright the world is here!
The sky surges in purple turbulence,
At my back the town in a golden haze;
How the alder stream murmurs, how the mill roars below!

I am as if drunken, led astray—
Oh muse, you have touched my heart,
With a breath of love!]

Up surges the image of the promise of happiness which the small
south German town still grants its guests on the right day, but not the
slightest concession is made to the pseudo-Gothic small-town idyll. The
poem gives the feeling of warmth and security in a confined space, yet at
the same time it is a work in the elevated style, not disfigured by
Gemütlichkeit and coziness, not sentimentally praising narrowness in
opposition to the wide world, not happiness in one's own little corner.
Language and the rudimentary plot both aid in skillfully equating the
utopia of what is close at hand with that of the utmost distance. The town
appears in the narrative only as a fleeting scene, not as a place of
lingering. The magnitude of the feeling that results from the speaker's
delight in the girl's voice, and not that voice alone but the voice of all of
nature, the choir, emerges only outside the confined arena of the town,
under the open purple-billowing sky, where the golden town and the
rushing brook come together in the *imago*. Linguistically, this is aided
by an inestimably subtle, scarcely definable *classical*, ode-like element.
As if from afar, the free rhythms call to mind unrhymed Greek stanzas,
as does the sudden pathos of the closing line of the first stanza, which is
effected with the most discreet devices of transposition of word order:
"Daβ in höherem Rot die Rosen leuchten vor." The single word "Muse"
at the end of the poem is decisive. It is as if this word, one of the most
overused in German classicism, gleamed once again, truly as if in the
light of the setting sun, by being bestowed upon the *genius loci* of the
friendly little town, and as though even in the process of disappearing it
were possessed of all the power to enrapture which an invocation of the
muse in the modern idiom, comically inept, usually fails to capture. The
poem's inspiration proves itself perhaps more fully in this than in any of
its other features: that the choice of this most objectionable word at a
critical point, carefully prepared by the latent Greek linguistic demeanor,
resolves the urgent dynamic of the whole like a musical *Abgesang*.* In the
briefest of spaces, the lyric succeeds in doing what the German epic
attempted in vain, even in such projects as Goethe's *Hermann und Dorothea*.

---

*The *Abgesang* was the closing portion of a stanza in medieval lyric poetry.

The social interpretation of a success like this is concerned with the stage of historical experience evidenced in the poem. In the name of humanity, of the universality of the human, German classicism had undertaken to release subjective impulses from the contingency that threatens them in a society where relationships between human beings are no longer direct but instead mediated solely by the market. It strove to objectify the subjective as Hegel did in philosophy and tried to overcome the contradictions of men's real lives by reconciling them in spirit, in the idea. The continued existence of these contradictions in reality, however, had compromised the spiritual solution: in the face of a life not grounded in meaning, a life lived painstakingly amid the bustle of competing interests, a prosaic life, as artistic experience sees it; in the face of a world in which the fate of individual human beings works itself out in accordance with blind laws, art, whose form gives the impression of speaking from the point of view of a realized humanity, becomes an empty word. Hence classicism's concept of the human being withdrew into private, individual existence and its images; only there did humanness seem secure. Of necessity, the idea of humankind as something whole, something self-determining, was renounced by the bourgeoisie, in aesthetic form as in politics. It is the stubborn clinging to one's own restricted sphere, which itself obeys a compulsion, that makes ideals like comfort and *Gemütlichkeit* so suspect. Meaning itself is linked to the contingencies of human happiness; through a kind of usurpation, individual happiness is ascribed a dignity it would attain only along with the happiness of the whole. The social force of Mörike's genius, however, consists in the fact that he combined the two experiences—that of the classicistic elevated style and that of the romantic private miniature—and that in doing so he recognized the limits of both possibilities and balanced them against one another with incomparable tact. In none of his expressive impulses does he go beyond what could be genuinely attained in his time. The much-invoked organic quality of his work is probably nothing other than this tact, which is philosophically sensitive to history and which scarcely any other poet in the German language possessed to the same degree. The alleged pathological traits in Mörike reported by psychologists and the drying up of his production in later years are the negative aspect of his very highly developed understanding of what is possible. The poems of the hypochondriacal clergyman from Cleversulzbach, who is considered one of our naive artists, are virtuoso pieces unsurpassed by the masters of *l'art pour l'art*. He is as aware of the empty and ideological aspects of elevated style as of the mediocrity, petit-bourgeois dullness, and obliviousness to totality of the Biedermeier period, in which the greater part of his lyric work falls. The spirit in him is driven to create, for the last time, images that would betray themselves neither by their classical drapery nor by local color, neither by their manly tones nor by their lipsmacking. As if walking a fine line, the residues of the elevated style that survive in memory echo in him, together with the signs of an immediate life that promised fulfillment precisely at the time when they were already condemned by the direction history was taking; and both greet the poet on his wandering only as they are about to vanish. He already shares in the paradox of lyric poetry in the ascending industrial age. As indeterminate and fragile as his solutions are the solutions of all the great lyric poets who come afterwards, even those who seem to be separated from him by an abyss—like Baudelaire, of whom Claudel said that his style was a mixture of Racine's and that of the journalists of his time. In industrial society the lyric idea of a self-restoring immediacy becomes— where it does not impotently evoke a romantic past—more and more something that flashes out abruptly, something in which what is possible transcends its own impossibility.

The short poem by Stefan George I would now like to discuss derives from a much later phase in this development. It is one of the celebrated songs from the *Seventh Ring,* a cycle of extremely condensed works which for all their lightness of rhythm are over-heavy with substance and wholly without *Jugendstil* ornament. Their eccentric boldness was rescued from the frightful cultural conservativism of the George circle only when the great composer Anton von Webern set them to music; in George, ideology and social substance are very far apart. The song reads:

Im windes-weben
War meine frage
Nur träumerei.
Nur lächeln war
Was du gegeben.
Aus nasser nacht
Ein glanz entfacht—
Nun drängt der mai
Nun muss ich gar
Um dein aug und haar
Alle tage
In sehnen leben.

[In the winds-weaving
My question was
Only daydreaming.
Only a smile was
What you gave.
From a moist night
A gleam ignites—
Now May urges
Now I must
For your eyes and hair
Every day
Live in yearning.]

Unquestionably, this is elevated style. Delight in things close at hand, something that still colors Mörike's much earlier poem, has fallen under a prohibition. It has been banished by the Nietzschean pathos of detached reserve which George conceives himself to be carrying on. The remains of Romanticism lie, a deterrent, between him and Mörike; the remains of the idyll are hopelessly outdated and have degenerated to heartwarmers. While George's poetry, the poetry of an imperious individual, presupposes individualistic bourgeois society and the autonomous individual as its preconditions, a curse is put on the bourgeois element of conventional form no less than on the bourgeois contents. But because this poetry can speak from no overarching framework other than the bourgeois, which it rejects not only tacitly and a priori but also expressly, it becomes obstructed: on its own initiative and its own authority, it simulates a feudal condition. Socially this is hidden behind what the cliché refers to as George's aristocratic stance. This stance is not the pose that the bourgeois, who cannot reduce these poems to objects of fondling, waxes indignant about. Rather, despite its demeanor of hostility to society, it is the product of the social dialectic that denies the lyric subject identification with what exists and its world of forms, while that subject is nevertheless allied with the status quo in its innermost core: it has no other locus from which to speak but that of a past seigneurial society. The ideal of nobility, which dictates the choice of every word, image, and sound in the poem, is derived from that locus, and the form is medieval in an almost undefinable way, a way that has been virtually imported into the linguistic configuration. To this extent the poem, like George altogether, is neoromantic. But it is not real things and not sounds that are evoked but rather a vanished condition of the soul. The artistically effected latency of the ideal, the absence of any crude archaicism, raises the song above the hopeless fiction it nonetheless offers. It no more resembles the medieval imitations used on wall plaques than it does the repertoire of the modern lyric; the poem's stylistic principle saves it from conformity. There is no more room in it for organic reconciliation of conflicting elements than there was for their pacification in the reality of George's time; they are mastered only through selection, through omission. Where things close at hand, the things one commonly calls concrete immediate experiences, are admitted into George's lyric poetry at all, they are allowed only at the price of mythologization: none may remain what it is. Thus in one of the landscapes of the *Seventh Ring* the child picking berries is transformed, wordlessly, as if with a magic wand, through a magical act of violence, into a fairy-tale child. The harmony of the song is wrested from an extreme of dissonance: it rests on what Valéry called *refus*, on an unyielding renunciation of everything through which the conventions of lyric poetry imagine that they have captured the aura of things. The method retains only the patterns, the pure formal ideas and schemata of lyric poetry itself, which speak with an intensity of expression once again in divesting themselves of all contingency. In the midst of Wilhelmine Germany the elevated style from which that lyric poetry emerged as polemic has no tradition at all to which it may appeal, least of all the legacy of classicism. It is achieved not by making a show of rhetorical figures and rhythms but by an ascetic omission of whatever might diminish its distance from a language sullied by commerce. If the subject is to genuinely resist reification in solitude here, it may no longer even try to withdraw into what is its own as though that were its property; the traces of an individualism that has in the meantime delivered itself over to the market in the form of the feuilleton are alarming. Instead, the subject has to step outside itself by keeping quiet about itself; it has to make itself a vessel, so to speak, for the idea of a pure language. George's greatest poems are aimed at rescuing that language. Formed by the Romance languages, and especially by the extreme simplification of the lyric through which Verlaine made it an instrument of what is most differentiated, the ear of George, the German student of Mallarmé, hears his own language as though it were a foreign tongue. He overcomes its alienation, which is an alienation of use, by intensifying it until it becomes the alienation of a language no longer actually spoken, even an imaginary language, and in that imaginary language he perceives what would be possible, but never took place, in its composition. The four lines "Nun muss ich gar / Um dein aug und haar / Alle tage / In sehnen leben," which I consider some of the most irresistible lines in German poetry, are like a quotation, but a quotation not from another poet but from something language has irrevocably failed to achieve: the medieval German poetry of the *Minnesang* would have succeeded in achieving it if it, if a tradition of the German language—if the German language itself, one is tempted to say—had succeeded. It was in this spirit that Borchardt tried to translate Dante. Subtle ears have taken umbrage at the elliptical "gar," which is probably used in place of "ganz und gar" [completely] and to some extent for the sake of the rhyme. One can concede the justice of this criticism and the fact that as used in the line the word has no proper meaning. But great works of art are the ones that succeed precisely where they are most problematic. Just as the greatest works of music may not be completely reduced to their structure but shoot out beyond it with a few superfluous notes or measures, so it is with the "gar," a Goethean "residue of the absurd" in which language escapes the subjective intention that occasioned the use of the word. It is probably this very "gar" that establishes the poem's status with the force of a déjà vu: through it the melody of the poem's language extends beyond mere signification. In the age of its decline George sees in language the idea that the course of history has denied it and constructs lines that sound as though they were not written by him but had been there from the beginning of time and would remain as they were forever. The quixotism of this enterprise, however, the impossibility of this kind of restorative writing, the danger of falling into arts and crafts, enriches the poem's substance: language's chimerical yearning for the impossible becomes an expression of the subject's insatiable erotic longing, which finds relief from the self in the other. This transformation of an individuality intensified to an extreme into self-annihilation—and what was the Maximin cult in the late George but a desperate renunciation of individuality construing itself as something positive—was necessary in creating the phantasmagoria of the folksong, something the German language had been groping for in vain in its greatest masters. Only by virtue of a differentiation taken so far that it can no longer bear its own difference, can no longer bear anything but the universal, freed from the humiliation of isolation, in the particular does lyrical language represent language's intrinsic being as opposed to its service in the realm of ends. But it thereby represents the idea of a free humankind, even if the George School concealed this idea from itself through a base cult of the heights. The truth of George lies in the fact that his poetry breaks down the walls of individuality through its consummation of the particular, through its sensitive opposition both to the banal and ultimately also to the select. The expression of his poetry may have been condensed into an individual expression which his lyrics saturate with substance and with the experience of its own solitude; but this very lyric speech becomes the voice of human beings between whom the barriers have fallen.

In Memory of Eichendorff

Je devine, à travers un murmure
Le contour subtil des voix anciennes
Et dans les lueurs musiciennes,
Amour pâle, une aurore future!
Verlaine, "Ariettes oubliées"

*I*n a culture that has been resurrected on a false basis, one's rela-
tion to the cultural past is poisoned. Love for the past is frequently
accompanied by resentment toward the present; by belief in the possession of a heritage that one loses the moment one imagines it cannot be
lost; by a feeling of comfort in familiar things that have been handed
down and under whose aegis those whose complicity helped pave the way
for the horror hope to escape it. The alternative to all that seems to be an
incisive gesture of "that's no longer acceptable." Sensitivity to the false
happiness of a cozy security zealously seizes upon the dream of a true
happiness, and heightened sensitivity to sentimentality contracts until it
is focused on the abstract point of the mere present, in the face of which
what once existed counts no more than if it had never existed. One might
say that experience is the union of tradition with an open yearning for
what is foreign. But the very possibility of experience is in jeopardy. The
break in the continuity of historical consciousness that Hermann Heimpel saw results in a polarization: on the one hand, cultural goods that are
antiquarian, and perhaps even shaped for ideological purposes; and on
the other, a contemporary historical moment that, precisely because it is
lacking in memory, is ready to subscribe to the status quo, even by
mirroring it where it opposes it. The rhythm of time has become
distorted. While the streets of philosophy are echoing with the metaphysics of time, time itself, once measured by the steady course of a person's
life, has become alienated from human beings; this is probably why it is
being discussed so feverishly. Something in the past that had truly been
handed down would have been sublated in its opposite, in the most

advanced form of consciousness; but an advanced consciousness that was in command of itself and did not have to worry about being negated by the most recent information would also have the freedom to love what is past. Great avant-garde artists like Schönberg did not have to prove to themselves that they had escaped from the spell of their forebears by experiencing anger toward those forebears. Having escaped and become emancipated, they could perceive the tradition as their equal instead of insisting on a distinction from tradition that only drowns out one's bondage to history in the demand for a radical and natural, as it were, new beginning. They knew that they were fulfilling the secret purpose of the tradition they were shattering. Only when one no longer breaks with tradition because one no longer senses it and hence does not try one's strength against it does one deny it; something that is different does not shrink from its affinity with its point of departure. It is not the timeless Now that would be contemporary but a Now saturated with the force of the past and therefore not needing to idolize it. It is up to advanced consciousness to correct the relationship to the past, not by glossing over the breach but by wresting what is contemporary away from what is transient in the past and granting no tradition authority. Tradition no longer has any more validity than does the converse belief that the living are right and the dead wrong, or that the world began when those now alive were born.

Joseph von Eichendorff resists such efforts. Those who sing his praises are primarily cultural conservatives. Many invoke him as the chief witness to a positive religiosity of the kind he set forth in rigid dogmatic fashion, especially in the literary-historical works of his late period. Others lay claim to him in the name of a regionalist spirit, a kind of poetics of ancestry along the lines of Joseph Nadler. They would like to resettle him in his native region; their "he was ours" is intended to support patriotic claims, with whose most recent form Eichendorff's restorationist universalism would have little in common. Given such adherents, an opportune reference to what is not up to date in Eichendorff is only too understandable. I remember clearly how when I was a student at the Gymnasium a teacher who had an important influence on me pointed out how trivial the image was in Eichendorff's lines "Es war, als hätt' der Himmel / Die Erde still geküsst" ["It was as though the sky / had quietly kissed the earth"], lines that I took as much for granted as Schumann's setting for them. I was incapable of countering the criticism even though it had not really convinced me; in just this way, Eichendorff is open to all objections but at the same time immune to each of them. What every ass hears, as Brahms put it, does not touch the quality of Eichendorff's poems. But if that quality is declared to be a mystery that one must respect, what hides behind such humble irrationalism is a lazy unwillingness to muster up the energetic receptivity the poem requires; and ultimately also a readiness to go on admiring what has already found approval and to content oneself with the vague conviction that there is something there that goes beyond the lyric poetry preserved in anthologies or editions of the classics. But at a time when no artistic experience is accepted unquestioningly any more, when, as children, no textbook authority can appropriate beauty for us any more—the beauty we understand precisely because we do not yet understand it—every act of contemplating beauty demands that we know why the object of our contemplation is called beautiful. A naiveté that would exempt itself from this demand is self-righteous and false; the substance of the work of art, which is itself spirit, does not need to be afraid of the mind that seeks to comprehend it; rather, it seeks out such a mind.

Rescuing Eichendorff from both friends and foes by understanding him is the opposite of a sullen apology. The element in his poems that became the property of men's glee clubs is not immune to its fate and to a large extent brought that fate upon itself. An affirmative tone in his work, a tone that glorifies existence as such, led straight to those anthologies. The apocryphal immortality he achieved there, however, should not be despised. Anyone who did not learn his "Wem Gott will rechte Gunst erweisen, / Den schickt er in die weite Welt" ["Whom God would truly favor / he sends out into the wide world"] by heart as a child is unfamiliar with a level of elevation of the word above everyday life, a level with which anyone who wants to sublimate that elevation and express the cleft between what human beings are meant to be and what the order of the world has made of them must be familiar. Similarly, Schubert's song cycle "Die schöne Müllerin" is truly accessible only to those who have sung the popular setting of "Das Wandern ist des Müllers Lust" ["Wandering is the Miller's Delight"] in the school chorus. When one first hears many of Eichendorff's lines—"Am liebsten betracht' ich die Sterne, / Die schienen, wenn ich ging zu ihr" ["The stars I like to look at best / are those that shone when I went to her"]—they sound like quotations, quotations learned by heart from God's primer.

But this is no reason to defend the all too unbroken tones in which Eichendorff sings praises and gives thanks. In the generations that have come and gone since his days, the ideological elements in the cheerful

and gregarious Eichendorff have emerged, with the result that his prose
often provokes a snicker. But even here the matter is not so simple. A
convivial song with a Goethean tone contains these lines:

> Das Trinken ist gescheiter,
> Das schmeckt schon nach Idee,
> Da braucht man keine Leiter,
> Das geht gleich in die Höh'.

[Drinking is smarter, / it even tastes like ideas; / you don't need a ladder,
/ it takes you right to the heights.]

Not only does the studentesquely casual mention of the word "idea"
allude to the great philosophy to whose era Eichendorff belonged; there
is also an impulse toward the spiritualization of the sensuous that extends
far beyond that era, one that has nothing in common with a late anacreon-
tic poetry and did not come into its own until Baudelaire's lethal wine
poems: from this time forth the Idea, the absolute, is as fleeting and
ephemeral as the bouquet of wine. It is probably not appropriate to
justify Eichendorff's affirmative tone as something wrested from the
darkness, as a widespread literary-historical cliché would have it; the
poems and prose show little evidence of such darkness. But they are
unquestionably related to European *Weltschmerz*. Eichendorff's forced
courage, his resolve to be of good cheer, are a response to that *Weltschmerz*, as he announces with strangely paradoxical force at the end of
one of his greatest poems, the one about the twilight: "Hüte dich, sei
wach und munter" ["Take care, be alert and of good cheer"]. What
Schumann at one point indicates as "im fröhlichen Ton," in a merry
tone, already resembles, in both Schumann and Eichendorff, Rilke's
"Als ob wir noch Fröhlichkeit hätten" ["As if we still had gladness"]:

> Hinaus, o Mensch, weit in die Welt
> Bangt dir das Herz in krankem Mut;
> Nichts ist so trüb in Nacht gestellt,
> Der Morgen leicht macht's wieder gut.

[Out, oh man, into the wide world / when your heart is fearful in your
sick spirit; / nothing is so bad at night / that morning cannot perhaps put
it right.]

The impotence of stanzas like these is not that of a restricted happiness
but that of futile invocation, and the expression of its futility, with the

Viennese "leicht" [easy] for "vielleicht" [perhaps], which is no doubt intended skeptically, is at the same time the force that reconciles us to them. The concluding lines of "Zwielicht" ["Twilight"] want to drown out childish fear, but "Manches bleibt in Nacht verloren" ["much remains lost in night"]. The late Eichendorff brought the precocious gratitude of the early Eichendorff to maturity in such a way that it becomes aware of its own deceitfulness and yet retains its own truth:

Mein Gott, dir sag' ich Dank,
Daβ du die Jugend mir bis über alle Wipfel
In Morgenrot getaucht und Klang,
Und auf des Lebens Gipfel,
Bevor der Tag geendet,
Vom Herzen unbewacht
Den falschen Glanz gewendet,
Daβ ich nicht taumle ruhmgeblendet,
Da nun herein die Nacht
Dunkelt in ernster Pracht.

[My God, I give thanks you to you / for dipping youth in dawn and sound / up to the tops of its trees, / and at the peak of life, / before the day was ended, / and quietly turning away / false brilliance from my heart, / so that I do not stagger now, blinded by fame, / now that night / is darkening in solemn splendor.]

Although the quality of peaceful reconciliation in these lines has now been irrevocably lost, it continues to shine radiantly, and not only on the night of the individual's death. Eichendorff glorifies what is, but he does not mean what exists. He was not a poet of the homeland but a poet of homesickness, as was Novalis, to whom he knew he was akin. Even in the poem that begins "Es war als hätt' der Himmel" ["It was as though the sky"], which he included in his *Geistliche Gedichte [Spiritual Poems]*, the feeling of an absolute homeland is conveyed successfully only because it does not refer directly to an animated nature but is merely expressed metaphorically, in the accents of an infallible metaphysical tact:

Und meine Seele spannte
Weit ihre Flügel aus,
Flog durch die stillen Lande,
Als flöge sie nach Haus.

["And my soul spread / her wings wide, / flew through the silent countryside / as though she were flying home."] At another point the poet's Catholicism does not balk at the mournful line "Das Reich des Glaubens ist geendet" ["The kingdom of faith is at an end"].

Still, Eichendorff's positiveness is intimately related to his conservatism, and his praise of what is is intimately related to the notion of something abiding. But if anywhere, it is in poetry that the status of conservatism has changed in the extreme. While today, after the disintegration of tradition, conservatism merely aids in justifying a bad status quo, with its arbitrary praise of binding ties, at one time it intended a very different status quo, one that can be fully judged only in relation to its opposite, an emerging barbarism. It is so obvious that much in Eichendorff has its origins in the perspective of the dispossessed feudal lord that it would be silly to criticize him in social terms; what Eichendorff had in mind, however, was not only the restoraton of a vanished order but also resistance to the destructive tendencies of the bourgeois. His superiority to all the reactionaries who are claiming him today is shown by the fact that like the great philosophy of his time he understood the necessity of the revolution he was terrified of: he embodies something of the critical truth of the consciousness of those who have to pay the price for the advance of the *Weltgeist*. Certainly there is much in his work on the nobility and the revolution that is narrow-minded, and his reservations about his own class are not free of a puritanical lament over the "plague of addiction to fame and pleasure," which he lumps together with the capitalist mentality that was spreading among the feudal class, with their tendency to turn their land "into a common commodity through their desperate speculations in their perpetual need of money." But he not only talked about the "swaggering bruisers of the Seven Years' War," "who made a profession of a certain upstandingness with an inimitably ridiculous masculine honor"; he also charged the German nationalists of the Napoleonic era with the "terrorism of a crude jingoism." While Eichendorff the feudal aristocrat may share, with the addition of some social criticism, the arguments against cosmopolitan leveling current among the right-wingers of his time, he by no means made common cause with those who advocate a return to the land, the "Jahns" and the "Fries." He is surprisingly sensitive to the aristocracy's sympathies with revolution and disintegration; he affirms them:

> An uncanny atmosphere, as of a thunderstorm, lay brooding . . . over the
> entire country; everyone sensed that something great was on the way; a

fearful unexpressed expectation of something, no one knew what, had
crept into almost everyone's spirits. In this atmosphere there appeared, as
always prior to an imminent catastrophe, strange figures and outrageous
adventurers like the Count St. Germain, Cagliostro, and others—emissaries, so to speak, of the future.

And he made statements about figures like Baron Grimm and the radical
emigré Count Schlabrendorf that fit no better with the stereotype of the
conservative than do the parts of Hegel's *Philosophy of Right* that deal
with the self-transcending forces of bourgeois society. These statements
read:

> Later, when the revolution became a fact, there emerged from these
> separatists certain highly questionable characters, such as the Baron Grimm,
> a restless, fanatical advocate of freedom, indefatigably fanning and turn-
> ing the flames until they closed over him and consumed him, and the
> famous Count Schlabrendorf, a settler in Paris, who let the whole social
> upheaval pass him by unchallenged in his cell like a great world tragedy,
> contemplating, directing and frequently steering it. For he stood so high
> above all the parties that he was always able to survey the battle of minds
> without being touched by its confused noise. This prophetic magician
> appeared before the great stage when he was still young, and when the
> catastrophe had run its course his gray beard had grown to his waist.

Here, certainly, sympathy for the Revolution has already been neutral-
ized to become the cultured humanitarianism of the spectator, but even
that rises commandingly above the current cult of the healthy, the
organic, and the whole: Eichendorff's traditionalism is broad enough to
embrace its own opposite. His freedom to see what is irrrevocable in the
historical process has been completely lost by the conservatism of the late
bourgeois phase; the less the precapitalist order is capable of being
restored, the more stubbornly ideology clings to the notion that it is
ahistorical and absolute.

The prebourgeois yeast in Eichendorff's conservatism, however, which
brings the unrest of longing, adventure, and blissful idleness to the
bourgeois element in him, extends deep into his lyric poetry. In *One-
Way Street* Benjamin writes: "The man . . . who knows himself to be in
accord with the most ancient heritage of his class or nation will sometimes
bring his private life into ostentatious contrast to the maxims that he
unrelentingly asserts in public, secretly approving his own behavior,
without the slightest qualms, as the most conclusive proof of the unshak-

able authority of the principles he puts on display."[1] That could have been based on Eichendorff; not, to be sure, on his private life, but on his conduct as a poet. To this we should add the question whether this lack of reliability expresses not only security but also a corrective to security, transcendence of the bourgeois society in which the conservative is never fully at home and in whose opponents something attracts him. In Eichendorff they are represented by the vagrants, the homeless of that era, as the messengers to the future of those who, as philosophy was to be in Novalis, are at home everywhere. One does not find Eichendorff praising the family as the nucleus of society. If some of his novellas— not *Ahnung und Gegenwart,* [*Intimation and Presence*] the great novel of his youth—end conventionally, with the hero's marriage, in the lyric poetry the poet, with unmistakable contempt for binding ties, confesses to having no place of his own. The motif comes from the folksong, but the insistence with which Eichendorff repeats it says something about him himself. The soldier sings: "Und spricht sie vom Freien: / So schwing ich mich auf mein Ross— / Ich bleibe im Freien, / Und sie auf dem Schloss" ["And if she talks about courting, / I jump on my horse— / I stay out of doors / and she in the castle"]. And the wandering musician sings: "Manche Schöne macht wohl Augen, / Mei-net, ich gefiel' ihr sehr, / Wenn ich nur was wollte taugen, / So ein armer Lump nicht wär. — / Mag dir Gott ein'n Mann bescheren, / Wohl mit Haus und Hof versehn! / Wenn wir zwei zusammen wären, / Möcht mein Singen mir vergehn" ["Many a beauty makes eyes at me, / says she likes me very much. / If only I were good for something / and not such a poor chump. — / God grant you a man / well provided with hearth and home! / If the two of us were together, / it would be all over with my singing"]. And the famous poem about the two traveling apprentices would be misunderstood by anyone who thought that the stanza about the first one, who found a sweetheart and founded his family in comfort in the home his father-in-law bought for him, sketches a picture of the proper way to live. The concluding stanza with its precip-itous weeping "Und seh ich so kecke Gesellen" ["And when I see such bold fellows"] refers to the mediocre happiness of the first apprentice as much as the lost happiness of the second; the right mode of life is concealed, perhaps already impossible, and in the last line, "Ach Gott, führ uns liebreich zu dir!" ["Oh God, lead us lovingly to you!"] an onrush of despair bursts the poem open.

The opposite of that despair is utopia: "Es redet trunken die Ferne / Wie von künftigem, grossem Gluck!" ["What is far away speaks to us drunkenly, / as of a great future happiness!"] —and not of a past happiness; so unreliable was Eichendorff's conservatism. But it is a rambling erotic utopia. Just as the heroes in his prose waver between feminine images that shade off into one another and are never sharply outlined against one another, so too Eichendorff's lyric poetry does not seem tied to a concrete image of a beloved woman: any particular beautiful woman would be a betrayal of the idea of boundless fulfillment. Even in "Übern Garten durch die Lüfte" ["Over the garden through the breezes"], one of the most passionate love poems in the German language, the beloved does not appear, nor does the poet speak about himself. Only the rejoicing is made known: "Sie ist Deine, sie ist dein!" ["She is yours, she is yours!"] Name and fulfillment fall under a ban on images. In contrast to the French tradition, undisguised depiction of sexuality was alien to the older tradition in German literature, and the penalty the average run of German literature has had to pay for that has been prudishness and an idealistic philistinism. But in its greatest representatives this silence has become a blessing; the force of what is left unsaid has permeated the language and given it its sweetness. In Eichendorff what was nonsensuous and abstract became a metaphor for something formless: an archaic heritage, something earlier than form and at the same time a late transcendence, something unconditioned, beyond form. The most sensuous of Eichendorff's poems remains within the invisibility of night:

Über Wipfel und Saaten
In den Glanz hinein —
Wer mag sie erraten?
Wer holte sie ein?
Gedanken sich wiegen,
Die Nacht ist verschwiegen,
Gedanken sind frei.

Errät es nur eine,
Wer an sie gedacht,
Beim Rauschen der Haine,
Wenn niemand mehr wacht,
Als die Wolken, die fliegen —
Mein Lieb ist verschwiegen
Und schön wie die Nacht.

[Over treetops and fields / into the gleam —/ Who could guess them? / Who could catch them? / Thoughts hover, / the night is discreet, /

thoughts are free. / May only one woman guess / who thought of her / with the rustling in the groves / when no one is awake / but the clouds that fly —/ my love is discreet / and as beautiful as night.]

Eichendorff, a contemporary of Schelling, is groping toward the *Fleurs du mal*, toward the line "O toi que la nuit rend si belle" ["Oh you whom night makes so beautiful"]. Without realizing it, Eichendorff's uncontained Romanticism leads to the threshold of modernity.

The experience of the modern element in Eichendorff, which has only now become accessible, leads directly to the center of his poetic substance. It is genuinely anti-conservative: a renunciation of the aristocratic, a renunciation even of the dominion of one's own ego over one's psyche. Eichendorff's poetry confidently lets itself be borne along by the steam of language, without fear that it will drown in it. For this generosity, which is not stingy with its own resources, the genius of language thanks him. The line "Und ich mag mich nicht bewahren" ["And I don't care to preserve myself"], which appears in one of the poems he placed at the head of his collected poems, is in a fact a prelude to his whole oeuvre. Here he is most intimately akin to Schumann, gracious and refined enough to disdain even his own right to exist: in the same way, the rapture in the third movement of Schumann's *Piano Fantasia* flows away into the ocean. Love is in bondage to death and oblivious of itself. In it the ego no longer becomes callous and entrenched within itself. It wants to make amends for some of the primordial injustice of being ego at all. Eichendorff is already a *bateau ivre*, but one that is still flying colored pennants on a river with green banks. "Nacht, Wolken, wohin sie gehen, / Ich weiss es recht gut" ["Night, clouds, I know full well / where they are going"]—these turbulently expressionistic lines occur in the poem "Nachtigallen" ["Nightingales"], which is modeled on a folksong: this constellation is Eichendorff. The itinerant musician says, "In der Nacht dann Liebchen lauschte / An dem Fenster süss verwacht" ["Then in the night my darling listened / at the window, sweetly half-awake"], an image of a woman with wild hair, enmeshed in dream, an image that cannot be captured by any precise conception but which is made more magical than any description could be by the syncopation of expression that merges the girl's sweetness with her fatigue. In the same spirit, she is elsewhere called "a sweet dreamy child". At times in Eichendorff words are simply babbled out without control, and in their extreme looseness they approach the archaic past: "Lied, mit Tränen halb geschrieben" ["A song half written with tears"].

A concept of culture that reduces the arts to a single common denominator is not worth much; we can see this in German literature, which,
since Lessing pitted Shakespeare against classicism, has, in complete
opposition to the great classical German music and philosophy, aimed
not at integration, system, a subjectively created unity in multiplicity,
but at relaxation and dissociation. Eichendorff secretly participates in this
undercurrent in German literature, which flows from *Sturm und Drang*
and the young Goethe through Georg Büchner and much in Gerhart
Hauptmann to Franz Wedekind, Expressionism, and Brecht. His poetry
is not "subjectivistic" in the way one tends to think of Romanticism as
being: it raises a mute objection to the poetic subject, a sacrifice to the
impulses of language. There is scarcely any writer whom Dilthev's
schema of experience and poetry fits worse than Eichendorff. The word
"wirr" [confused, chaotic], one of his favorites, means something completely different than the young Goethe's "dumpf" [dull, torpid, stale]:
it signals the suspension of the ego, its surrender to something surging
up chaotically, whereas Goethean dullness always referred to a self-
assured spirit in the process of formation. One of Eichendorff's poems
begins: "Ich hör die Bächlein rauschen / Im Walde her und hin, / Im
Walde in dem Rauschen / Ich weiss nicht, wo ich bin" ["I hear the little
brooks rustling / to and fro in the woods, / in the woods in the rustling /
I know not where I am"]; this poetry never knows where "I" am, because
the ego squanders itself on what it is whispering about. The metaphor of
the little brooks that rustle "to and fro" is brilliantly false, for brooks
flow in one direction only, but the back and forth movement mirrors the
agitated quality of what the sound says to the ego, which listens instead
of localizing it; such expressions anticipate a bit of Impressionism as
well. The poem "Zwielicht," a special favorite of Thomas Mann, takes
this to an extreme. In the hunting scene in Eichendorff's novel *Ahnung
und Gegenwart,* in which it is embedded, the poem retains a certain
surface intelligibility, motivated by jealousy. But that does not go very
far. The line "Wolken ziehn wie schwere Träume" ["clouds move like
heavy dreams"] procures for the poem the specific kind of meaning
contained in the German word *Wolken,* as distinguished for example
from the French *nuage:* in this line it is the word *Wolken* and what
accompanies it, and not merely the images the words signify, that move
past like heavy dreams. And in the continuation especially, the poem,
isolated from the novel, bears witness to the self-estrangement of the ego
that has divested itself of itself until it reaches the madness of the schizoid
warning "Hast ein Reh du lieb vor andern, / Lass es nicht alleine grasen"

["If you love one doe above others / do not let it graze alone"], and the isolate's delusions of persecution, which turn his friend into an enemy for him.

Eichendorff's renunciation of self has nothing in common with the power of material contemplation, the capacity for concreteness which the stereotype equates with poetic capacity. It is not only in the *imago* of love that his lyric poetry tends to abstractness. It scarcely ever obeys the criteria of intense sensuous experience of the world that have been derived from Goethe, Stifter, and Mörike. It thereby casts doubt on the unconditional rightness of those criteria themselves; they may be a reaction formation, an attempt to compensate for what Idealist philosophy withheld from the German spirit. In the fairy tales in the Grimm collection no forest is ever described or even given a characterization; but what forest was ever so much a forest as the one in the fairy tales? Wolfdietrich Rasch has correctly noted how infrequently lines of "heightened graphic vividness, with special optical charms," like the line "Schon funkelt das Feld wie geschliffen" ["the field sparkles as though polished"], occur in Eichendorff. But one cannot simply pose the rhetorical question whether it is really necessary to demonstrate wherein the fascination of his verses lies. For Eichendorff achieves the most extraordinary effects with a stock of images that must have been threadbare even in his day. The castle that forms the object of Eichendorff's longing is spoken of only as the castle; the obligatory stock of moonlight, hunting horns, nightingales, and mandolins is provided, but without doing much harm to Eichendorff's poetry. The fact that Eichendorff was probably the first to discover the expressive power in fragments of the *lingua mortua* contributes to this. He liberates the lyrical tonal values of foreign words. In the utopian poem "Schöne Fremde" ["Beautiful Foreigner"] the words "phantastische Nacht" ["fantastic night"] occur immediately after "Wirr wie in Träumen" ["Confused as in dreams"], and the abstract word "fantastic," archaic and virginal at the same time, evokes the whole feeling of the night, which a more exact epithet would cut to shreds. But these stage properties are brought to life not through discoveries of this kind, not by being seen in a new way, but through the constellation into which they enter. Eichendorff's lyric poetry as a whole wants to arouse the dead, as the motto at the end of the section entitled "Sängerleben" ["the life of the poet"] —a motto which is in need of a respite—postulates: "Schläft ein Lied in all Dingen, / Die da träumen fort und fort, / Und die Welt hebt an zu singen, / Triffst du nur das

Zauberwort" ["There is a song sleeping in all things / that dream on and on, / and the world begins to sing / if you only find the magic word"]. The word for which these lines, no doubt inspired by Novalis, yearn is no less than language itself. What decides whether the world sings is whether the poet manages to hit the mark, to attain the darkness of language, as if that were something already existing in itself. This is the anti-subjectivism of Eichendorff the Romantic. Here in the poet of nostalgia, in whose work much that is baroque lives on intact, there is much that recalls allegory. There are two stanzas that capture the fulfillment of his allegorical intention in almost paradigmatic fashion:

Es zog eine Hochzeit den Berg entlang,
Ich hörte die Vögel schlagen,
Da blitzten viel Reiter, das Waldhorn klang,
Das war ein lustiges Jagen!

Und eh' ich's gedacht, war alles verhallt,
Die Nacht bedecket die Runde,
Nur von den Bergen noch rauschet der Wald,
Und mich schauert im Herzensgrunde.

[A wedding party was coming along the mountain, / I heard the birds calling, / many riders flashed by, the hunting horn sounded, / that was a merry hunt! / And before I knew it, / all had died out, / night fell on the group, / only the forest still rustled from the mountains, / and I trembled deep in my heart.]

In this vision of the wedding party that appears and then vanishes suddenly, Eichendorff's allegory, completely unexpressed and thereby all the more emphatic, aims at the very center of the nature of allegory, transience; the shudder that comes over him in the face of the ephemerality of this celebration, whose meaning is permanence, transforms the wedding back into a spirit wedding and freezes the abruptness of life into something ghostly. If the speculative philosophy of identity, in which the concrete world is spirit and spirit is nature, stood at the beginnings of German Romanticism, now, in freezing them, Eichendorff once more endows things, which have become reified, with the power to signify, to point beyond themselves. This momentary lightning flash from a thing-world that is still quivering with life internally may explain to some extent the unfading quality of the process of fading in Eichendorff. One poem begins, "Aus der heimat hinter den Blitzen rot" ["Out of the homeland behind the red lightning"], as though the lightning were a congealed piece of the landscape in which father and mother have long lain dead, an indicator of mourning. In the same way, the bright bands of sunlight between thunderclouds resemble lightning that might flash from them. None of Eichendorff's images is only what it is, and yet none can be reduced to a single concept: this lack of resolution of allegorical moments is his poetic medium.

Only the medium, of course. In Eichendorff's poetry the images are truly only elements, consigned to annihilation within the poem itself. Fifty years ago, in his book *Das Stilgesetz der Poesie* [*The Stylistic Law of Poetry*], a project whose execution is as humble as its conception is daring, the now forgotten German aesthetician Theodor Meyer, who was certainly not familiar with Mallarmé, developed a theory directed against Lessing's *Laocoon* and the tradition derived from it. These sentences from the book provide a fair summary of it:

> If we look more closely, we might find that such sensory images [*Sinnenbilder*] cannot be created with language, that language puts its own stamp on everything that passes through it, including the sensory; that it thus presents us the life the poet offers us for our vicarious enjoyment in the form of psychic structures [*psychische Gebilde*] that, in contrast to the phenomena of sensory reality, are suitable only for our faculty of inner representation [*Vorstellung*]. In that case language would be not the vehicle but the representational means [*Darstellungsmittel*] of poetry. For we would receive the substance of poetry not in sensory images that language would suggest but in language itself and in the structures created by it and peculiar to it alone. One sees that the question of the representational means of poetry is not an idle one; it immediately becomes the question of art's ties to sensory phenomena. If it should be the case that the doctrine of language as vehicle is an error which must fall by the wayside, then the definition of art as contemplation [*Anschauung*] will fall with it.[2]

This fits Eichendorff exactly. "Language as the representational means of poetry," as something autonomous, is his divining rod. The subject's self-extinction is in the service of language. Someone who does not wish to preserve himself discovers these lines for himself: "Und so muss ich, wie im Strome dort die Welle, / Ungehört verrauschen an des Frühlings Schwelle" ["And so like the wave there in the flood I must / die away, unheard, on the threshold of spring"]. The subject turns itself into

Rauschen, the rushing, rustling, murmuring sound of nature: into language, living on only in the process of dying away, like language. The act in which the human being becomes language, the flesh becomes word, incorporates the expression of nature into language and transfigures the movement of language so that it becomes life again. "Rauschen" was Eichendorff's favorite word, almost a formula; Borchardt's "Ich habe nichts als Rauschen" ["I have nothing but murmuring"] could stand as the motto of Eichendorff's poetry and prose. To associate it all too quickly with music, however, would be to miss the sense of this *Rauschen*. *Rauschen* is not a sound [*Klang*] but a noise [*Geräusch*], more closely akin to language than to sound, and Eichendorff himself presents it as similar to language. "He quickly left the place," the narrator says of the hero of Eichendorff's novella *Das Marmorbild* [*The Marble Statue*], "and without stopping to rest he hurried out again through the gardens and vineyards to the peaceful city; for now the rustling of the trees as well appeared to him as a continual secret perceptible whispering, and the tall spectral poplars seemed to reach out for him with their long stretched-out shadows." This again is allegorical in nature: as though nature had become a meaningful language for this melancholy man. But in Eichendorff's writing the allegorical intention is borne not so much by nature, to which he ascribes it in this passage, as by his language in its distance from meaning. It imitates *Rauschen* and solitary nature. It thereby expresses an estrangement which no thought, only pure sound can bridge. But also the opposite. Things, which have grown cold, are brought back to themselves by the similarity of their names to themselves, and the movement of language awakens that resemblance. A potential contained in the work of the young Goethe, the nocturnal landscape in his poem "Willkommen und Abschied" ["Welcome and Farewell"], becomes a law of form in Eichendorff's work: the law of language as a second nature, in which the objectified nature that has been lost to the subject returns as an animated nature. It is hardly accidental that Eichendorff came very close to being aware of this in a song he wrote for Goethe's birthday celebration in 1831, his last: "Wie rauschen nun Wälder und Quellen / Und singen vom ewigen Port" ["How the forests and springs murmur / and sing of the eternal port"]. Proust says that the world itself looks different since Renoir painted his paintings. Here, in a profound look at Goethe's poetry, something of immense significance is celebrated: through his poetry, nature itself has changed; through Goethe, nature has become a murmuring, rustling nature, that which murmurs [*die Rauschende*]. But the "port" which, in Eichendorff's interpretation, the woods and springs are singing of is reconciliation with things through language. Language transcends itself to become music only by virtue of that reconciliation. The stage-prop quality of the linguistic elements in Eichendorff does not contradict this; it is the prerequisite for it. In Eichendorff's writing the stereotypical symbols of an already reified Romanticism represent the disenchantment of the world, and it is precisely in them that this awakening through self-sacrifice is achieved. As in Brecht's poem about Lao Tse, only what is most delicate has the strength to oppose what is most rigid: "Daβ das weiche Wasser in Bewegung mit der Zeit den Stein besiegt. Du verstehst" ["That the soft water in time conquers the stone with its movement. You understand"]. The soft water with its movement: that is the descending flow of language, the direction it flows of its own accord, but the poet's power is the power to be weak, the power not to resist the descending flow of language rather than the power to control it. It is as defenseless against the accusation of triviality as the elements are; but what it succeeds in doing—washing words away from their circumscribed meanings and causing them to light up when they come in contact with one another—demonstrates the pedantic poverty of such objections.

Eichendorff's greatness should be sought not where he is best defended but where the vulnerability of his demeanor is most exposed. The poem "Sehnsucht" ["Longing"] reads:

Es schienen so golden die Sterne,
Am Fenster ich einsam stand
Und hörte aus weiter Ferne
Ein Posthorn im stillen Land.
Das Herz mir im Leibe entbrennte,
Da hab' ich mir heimlich gedacht:
Ach, wer da mitreisen könnte
In der prächtigen Sommernacht!

Zwei junge Gesellen gingen
Vorüber am Bergeshang,
Ich hörte im Wandern sie singen
Die stille Gegend entlang:
Von schwindelnden Felsenschlüften,
Wo die Wälder rauschen so sacht,
Von Quellen, die von den Klüften
Sich stürzen in die Waldesnacht.

Sie sangen von Marmorbildern,
Von Gärten, die überm Gestein
In dämmernden Lauben verwildern,
Palästen im Mondenschein,
Wo die Mädschen am Fenster lauschen,
Wann der Lauten Klang erwacht
Und die Brunnen verschlafen rauschen
In der prächtigen Sommernacht.

[The stars were shining so golden, / I stood alone at the window / and
heard from far in the distance / a posthorn in the quiet countryside. / My
heart caught fire in my body / and I secretly thought to myself: / Oh, if
one could journey alone / in the magificent summer night! / Two young
journeymen were passing by / on the mountain slope, / I heard them sing
as they wandered / through the silent region: / of dizzying ravines / where
the woods rustle so gently, / of springs that plunge from gorges / into the
forest night. / They sang of marble statues, / of gardens running wild on
rocky ground / in twilit bowers, / palaces in the moonlight, / where the
maidens listen at the window / when the sound of the lutes awakens / and
the fountains murmur sleepily / in the magnificent summer night.]

This poem, as immortal as any ever written, contains almost no feature
that is not demonstrably derivative, but each of these features is transformed in character through its contact with the others. What could one
say of a nocturnal landscape that is less compelling than that it is quiet,
and what is more cliched than the posthorn; but the posthorn in the quiet
countryside, the profound paradox that the sound, the aura of silence,
does not kill the silence so much as make it silence, carries us giddily
beyond the familiar, and through its contrast with the one that precedes
it, the very next line, "Das Herz mir im Leibe entbrennte," with its
unusual imperfect ["entbrennte" for "entbrannte"] which seems unable to
free itself of the violent throbbing of the present, vouchsafes a dignity
and forcefulness completely foreign to any of the words in isolation. Or:
how weak by any criterion of refinement is the attribute "magnificent"
for the summer night. But this adjective's associational field encompasses
humanly created beauty, all the riches of fabric and embroidery, and
thereby brings the image of the starry sky close to the archaic image of
the cloak and the tent: the portentous reminder of those archaic images
makes it glow. The four lines about the mountains obviously depend on
those in Goethe's "Kennst du das Land," but how far from Goethe's
powerful and spellbinding "Es stürzt der Fels und über ihn die Flut"

["The rock plunges and over it the torrent"] is the *pianissimo* of Eichendorff's "where the woods rustle so softly," the paradox of a light rustling still perceptible virtually only in an inner acoustical space, into which the heroic landscape dissolves, sacrificing the sharpness of the images to their dissolution in open infinity. Similarly, the Italy of the poem is not the confirmed goal of the senses but only an allegory of longing, full of the expression of transience, of "something that has run wild"; it is hardly the present. But the transcendence of longing is captured in the end of the poem, a brilliant formal idea that springs from the poem's metaphysical substance. The poem circles back to close up as in a musical recapitulation. The magnificent summer night appears once again, as the fulfillment of the longing of the one who wanted to journey along in the magnificent summer night—longing itself. The poem twines, as it were, around Goethe's title "Selige Sehnsucht" ["Blessed longing"]: longing opens out onto itself as its proper goal, just as the one who yearns experiences his own situation in the infinity of longing, its transcendence beyond all specificity; just as love is always directed as much to love itself as to the beloved. For when the last image of the poem reaches the maidens listening at the window, the poem reveals itself to be an erotic one; but the silence in which Eichendorff always cloaks desire is transformed into that supreme idea of happiness in which fulfillment reveals itself to be longing, the eternal contemplation of the godhead.

⧓

Both in the periodization of intellectual history and in terms of his own character, Eichendorff belongs to the declining phase of German Romanticism. He was acquainted with many of those in the first generation of Romantics, Clemens Brentano among them, but the bond seems to have been broken; it is no accident that he confused German Idealism, in Schlegel's words one of the great currents of the age, with rationalism. Misunderstanding them completely, he accused Kant's succcessors—he had insightful and respectful things to say about Kant himself—of "a kind of decorative Chinese painting without the shadows that make the image come alive," and he criticized them for simply "negating as disturbing and superfluous the mysterious and inscrutable elements that permeate all of human existence." The break in tradition indicated by these uninformed sentences, written by one who had himself studied in Heidelberg during its years of greatness, is in accordance with Eichendorff's attitude toward the legacy of Romanticism. Far from diminishing the worth of Eichendorff's poetry, however, these historical reflections only demonstrate the silliness of a point of view based on the schema of rise, high point, and decline. More devolved upon Eichendorff's writings than upon those of the initiators of German Romanticism, who were already a historical phenomenon to him and whom he scarcely understood. If Romanticism, as Kierkegaard, another of its epigones, said, baptizes every experience with oblivion and dedicates it to the eternity of remembrance, then in order to do full justice to the idea of Romanticism, a memory that was in contradiction to Romanticism's own immediacy and presence would be needed. It is only words now defunct, spoken by Eichendorff's own mouth, that have returned to nature; only mourning for the lost moment has preserved what the living moment continues, even today, to miss.

Coda: Schumann's Lieder

Schumann's *Liederkreis* opus 39, on poems by Eichendorff, is one of the great lyric song cycles in music. From Schubert's *Schöne Müllerin* and *Winterreise* through Schönberg's *Georgelieder* opus 15, the song cycle constitutes a form unto itself, one that avoids the danger inherent in all song, that of prettifying the music by putting it into small genre-like formats, through a process of construction: the whole emerges from the complex of miniature-like elements. The quality of Schumann's cycle has never been in doubt, any more than the fact that its quality is linked to his felicitous choice of great poetry. Many of Eichendorff's most important poems are among those included, and the few that are not inspired composition through certain unique features. These songs have rightly been called "congenial," equally great in words and music. But that does not mean that they merely reproduced the lyric content of the texts; if they had, they would be superfluous by the criterion of utmost artistic economy. Rather, they bring out a potential contained in the poems, the transcendence into song that arises in the movement beyond all specificity of image and concept, in the rustling and murmuring of language's flow. The brevity of the texts selected—no composition other than the virtually extraterritorial third song is longer than two pages—permits extreme precision in each one and precludes mechanical repetition from the outset. For the most part we are dealing with songs in stanzas with variations; occasionally we have tripartite song forms of the a-b-a-b type, and in some cases completely unconventional forms ending in an *Abge-sang*. The specific characters of the songs are balanced against one another with great precision, whether through increasingly emphatic contrasts or through transitions that link them to one another. It is precisely the sharp contouring of the individual characteristics that makes an overall plan necessary if the whole is not to splinter off into details; the perennial question of whether the composer was conscious of such a plan becomes irrelevant in the face of the actual composition. Critics are constantly referring to Schumann's formalism, and where it is a question of the traditional forms from which he was already alienated they are partially correct; where he creates his own forms, as in his early instrumental and vocal cycles, Schumann demonstrates not only an extremely subtle sense of form but above and beyond that a sense of form that is extremely original. Alban Berg was the first to call attention to this—very convinc-ingly—is his exemplary analysis of Schumann's "Träumerei" and its place within the *Kinderszenen* [*Scenes from Childhood,* opus 15]. The structure of the Eichendorff songs, which are related to the *Kinderszenen* in many respects, demands similar analysis if we are to go beyond merely reaffirming their beauty.

The structure of Schumann's *Liederkreis* is intimately related to the content of the texts. The title *Liederkreis* [*Song Cycle*], which originated with Schumann, must be taken literally: the sequence is linked together in terms of the keys of the individual songs and at the same time follows a modulatory course from the melancholy of the first song, in F sharp minor, to the ecstasy of the last in F sharp major. Like the *Kinderszenen,* the whole is divided into two parts; an extremely simple symmetrical relationship with the caesura after the sixth song. The caesura should be marked with a definite break. The last song in the first part, "Schöne Fremde" ["Beautiful Stranger"], is in B major, with a marked ascent into the region of the dominant; the last song in the whole cycle is in F sharp major, a fifth up from B major. This architectonic relationship expresses a poetic one: the sixth song ends in the utopia of a great future happiness, in anticipation; the last song, "Frühlingsnacht" ["Spring Night"], ends in rejoicing: "Sie ist Deine, sie ist dein" ["She is yours, she is yours"], in the present. The caesura is made more emphatic through the arrangement of the keys of the individual songs. The songs in the first part are all written in keys with sharps. At the beginning of the second part there are two songs in the key of A minor, without a key signature. The songs then take up the key signatures that were dominant in the first part, as in a recapitulation, until the original key of F sharp is reached, while at the same time the strongest possible modulatory intensification is effected through the shift of the key into major. The sequence of keys is balanced down to the smallest detail. The second song, in A major, presents the parallel major to the first, in A minor, and the third, in E major, the dominant of the second song's A major. The fourth sinks to G major, related to the third song's E major as its mediant, the fifth restores the preceding E major, and the sixth ascends again, to B major. Of the two A minor songs in the second part, the first closes on a dominant chord that evokes the memory of E major. The following song, "In der Fremde" ["Abroad"], is in A major instead of A minor, and the next one again reaches E major as the dominant of A major, in analogy to the architectonic relationship of the third to the second song. Similarly, the tenth song, in E minor, corresponds to the fourth, in G major, both in keys with only one sharp. In place of the E major of the fifth song, however, the eleventh song offers only A major and thereby gives the utmost modulatory emphasis to the transition into the extreme key of F sharp major through the great distance between them.

These harmonic proportions provide the cycle with its internal form. It begins with two lyrical pieces, the first sad and the second in a tone of forced cheerfulness. The third, "Waldesgespräch" ["Forest Dialogue"], the Lorelei ballad, presents a contrast, both in its narrative tone and in its broader scope and two-stanza structure; it occupies a special position in the first part, similar to that of "Wehmut" ["Melancholy"] in the second. The fourth and fifth songs return to the intimate tone but intensify its delicacy, "Die Stille" ["Silence"] being a *piano* song and "Mondnacht" ["Moonnight"] a *pianissimo* song. The sixth song, "Schöne Fremde" brings the first great outburst. The second part of the cycle is opened by a piece that lies between song and ballad, and in the song that follows it the lyric expression is also given in the medium of narrative. Formally, "Wehmut," which follows, is an intermezzo, as "Waldgespräch" was, but a thoroughly lyrical one—the self-reflection, as it were, of the cycle. The tenth song, "Zwielicht" ["Twilight"] reaches, as the poem demands, the center of gravity of the whole cycle, the deepest, darkest point of feeling. It continues to reverberate in the eleventh song, "Im Walde" ["In the Forest"], a vision of the hunt. Followed, finally, in the starkest contrast of the whole cycle, by the exaltation of "Frühlingsnacht."

A few comments on the individual songs: the first, "In der Heimat hinter den Blitzen rot" is marked "Nicht schnell" [not fast] and for that reason is almost always taken too slowly; one should think of it in terms of peaceful half notes, not quarter notes. Especially striking are the dissonant chordal accents; the short middle section has a pale, shimmering major, with short motivic spurts in the piano part; an indescribably expressive harmonic variation occurs on the words "Da ruhe ich auch" ["Then I will rest too"]. In the cycle as a whole this song has an introductory function. It does not extend beyond itself melodically and works primarily with intervals of seconds. The second song, "Dein Bildnis wunderselig" ["Your Divinely Lovely Likeness"], the song most like Schumann's Heine songs, has an urgent middle section whose impulse achieves fulfillment in the recapitulation. The recapitulation begins with an extension of the dominant in the absence of the tonic, so that the harmonic stream flows out over the formal divisions. Once again we see the beginnings of independent secondary voices, a kind of sketched-in harmonic counterpoint characteristic of the style of the work as a whole; the postlude is consistent, working with imitations of the theme through its inversion. The third song, "Waldesgespräch" is one of those prototypical Schumann forms that gave rise to Brahms. The form is organized through the contrast between the ballad narrative and the ghostly voice. Most original, musically speaking, are the discordant, chromatically altered chords that express the menacing attraction. The fourth song, which is sung as a monologue, has an abrupt outburst in the middle section and immediately becomes soft again. A subdominant chord is struck on the word "wissen"; the double suspended notes give it the tonal quality of a triangle. As Goethe said, it is difficult to speak about things that have been extremely influential, and this is true of "Mondnacht," the fifth song. But one can at least point out the features in its composition, which is clarity itself become sound, through which it avoids monotony, such as the additional friction provided by the seconds on the words "durch die Felder" in the second stanza. The song's trademark is the great ninth chord with which it begins. Through the way it is set and the way it is resolved in figuration, the chord avoids the opulent quality it often takes on in Wagner, Strauss, and later composers. Instead, the layered thirds suggest the feeling of the poem: the ear extends the intervals on beyond what is really sounding, as if into infinity, while at the same time the continuation of the third interval preserves the clarity whose relationship to the infinite produces the song's tonality. The form approaches the structure of the medieval lyric and *Meistergesang;* like an *Abgesang,* the last stanza reproduces the poem's expansive gesture, while the last two lines recapitulate the beginning and close off the transcendent structure. No ear that has once heard the rhythmical extension on the closing word "Als flöge sie nach Haus" ["As though it were flying home"], where two measures in ⅜ time are made into one measure in ¾ time, can resist it. This *ritardando,* effected through the composition, gave rise to a technique of Brahms that eventually broke Schumann's unchallenged superiority in the eight-measure period. The sixth song, "Schöne Fremde" begins on the mediant in a kind of floating tonality, so that the A major of the ecstatic conclusion sounds as though it had not been there from the beginning but had been produced by the course of the melody; the word "phantastisch" is mirrored in a dissonance that is sweetly urgent. Here too the concluding stanza is clearly of the nature of an *Abgesang;* but the song as a whole abstains from the symmetry of repetition; with truly unheard-of freedom, it flows in the directions its melodic and harmonic intentions take it.

"Auf einer Burg" ["In a Castle"], the Gothic piece with which the second half of the *Liederkreis* begins, is distinguished by its bold dissonances, probably unique in Schumann and the early nineteenth century, which result from the collision of the melodic line and the chorale-like ties in the accompaniment, which moves step-wise; it is as though the modernity of this harmonization were an attempt to protect the poem from aging. The eighth song "Ich hör die Bächlein rauschen" ["I hear the little brooks rushing"], with its subdued haste, is composed of utterly simple two-beat measures without any rhythmical variation, but it has such expressive harmonic nuances and such a sharp accent at the end that it emanates the wildest kind of agitation. The adagio intermezzo "Wehmut," the ninth song, maintains an unbroken legato of harmonic instrumental voices; the modulatory detour into the subdominant region on the word "Sehnsucht," however, casts an oblique, melancholy light on it for a second, a light that seems to come from outside; against the D major which it suggests, the tonic key E major seems to glow with a sickly light. In stark contrast to the preceding song, "Zwielicht," the tenth song, a simple stanzaic song in form and perhaps the most wonderful piece in the cycle, is contrapuntal, in that infinitely productive reinterpretation of Bach to which historicism objects while in fact Bach thus transformed enjoys a genuine afterlife. The prototype which has been reconceived here is no doubt the theme from the B minor fugue in the first volume of the *Well-Tempered Clavier*. The C in the counterpoint in the second measure, taken from the harmonic minor scale, has a kind of heaviness that is then communicated to the whole, horizontally and vertically, pulling the music as a whole down into the depths. The first and second stanzas end with the dark sound of a long echoing chord, as though the song were sounding in a hollow space; the third stanza, "Hast du einen Freund hienieden" ["If you have a friend here below"] strengthens the contrapuntal fabric by adding a third independent voice; the fourth, finally, simplifies the song by making it homophonic, keeping the identical melody, and the remarkable last line, "Hüte dich, sei wach und munter," is made as concise as possible, like a recitative. The song that follows, "Im Walde" ["In the Forest"], is produced by the repetition of the horn sound and the repeated opposition of *ritardando* and *a tempo*, which, incidentally, creates extraordinary difficulties in performance. Schumann's sense of form triumphs: as though to balance out the stubborn retarding moments, he writes an extremely haunting *Abgesang*, which glides with utter smoothness and yet keeps time to the rhythm of the horn, down to the last two notes in the vocal part. The "Frühlingsnacht," finally, as famous as "Es wär, als hätt' der Himmel," seems to have been created with a single stroke, as if in mockery of analytic examination; but its unity is produced precisely by the articulation of its compressed course. As in the "Mondnacht," the idea of the song—here that of the person reaching out beyond himself in ecstasy—is implicit in the opening material. The melody has as its nucleus a transcribed seventh chord. The seventh interval in the chord has melodic import; its impetus moves beyond the triadic thirds and interspersed seconds and, in a compositional space that is otherwise defined by the latter, helps to give voice to a subjectivity that breaks its bonds. But Schumann's genius did not stop at the symbolism of affects but rather moved the critical seventh interval back into the center structurally. The interval is hinted at in the sequence of beginnings and endings of phrases in "Jauchzen möcht' ich, möchte weinen" ["I would like to shout with joy, would like to weep"]; at the word "Sterne" [stars] it takes hold of the vocal part, and finally, before the words "Sie ist Deine," it is varied in the accompanying phrase in the piano accompaniment so that the motivic sequence matches the curve of feeling. This song of the most extreme explosion of feeling is a *piano* song, returning to its quiet basis after each wave, and it owes its breathless quality, which is discharged only in the *forte* of these two lines, to this. The middle movement, "Jauchzen möcht' ich, möchte weinen," sets up an opposing voice, once again only hinted at, to the coursing chordal accompaniment without interrupting its movement. The breathless quality reaches its climax at the point immediately before the words "Mit dem Mondesglanz herein" ["In with the moonlight"], where a good portion of the measure is left vacant. The repetition of the first stanza leads to the climax, not only through the harmonic and melodic variants but because at the decisive point the counterpoint in the middle section is added, now completely free and fulfilling, and it carries over into the postlude, where the motif, true rejoicing, leaves everything else behind, forgotten.

Heine the Wound

*A*nyone who wants to make a serious contribution to remembering Heine on the centennial of his death and not merely deliver a formal speech will have to speak about a wound; about what in Heine and his relationship to the German tradition causes us pain and what has been repressed, especially in Germany since the Second World War. Heine's name is an irritant, and only someone who addresses that without white-washing it can hope to be of aid.

The National Socialists were not the first to defame Heine. In fact, they almost honored him when they put the now famous words "Author Unknown" under his poem "Die Loreley," thus unexpectedly sanction-ing as a folksong the secretly scintillating verses that remind one of Parisian Rhine nymphs from a long-lost Offenbach opera. Heine's *Book of Songs* had a stupendous influence, extending far beyond literary circles. In its train lyric poetry was ultimately drawn down into the language of commerce and the press. This is why Heine came to have such a bad name among those responsible for culture around 1900. The George Circle's verdict may be ascribed to nationalism, but that of Karl Kraus cannot be erased. Since that time Heine's aura has been painful and guilt-laden, as though it were bleeding. His own guilt became an alibi for those of his enemies whose hatred for the Jewish middleman ultimately paved the way for the unspeakable horror.

One who confines himself to Heine as a prose writer avoids the annoyance; Heine's stature as a prose writer in the utterly dismal level of the era between Goethe and Nietzsche is immediately evident. This prose is not limited to Heine's capacity for conscious pointed linguistic formulation, a polemical power extremely rare in Germany and in no way inhibited by servility. August von Platen had the opportunity to experience it when he made an anti-Semitic attack on Heine and was disposed of in a way that would probably be called existential nowadays—if the concept of the existential were not so carefully preserved from contamination by the real existence of human beings. But in its substance Heine's prose goes far beyond such bravura pieces. After Leibniz gave Spinoza the cold shoulder, the whole German Enlightenment failed, at least in that it lost its social sting and confined itself to subservient affirmation; of all the famous names in German literature, Heine alone, for all his affinities with Romanticism, retains an undiluted concept of enlightenment. The discomfort he arouses despite his conciliatory stance comes from that harsh climate. With polite irony he refuses to smuggle right back in through the back door—or the basement door to the depths—what he has just demolished. It is questionable whether he had such a strong influence on the young Marx as many young sociologists would like to think. Politically, Heine was not a traveling companion one could count on: even of socialism. But in contrast to socialism he held fast to the idea of uncurtailed happiness in the image of a just society, an idea quickly enough disposed of in favor of slogans like "Anyone who doesn't work won't eat." His aversion to revolutionary purity and stringency is indicative of Heine's distrust of mustiness and asceticism, elements whose traces are already evident in many early socialist documents and which, much later, worked in favor of disastrous developmental tendencies. Heine the individualist—and he was so much an individualist that even in Hegel he heard only individualism—did not bow to the individualistic concept of inwardness. His idea of sensuous fulfillment encompasses fulfillment in external things, a society without coercion and deprivation.

The wound, however, is Heine's lyric poetry. At one time its immediacy was enchanting. It interpreted Goethe's dictum on the occasional poem to mean that every occasion found its poem and everyone considered the opportunity to write to be something favorable. But at the same time, this immediacy was thoroughly mediated. Heine's poems were ready mediators between art and an everyday life bereft of meaning. For them as for the feuilletonist, the experiences they processed secretly became raw materials that one could write about. The nuances and tonal values which they discovered, they made interchangeable, delivered them into the power of a prepared, ready-made language. For them the life to which they matter-of-factly bore witness was venal; their spontaneity was one with reification. In Heine commodity and exchange seized control of sound and tone, whose very nature had previously consisted in the negation of the hustle and bustle of daily life. So great had the power of a mature capitalist society become at that time that lyric poetry could no longer ignore it without descending into provincial folksiness. In this respect, Heine, like Baudelaire, looms large in the modernism of the nineteenth century. But Baudelaire, the younger of the two, heroically wrests dream and image from modernity itself, from the experience of implacable destruction and dissolution, which by then was further advanced; indeed he transfigures the loss of all images, transforming that loss itself into an image. The forces of this kind of resistance increased along with those of capitalism. In Heine, whose poems were still set to music by Schubert, they had not reached such a high level of intensity. He surrendered more willingly to the flow of things; he took a poetic technique of reproduction, as it were, that corresponded to the industrial age and applied it to the conventional romantic archetypes, but he did not find archetypes of modernity.

It is just this that later generations find embarrassing. For since the existence of a bourgeois art in which artists have to earn their livelihoods without patrons, they have secretly acknowledged the law of the marketplace alongside the autonomy of their laws of form, and have produced for consumers. It was only that this dependency was not visible behind the anonymity of the marketplace. It allowed the artist to appear pure and autonomous in the eyes of himself and others, and this illusion itself was accepted at face value. Heine the advocate of enlightenment unmasked Heine the Romantic, who had been living off the good fortune of autonomy, and brought the commodity character of his art, previously latent, to the fore. He has not been forgiven for that. The ingratiating quality of his poems, which is over-acted and hence becomes self-critical, makes it plain that the emancipation of the spirit was not the emancipation of human beings and hence was also not that of the spirit.

But the rage of the person who sees the secret of his own degradation in the confessed degradation of someone else is directed with sadistic assurance to Heine's weakest point, the failure of Jewish emancipation. For Heine's fluency and self-evidence, which is derived from the language of communications, is the opposite of a native sense of being at home in language. Only someone who is not actually inside language can manipulate it like an instrument. If the language were really his own, he would allow the dialectic between his own words and words that are pre-given to take place, and the smooth linguistic structure would disintegrate. But for the person who uses language like a book that is out of print, language itself is alien. Heine's mother, whom he loved, did not have full command of German. His lack of resistance to words that are in fashion is the excessive mimetic zeal of the person who is excluded. Assimilatory language is the language of unsuccessful identification. There is a well-known anecdote according to which the youthful Heine, when asked by the elderly Goethe what he was working on, replied "a Faust" and was thereupon ungraciously dismissed. Heine explained this incident in terms of his shyness. His impertinence sprang from the impulse of the person who wants for the life of him to be accepted and is thereby doubly irritating to those who are already established, who drown out their own guilt at excluding him by holding the vulnerability of his adaptation up to him. This continues to be the trauma of Heine's name today, and it can be healed only if it is recognized rather than left to go on leading an obscure, preconscious existence.

The possibility of that, however, is contained, as a potential for rescue, within Heine's poetry itself. For the power of the one who mocks impotently exceeds his impotence. If all expression is the trace left by suffering, then Heine was able to recast his own inadequacy, the muteness of his language, as an expression of rupture. So great was the virtuosity of this man, who imitated language as if he were playing it on a keyboard, that he raised even the inadequacy of his language to the medium of one to whom it was granted to say what he suffered. Failure, reversing itself, is transformed into success. Heine's essence is fully revealed not in the music composed to his poems but only in the songs of Gustav Mahler, written forty years after his death, songs in which the brittleness of the banal and the derivative is used to express what is most real, in the form of a wild, unleashed lament. It was not until Mahler's songs about the soldiers who flew the flag out of homesickness, not until the outbursts of the funeral march in his Fifth Symphony, until the folksongs with their harsh alternation of major and minor, until the convulsive gestures of the Mahlerian orchestra, that the music in Heine's verses was released. In the mouth of a stranger, what is old and familiar takes on an extravagant and exaggerated quality, and precisely that is the truth. The figures of this truth are the aesthetic breaks; it forgoes the immediacy of rounded, fulfilled language.

The following stanzas appear in the cycle of poems that Heine, the emigrant, called *Der Heimkehr* [*The Return Home*]:

Mein Herz mein Herz ist traurig,
Doch lustig leuchtet der Mai;
Ich stehe, gelehnt an der Linde,
Hoch auf der alten Bastei.

Da drunten fließt der blaue
Stadtgraben in stiller Ruh;
Ein Knabe fährt im Kahne,
Und angelt und pfeift dazu.

Jenseits erheben sich freundlich,
In winziger, bunter Gestalt,
Lusthäuser und Gärten und Menschen,
und Ochsen und Wiesen und Wald.

Die Mägde bleichen Wäsche,
Und springen im Gras herum:
das Mühlrad staubt Diamanten,
Ich höre sein fernes Gesumm.

Am alten grauen Turme
Ein Schilderhäuschen steht;
Ein rotgeröckter Bursche
Dort auf und nieder geht.

Er spielt mit seiner Flinte,
Die funkelt im Sonnenrot,
Er präsentiert und schultert—
Icht wollt, er schösse mich tot.

[My heart, my heart is heavy,
Though joyously shines the May,
As I stand 'neath the lime-tree leaning
High on the ramparts grey.

The moat winds far beneath me;
On its waters calm and blue
A boy in his boat is drifting,
Fishing and whistling too.

Beyond, like a smiling picture,
Little and bright, lie strewed
Villas and gardens and people
Cattle and meadows and wood.

The maidens are bleaching linen—
They skip on the grass and play;
The mill-wheel scatters diamonds,
Its drone sounds, far away.

A sentry-box is standing
The old grey keep below,
And a lad in a coat of scarlet
Paces there to and fro.

He handles and plays with his musket—
It gleams in the sunset red,
He shoulders and presents it—
I would that he shot me dead!
(translation by M. M. B., in *Heine's Prose and Poetry*, [New York:
    Dutton, 1934], pp. 27–28)]

It has taken a hundred years for this intentionally false folksong to
become a great poem, a vision of sacrifice. Heine's stereotypical theme,
unrequited love, is an image for homelessness, and the poetry devoted to
it is an attempt to draw estrangement itself into the sphere of intimate
experience. Now that the destiny which Heine sensed has been fulfilled
literally, however, the homelessness has also become everyone's homelessness; all human beings have been as badly injured in their beings and
their language as Heine the outcast was. His words stand in for their
words: there is no longer any homeland other than a world in which no
one would be cast out any more, the world of a genuinely emancipated
humanity. The wound that is Heine will heal only in a society that has
achieved reconciliation.

Looking Back on Surrealism

The currently accepted theory of Surrealism, which was set down in Breton's manifestos but also dominates the secondary literature, links it with dreams, the unconscious, and perhaps Jungian archetypes, which are said to have found in collages and automatic writing an emancipated image-language uncontaminated by the conscious ego. Dreams, according to this theory, treat the elements of the real the way the method of Surrealism does. If, however, no art is required to understand itself—and one is tempted to consider art's self-understanding and its success almost incompatible—then it is not necessary to fall in line with this programmatic view, which is repeated by those who expound Surrealism. What is deadly about the interpretation of art, moreover, even philosophically responsible interpretation, is that in the process of conceptualization it is forced to express what is strange and surprising in terms of what is already familiar and thereby to explain away the only thing that would need explanation. To the extent to which works of art insist on explanation, every one of them, even if against its own intentions, perpetrates a piece of betrayal to conformity. Were Surrealism in fact nothing but a collection of literary and graphic illustrations of Jung or even Freud, it would not only duplicate, superfluously, what the theory itself says rather than giving it a metaphorical garb, but it would also be so innocuous that it would hardly leave room for the scandal that is Surrealism's intention and its lifeblood. Reducing Surrealism to psychological dream theory subjects it to the ignominy of something official. Companion piece to the well-versed "That is a father figure" is the self-satisfied "Yes, we know," and, as Cocteau well knew, something that is supposed to be a mere dream always leaves reality untouched, whatever damage is done to its image.

But that theory does not do justice to the matter. That is not the way people dream; no one dreams that way. Surrealist constructions are merely analogous to dreams, not more. They suspend the customary logic and the rules of the game of empirical evidence but in doing so respect the individual objects that have been forcibly removed from their context and bring their contents, especially their human contents, closer to the form of the object. There is a shattering and a regrouping, but no dissolution. The dream, to be sure, does the same thing, but in the dream the object world appears in a form incomparably more disguised and is presented as reality less than it is in Surrealism, where art batters its own foundations. The subject, which is at work much more openly and uninhibitedly in Surrealism than in the dream, directs its energy toward its own self-annihilation, something that requires no energy in the dream; but because of that everything becomes more objective, so to speak, than in the dream, where the subject, absent from the start, colors and permeates everything that happens from the wings. In the meantime the Surrealists themselves have discovered that people do not free associate the way they, the Surrealists, write, even in psychoanalysis. Furthermore, even the spontaneity of psychoanalytic associations is by no means spontaneous. Every analyst knows how much trouble and exertion, how much effort of will is required to master the involuntary expression that occurs through these efforts, even in the psychoanalytic situation, to say nothing of the artistic situation of the Surrealists. It is not the unconscious in itself that comes to light in the world-rubble of Surrealism. Assessed in terms of their relationship to the unconscious, the symbols would prove much too rationalistic. This kind of decoding would force the luxuriant multiplicity of Surrealism into a few patterns and reduce it to a few meager categories like the Oedipus complex, without attaining the power that emanated from the idea of Surrealism if not from its works of art; Freud too seems to have responded to Dali this way.

After the European catastrophe the Surrealist shocks lost their force. It is as though they had saved Paris by preparing it for fear: the destruction of the city was their center. To conceptualize Surrealism along these lines, one must go back not to psychology but to Surrealism's artistic techniques. Unquestionably, they are patterned on the montage. One could easily show that even genuine Surrealist painting works with its motifs and that the discontinuous juxtaposition of images in Surrealist lyric poetry is montage-like. But these images derive, as we know, in part literally and in part in spirit from the late nineteenth-century illustrations that belonged to the world of the parents of Max Ernst's generation. There were collections in existence as early as the 1920s, outside the sphere of Surrealism, like Alan Bott's *Our Fathers*, which partook—parasitically—of Surrealist shock and by doing so dispensed with the strain of alienation through montage as a kindness to the audience. Authentic Surrealist practice, however, replaced those elements with unfamiliar ones. It is precisely the latter which, through fright, gave that material the aspect of something familiar, the quality of "Where have I seen that before?" Hence one may assume that the affinity with psychoanalysis lies not in a symbolism of the unconscious but in the attempt to uncover childhood experiences by means of explosions. What Surrealism adds to illustrations of the world of objects is the element of childhood we lost; when we were children, those illustrated papers, already obsolete even then, must have leaped out at us the way Surrealist images do now. The subjective aspect in this lies in the action of the montage, which attempts—perhaps in vain, but the intention is unmistakable—to produce perceptions as they must have been then. The giant egg from which the monster of the Last Judgment can creep forth at any moment is so big because we were so small the first time we looked at an egg and shuddered.

Obsoleteness contributes to this effect. It seems paradoxical for something modern, already under the spell of the sameness of mass production, to have any history at all. This paradox estranges it, and in the "Children's Pictures for the Modern Age" it becomes the expression of a subjectivity that has become estranged from itself as well as from the world. The tension in Surrealism that is discharged in shock is the tension between schizophrenia and reification; hence it is specifically not a tension of psychological inspiration. In the face of total reification, which throws it back upon itself and its protest, a subject that has become absolute, that has full control of itself and is free of all consideration of the empirical world, reveals itself to be inanimate, something virtually dead. The dialectical images of Surrealism are images of a dialectic of subjective freedom in a situation of objective unfreedom. In them, European *Weltschmerz* turns to stone, like the pain of Niobe, who lost her children; in them bourgeois society abandons its hopes of survival. One can hardly assume that any of the Surrealists were familiar with Hegel's *Phenomenology*, but a sentence from it, which must be considered in conjunction with the more general thesis that history is progress in the consciousness of freedom, defines the substance of Surrealism: "The sole work and deed of universal freedom therefore is *death*, a death too which has no inner significance or filling."[1] Surrealism adopted this critique as its own; this explains its anti-anarchistic political impulses, which, however, were incompatible with its substance. It has been said that in Hegel's thesis the Enlightenment abolishes itself by realizing itself; the cost of comprehending Surrealism is equally high—it must be understood not as a language of immediacy but as witness to abstract freedom's reversion to the supremacy of objects and thus to mere nature. The montages of Surrealism are the true still lives. In making compositions out of what is out of date, they create *nature morte*.

These images are not images of something inward; rather, they are fetishes—commodity fetishes—on which something subjective, libido, was once fixated. It is through these fetishes, not through immersion in the self, that the images bring back childhood. Surrealism's models would be pornography. The things that happen in the collages, the things that are convulsively suspended in them like the tense lines of lasciviousness around a mouth, are like the changes that occur in a pornographic image at the moment when the voyeur achieves gratification. Breasts that have been cut off, mannequin's legs in silk stockings in the collages—these are mementos of the objects of the partial drives that once aroused the libido. Thinglike and dead, in them what has been forgotten reveals itself to be the true object of love, what love wants to make itself resemble, what we resemble. As a freezing of the moment of awakening, Surrealism is akin to photography. Surrealism's booty is images, to be sure, but not the invariant, ahistorical images of the unconscious subject to which the conventional view would like to neutralize them; rather, they are historical images in which the subject's innermost core becomes aware that it is something external, an imitation of something social and historical. "Come on Joe, imitate that old-time music."*

In this respect, however, Surrealism forms the complement to the *Neue Sachlichkeit*, or New Objectivity, which came into being at the same time. The *Neue Sachlichkeit*'s horror of the crime of ornamentation, as Adolf Loos called it, is mobilized by Surrealist shocks. The house has a tumor, its bay window. Surrealism paints this tumor: an excrescence of

---

*A line from the "Bilbao Song" in Brecht and Weill's *Happy End:* "Geh Joe, mach die Musik von damals nach."—Translator's note.

flesh grows from the house. Childhood images of the modern era are the quintessence of what the *Neue Sachlichkeit* makes taboo because it reminds it of its own object-like nature and its inability to cope with the fact that its rationality remains irrational. Surrealism gathers up the things the *Neue Sachlichkeit* denies to human beings; the distortions attest to the violence that prohibition has done to the objects of desire. Through the distortions, Surrealism salvages what is out of date, an album of idiosyncrasies in which the claim to the happiness that human beings find denied them in their own technified world goes up in smoke. But if Surrealism itself now seems obsolete, it is because human beings are now denying themselves the consciousness of denial that was captured in the photographic negative that was Surrealism.

⊟⁝⊟⁝⊟

Punctuation Marks

The less punctuation marks, taken in isolation, convey meaning or expression and the more they constitute the opposite pole in language to names, the more each of them acquires a definitive physiognomic status of its own, an expression of its own, which cannot be separated from its syntactic function but is by no means exhausted by it. When the hero of Gottfried Keller's novel *Der grüne Heinrich* was asked about the German capital letter P, he exclaimed, "That's pumpernickel!" That experience is certainly true of the figures of punctuation. An exclamation point looks like an index finger raised in warning; a question mark looks like a flashing light or the blink of an eye. A colon, says Karl Kraus, opens its mouth wide: woe to the writer who does not fill it with something nourishing. Visually, the semicolon looks like a drooping moustache; I am even more aware of its gamey taste. With self-satisfied peasant cunning, German quotation marks [»«] lick their lips.

All of them are traffic signals; in the last analysis, traffic signals were modeled on them. Exclamation points are red, colons green, dashes call a halt. But the George Circle was wrong in mistaking them for marks of communication because of this. On the contrary, they are marks of oral delivery; instead of diligently serving the interplay between language and the reader, they serve, hieroglyphically, an interplay that takes place in the interior of language, along its own pathways. Hence it is superfluous to omit them as being superfluous: then they simply hide. Every text, even the most densely woven, cites them of its own accord—friendly spirits whose bodiless presence nourishes the body of language.

⊟⁝⊟

There is no element in which language resembles music more than in the punctuation marks. The comma and the period correspond to the half-cadence and the authentic cadence. Exclamation points are like silent cymbal clashes, question marks like musical upbeats, colons dominant seventh chords; and only a person who can perceive the different weights of strong and weak phrasings in musical form can really feel the distinction between the comma and the semicolon. But perhaps the idiosyncratic opposition to punctuation marks that arose in the early part of this century, an opposition from which no observant person can completely dissociate himself, is not so much a revolt against an ornamental element as it is the expression of how sharply music and language diverge from one another. But it can hardly be considered an accident that music's contact with the punctuation marks in language was bound up with the schema of tonality, which has since disintegrated, and that the efforts of modern music could easily be described as an attempt to create punctuation marks without tonality. But if music is forced to preserve the image of its resemblance to language in punctuation marks, then language may give in to its resemblance to music by distrusting them.

❂

The distinction between the Greek semicolon [·], a raised point whose aim is to keep the voice from being lowered, and the German one, which accomplishes the lowering with its period and its hanging lower part and yet keeps the voice suspended by incorporating the comma—truly a dialectical image—seems to reproduce the distinction between classical antiquity and the Christian Era, finitude refracted through the infinite, although it may be the case that the Greek sign currently in use was invented by the sixteenth-century Humanists. History has left its residue in punctuation marks, and it is history, far more than meaning or grammatical function, that looks out at us, rigidified and trembling slightly, from every mark of punctuation. One is almost, therefore, tempted to consider authentic only the punctuation marks in German Gothic type, or *Fraktur*, where the graphic images retain allegorical features, and to regard those of Roman type as mere secularized imitations.

❂

The historical character of punctuation marks can be seen in the fact that what becomes outdated in them is precisely what was once modern in them. Exclamation points, gestures of authority with which the writer tries to impose an emphasis external to the matter itself, have become intolerable, while the *sforzato,* the musical counterpart of the exclamation point, is as indispensable today as it was in Beethoven's time, when it marked the incursion of the subjective will into the musical fabric. Exclamation points, however, have degenerated into usurpers of authority, assertions of importance. It was exclamation points, incidentally, that gave German Expressionism its graphic form. Their proliferation was both a protest against convention and a symptom of the inability to alter the structure of language from within; language was attacked from the outside instead. Exclamation points survive as tokens of the disjunction between idea and realization in that period, and their impotent evocation redeems them in memory: a desperate written gesture that yearns in vain to transcend language. Expressionism was consumed in the flames of that gesture; it used exclamation points to vouch for its effect, and it went up in smoke along with them. Seen in German Expressionist texts today, they look like the multiple zeros on the banknotes printed during the German inflation.

⧗

Literary dilettantes can be recognized by their desire to connect everything. Their products hook sentences together with logical connectives even though the logical relationship asserted by those connectives does not hold. To the person who cannot truly conceive anything as a unity, anything that suggests disintegration or discontinuity is unbearable; only a person who can grasp totality can understand caesuras. But the dash provides instruction in them. In the dash, thought becomes aware of its fragmentary character. It is no accident that in the era of the progressive degeneration of language, this mark of punctuation is neglected precisely insofar as it fulfills its function: when it separates things that feign a connection. All the dash claims to do now is to prepare us in a foolish way for surprises that by that very token are no longer surprising.

⧗

The serious dash: its unsurpassed master in nineteenth-century German literature was Theodor Storm. Rarely have punctuation marks been so deeply allied with content as the dashes in his novellas, mute lines into the past, wrinkles on the brow of his text. With them the narrator's voice falls into an uneasy silence: the span of time they insert between two sentences is that of a burdensome heritage: set bald and naked between the events they draw together, they have something of the fatefulness of the natural context and something of a prudish hesitancy to make reference to it. So discreetly does myth conceal itself in the nineteenth century; it seeks refuge in typography.

∎∎∎

Among the losses punctuation suffers through the decay of language is the slash mark or diagonal, as used, for instance, to separate lines of a stanza of verse quoted in a piece of prose. Set as a stanza, the lines would rip the fabric of the language apart; printed simply as prose, the effect of verse is ridiculous, because the meter and the rhyme seem like unintended wordplay. The modern dash, however, is too crude to accomplish what it should in such cases. But the capacity to perceive such differences physiognomically is a prerequisite for the proper use of punctuation marks.

∎∎∎

The ellipsis, a favorite way of leaving sentences meaningfully open during the period when Impressionism became a commercialized mood, suggests an infinitude of thoughts and associations, something the hack journalist does not have; he must depend on typography to simulate them. But to reduce the three dots borrowed from the repeating decimal fractions of arithmetic to two, as the George Circle did, is to imagine that one can continue with impunity to lay claim to that fictive infinitude by costuming as exact something whose inherent intention is to be inexact. The punctuation of the brazen hack is no better than that of the modest hack.

∎∎∎

Quotation marks should be used only when something is quoted and if need be when the text wants to distance itself from a word it is referring to. They are to be rejected as an ironic device. For they exempt the writer from the spirit whose claim is inherent in irony, and they violate the very concept of irony by separating it from the matter at hand and presenting a predetermined judgment on the subject. The abundant ironic quotation marks in Marx and Engels are the shadows that totalitarian methods cast in advance upon their writings, whose intention was the opposite: the seed from which eventually came what Karl Kraus called *Moskauderwelsch* [Moscow double-talk, from *Moskau*, Moscow, and *Kauderwelsch*, gibberish or double-talk]. The indifference to linguistic expression shown in the mechanical delegation of intention to a typographic cliché arouses the suspicion that the very dialectic that constitutes the theory's content has been brought to a standstill and the object assimilated to it from above, without negotiation. Where there is something that needs to be said, indifference to literary form always indicates dogmatization of the content. The blind verdict of ironic quotation marks is its graphic gesture.

◨⁝◧

Theodor Haecker was rightfully alarmed by the fact that the semicolon is dying out; this told him that no one can write a period, a sentence containing several balanced clauses, any more. Part of this incapacity is the fear of page-long paragraphs, a fear created by the marketplace—by the consumer who does not want to tax himself and to whom first editors and then writers accommodated for the sake of their incomes, until finally they invented ideologies for their own accommodation, like lucidity, objectivity, and concise precision. Language and subject matter cannot be kept separate in this process. The sacrifice of the period leaves the idea short of breath. Prose is reduced to the "protocol sentence," the darling of the logical positivists, to a mere recording of facts, and when syntax and punctuation relinquish the right to articulate and shape the facts, to critique them, language is getting ready to capitulate to what merely exists, even before thought has time to perform this capitulation eagerly on its own for the second time. It starts with the loss of the semicolon; it ends with the ratification of imbecility by a reasonableness purged of all admixtures.

◨⁝◧

The test of a writer's sensitivity in punctuating is the way he handles parenthetical material. The cautious writer will tend to place that material between dashes and not in round brackets [i.e., what is commonly called parentheses, ( )], for brackets take the parenthesis completely out of the sentence, creating enclaves, as it were, whereas nothing in good prose should be unnecessary to the overall structure. By admitting such superfluousness, brackets implicitly renounce the claim to the integrity of the linguistic form and capitulate to pedantic philistinism. Dashes, in contrast, which block off the parenthetical material from the flow of the sentence without shutting it up in a prison, capture both connection and detachment. But just as blind trust in their power to do so would be illusory, in that it would expect of a mere device something that only language and subject matter can accomplish, so the choice between dashes and brackets helps us to see how inadequate abstract norms of punctuation are. Proust, whom no one can lightly call a philistine and whose pedantry is nothing but one aspect of his wonderful micrological power, did not hesitate to use brackets, presumably because in the extended periods of his sentences the parenthetical material became so long that its sheer length would have nullified the dashes. The parentheses need more solid dams if they are not to flood the whole period and promote the chaos from which each of these periods was wrested, breathlessly. But the justification for Proust's use of punctuation marks lies solely in the approach of his whole novelistic oeuvre: the illusion of the continuity of the narrative is disrupted and the asocial narrator is ready to climb in through all the openings in order to illuminate the obscure *temps durée* with the bull's eye lantern* of a memory that is by no means all so involuntary. Proust's bracketed parentheses, which interrupt both the graphic image and the narrative, are memorials to the moments when the author, weary of aesthetic illusioin and distrustful of the self-contained quality of events which he is after all only making up, openly takes the reins.

⁕⁝⁕

The writer is in a permanent predicament when it comes to punctuation marks; if one were fully aware while writing, one would sense the impossibility of ever using a mark of punctuation correctly and would give up writing altogether. For the requirements of the rules of punctuation and those of the subjective need for logic and expression are not compatible: in punctuation marks the check the writer draws on language is refused payment. The writer cannot trust in the rules, which are often rigid and crude; nor can he ignore them without indulging in a kind of eccentricity and doing harm to their nature by calling attention to what is inconspicuous—and inconspicuousness is what punctuation lives by. But if, on the other hand, he is serious, he may not sacrifice any part of his aim to a universal, for no writer today can completely identify with anything universal; he does so only at the price of affecting the archaic. The conflict must be endured each time, and one needs either a lot of strength or a lot of stupidity not to lose heart. At best one can advise that

---

*A lantern that can be closed to conceal the source of the light.—Translator's note.

punctuation marks be handled the way musicians handle forbidden chord progressions and incorrect voice-leading. With every act of punctuation, like every such musical cadence, one can tell whether there is an intention or whether it is pure sloppiness. To put it more subtly, one can sense the difference between a subjective will that brutally demolishes the rules and a tactful sensitivity that allows the rules to echo in the background even where it suspends them. This is especially evident with the most inconspicuous marks, the commas, whose mobility readily adapts to the will to expression, only, however, to develop the perfidiousness of the object, *die Tücke des Objekts,* in such close proximity to the subject and become especially touchy, making claims one would hardly expect of them. Today, certainly, one will do best to adhere to the rule "better too few than too many." For through their logical-semantic autonomy, punctuation marks, which articulate language and thereby bring writing closer to the voice, have become separate from both voice and writing, and they come into conflict with their own mimetic nature. An ascetic use of punctuation marks attempts to compensate for some of that. In every punctuation mark thoughtfully avoided, writing pays homage to the sound it suppresses.

⊟⊟⊟⊟

The Artist as Deputy

*P*aul Valéry's reception in Germany —and he has not yet really been successfully received here—presents special difficulties because Valéry's claim rests primarily on his work in lyric poetry. It goes without saying that lyric poetry cannot be transposed into a foreign language in anything remotely like the way prose can; certainly not the *poésie pure* of Valéry, the disciple of Mallarmé, which is inplacably sealed off from all communication with a hypothetical readership. It was Stefan George who said, correctly, that the task of a translation of lyric poetry is not to introduce a foreign writer but to erect a monument to him in one's own langauge, or, in the turn Benjamin gave the idea, to extend and intensify one's own language through the incursion of the foreign literary work. Despite this, or perhaps precisely because of the intransigence of his great translator,* the historical material of German literature is unimaginable without Baudelaire. The case of Valéry is altogether different; moreover, Germany remained essentially closed to Mallarmé as well. If the selection of Valéry's poems that Rilke tried his hand at did not succeed in doing anything like what George's great translations did, or Rudolf Borchardt's Swinburne translations, the fault does not lie solely with the inaccessibility of the originals. Rilke violated the fundamental law of all legitimate translation, fidelity to the word, and when it came to Valéry he fell back into a practice of *Nachdichten*, or free rendering, that neither does justice to the original nor rises to full internal freedom through strict replication of the model. One need only compare Rilke's version of

---

*Stefan George translated Baudelaire into German.—Translator's note.

one of Valéry's most famous and in fact most beautiful poems, "Les Pas," with the original to see what an evil star presided over the encounter.

Now, as we know, Valéry's work consists by no means only of lyric poetry but also of prose of a truly crystalline variety that walks the fine line between aesthetic form and reflection on art in a provocative fashion. In France there are highly competent judges, André Gide among them, who accord even greater value to this part of Valéry's production. In Germany the prose too, aside from *Monsieur Teste* and *Epaulinos,* is scarcely known. If I discuss one of the prose works here, it is not simply to request for the well-known name of an author whose work is unknown something of the response he should not need to ask for, but to use the objective force inherent in his work to attack the stubborn antithesis of committed and pure art. That antithesis is a symptom of the disastrous tendency to stereotyping, to thinking in rigid and schematic formulas, that the culture industry produces everywhere and that has long since invaded the realm of aesthetic reflection as well. Production threatens to become polarized, with the sterile administrators of eternal values on the one side and on the other the poets of catastrophe, with whom one sometimes feels that the concentration camps suit them just fine as encounters with the void. I would like to show the kind of historical and social content that is inherent in the work of Valéry, work that forbids itself any kind of shortcut to praxis; I want to demonstrate that insisting on the formal immanence of the work of art need not have anything to do with praising ideas that are inalienable but damaged, and that a deeper knowledge of historical changes of essence is revealed in this kind of art and the thought that feeds on and resembles it than in utterances so adroitly aimed at changing the world that the burdensome weight of the world they want to change threatens to slip away from them.

The book I have in mind is readily accessible. It appeared in the series Bibliothek Suhrkamp and its German title is *Tanz, Zeichnung und Degas* [English *Degas Dance Drawing*].[1] The translation is by Werner Zemp. It is engaging, even if it does not always reproduce the painstakingly achieved grace of Valéry's text with the profundity the text requires. In return, the element of lightness in Valéry, the arabesque-like quality, and its paradoxical relationship to the extremely weighty thoughts is preserved; at least the terrors of unintelligibility do not emanate from this little volume. One envies Valéry's ability to formulate the subtlest and most complex experience in a playful and ethereal way; this is the program he sets for himself at the beginning of his book on Degas:

Just as a half-idle reader will scribble in the margins of a book, producing —as absent-mindedness or the pencil dictates—tiny figures or vague branch work around the mass of print, so I propose to follow my own fancy in writing around these drawings by Degas. My text to these illustrations may be left unread, or read discontinuously, since the connection and relationship between it and the drawings is of the loosest and least immediate kind. (5)

This ability of Valéry's cannot properly be reduced to the Gallic talent for form which is always brought in to fill the gaps, nor even to his own exceptional formal talent. It is nourished by his indefatigable drive for objectivation and realization, to use Cézanne's term, which does not tolerate anything obscure, anything unclarified or unresolved, and for which outward transparency becomes the criterion of inward success.

This might make it all the easier to take offense when a philosopher talks about a book by an esoteric poet about a painter obsessed with craft. I prefer to discuss this reservation at the outset rather than to provoke it naively; the more so in that the discussion opens up an avenue of access to the subject matter itself. I do not consider it my task to express my views on Degas, nor do I consider myself capable of doing so. Those of Valéry's ideas that I want to discuss all go beyond the great Impressionist painter. Yet they were achieved through the kind of proximity to the artistic object that only someone who himself produces with the utmost responsibility is capable of. Great insights into art come about either in utter detachment, deduced from a concept undisturbed by so-called connoisseurship, as in Kant or Hegel; or in absolute proximity, the attitude of the person behind the scenes, who is not an audience but rather follows the work of art from the point of view of how it is made, of technique. The average empathic connoisseur, the man of taste, is now and probably always has been in danger of missing works of art by degrading them to projections of his own contingency rather than subjecting himself to their objective discipline. Valéry provides an almost unique example of the second type, the person who knows about the work of art through his métier, the exacting work process, but in whom this process is immediately so felicitously reflected that it turns into theoretical insight, into that good universality that does not leave the particular out but rather preserves it and drives it, with the force of its own movement, to cogency. Valéry does not philosophize about art but breaks through the blindness of the artifact in the windowless, so to speak, activity of form-giving. In this way he expresses something of the obligation incumbent on every

self-conscious philosophy today: the same obligation whose opposite pole
—the speculative concept—was reached by Hegel a hundred and forty
years ago in Germany. In Valéry the principle of *l'art pour l'art*, taken to
its ultimate consequences, transcends itself, true to the maxim from
Goethe's *Elective Affinities* that everything perfect in its own kind points
beyond its own kind. To carry out the spiritual process that is strictly
immanent in the work of art itself means to overcome the blindness and
bias of the work of art. There is a good reason why Valéry's thoughts
keep circling around Leonardo da Vinci; in Leonardo, at the beginning
of an era, the same identity of art and knowledge was posited, in
unmediated fashion, that in Valéry at the end of an era found its way
through a hundred mediations to a magnificent self-awareness. The paradox around which Valéry's work is organized, a paradox which makes
itself felt again and again in the Degas book, is none other than that the
whole human being and the whole of humankind is intended in every
artistic utterance and every piece of scientific knowledge, but this intention can be realized only through a self-denying division of labor ruthlessly intensified to the point of the sacrifice of individuality, the self-
surrender of the individual human being.

I am not arbitrarily inserting these thoughts into Valéry: "What I call
'Great Art' is simply art that demands the employment of *all* of a man's
faculties, to produce works which invoke and bring into play *all* of
another man's faculties for their comprehension" (78). With a somber
glance from the historico-philosophical standpoint, and perhaps with
Leonardo in mind, Valéry demands the same thing of the artist:

> At this point, many a one may exclaim, What does it matter? But for my
> part, I believe it matters considerably that the work of art be the act of a
> *whole man*. But how is it that what was once considered so important
> should nowadays be considered negligible, as a matter of course? An
> amateur, a connoisseur of the days of Julius II or Louis XIV would be
> astonished to learn that almost everything he held to be essential in
> painting is today not only neglected, but is radically absent from the
> painter's considerations and the public's demands. In fact the more *refined*
> the public, the more advanced it is, the further away is it from the ancient
> ideals I was speaking of. But in this way we are withdrawing from human
> completeness. The whole man is dying out. (76–77)

It remains to be seen whether the expression "whole man" [in the
German translation Adorno is discussing, *Vollmensch*] is the appropriate
translation for what Valéry meant; in any case, Valéry's aim is the

undivided human being, whose capacities and modes of response have not been ripped apart, alienated from one another and congealed into valorizable functions in accordance with the schema of the social division of labor.

But Degas, whose insatiability in his demands on himself is equivalent, according to Valéry, to this idea of art, is depicted by Valéry as the extreme opposite of a universal genius, despite the fact that as we know, the painter not only sculpted but also wrote sonnets over which there were memorable controversies with Mallarmé. Valéry says of him:

> The sheer labor of Drawing had become a passion and a discipline to him, the object of a *mystique* and an ethic all-sufficient in themselves, a supreme preoccupation which abolished all other matters, a source of endless problems in precision which released him from any other form of inquiry. He was and wished to be a specialist, of a kind that can rise to a sort of universality. (64)

According to Valéry, this kind of intensification of specialization to the point of universality, the congealed intensification of production organized in terms of the division of labor, may contain the potential to counteract the deterioration of human capacities—what would be called "ego weakness" in current psychological terminology—that Valéry's speculation is concerned with. He cites a statement made by Degas at seventy: "You have to have a high conception, not of what you are doing, *but of what you may do one day:* without that, there's no point in working" (64). Valéry interprets this as follows:

> There speaks a real pride, an antidote to all vanity. The artist who is essentially an artist is like a player forever harried by new combinations of the game, haunted nightly by the specter of the chessboard or the cards alighting on the baize, obsessed with tactical images and solutions more living than real ones.
>
> A man not possessed by a *presence* of this intensity is an uninhabited man: an area in the void.
>
> No doubt love, ambition, or a thirst for lucre can powerfully fill up a lifetime. But the existence of a positive aim, the awareness (implicit in such an aim) of being near or far from it, of realizing it or not, reduces those passions to the status of *the finite*. Whereas the longing to create some work revealing more power and perfection than we know we possess, indefinitely removes that aim, which eludes and stands counter to our

every living moment. Each step forward makes it more beautiful and more remote.

The idea of completely mastering the technique of an art, of achieving the freedom to employ its means as confidently and as easily as we do our limbs and our senses in their ordinary functions, is one which inspires a few men to infinite determination, struggle, practice, and agony. (64–65)

And Valéry summarizes the paradox of the universal specialist: "Flaubert, Mallarmé, in very different kinds and styles, are literary examplars of the total consecration of a lifetime to the total demands which they invented and conferred on the art of writing." (65)

Permit me to recall my statement that Valéry, the notorious *artiste* and aesthete, is granted deeper insight into the social nature of art than is the doctrine of art's immediate utilitarian application in practical politics. That is confirmed here. For the current theory of committed art simply ignores a fact that irrevocably governs an exchange society, the fact that human beings are alienated from one another and that objective spirit is alienated from the society it expresses and regulates. This theory wants art to speak to human beings directly, as though the immediate could be realized directly in a world of universal mediation. But it thereby degrades word and form to a mere means, to an element in the context of the work's effect, to psychological manipulation; and it erodes the work's coherence and logic, which are no longer to develop in accordance with the law of their own truth but are to follow the line of least resistance in the consumer. Valéry has relevance for us today, and is the opposite of the aesthete which vulgar prejudice has stereotyped him as being, because he opposes the claims of a nonhuman cause to an overly hasty pragmatic spirit, and does so for the sake of what is human. That the division of labor cannot be banished by denying it, that the coldness of the rationalized world cannot be dispelled by recommending irrationality, however, is a social truth that has been demonstrated most emphatically by fascism. It is through more, not less, reason that the wounds dealt the irrational totality of humankind by the instrument that is reason can be healed.

Valéry did not naively take up the position of the isolated and alienated artist, nor did he abstract from history, nor deceive himself about the social process that terminated in alienation. Against those who have taken up residence in private inwardness, against the cleverness that often enough fulfills its commercial function by feigning the purity of someone who keeps his eyes to the front, Valéry cites a wonderful statement by Degas: "Another anchorite who knows the train times" (93). With full rigor and no admixture of ideology, as ruthlessly as any theoretician of society, Valéry expresses the contradiction between artistic work and the current social conditions of material production. As Carl Gustav Jochmann did in Germany more than a hundred years ago, he accuses art itself of archaism:

> It sometimes seems to me that the labor of the artist is of a very old-fashioned kind; the artist himself a survival, a craftsman or artisan of a disappearing species, working in his own room, following his own home-made empirical methods, living in untidy surroundings; using broken pots, kitchenware, any old castoffs that come to hand. . . . Perhaps conditions are changing, and instead of this spectacle of an eccentric individual using whatever comes his way, there will instead be a picture-making laboratory, with its specialist officially clad in white, rubber-gloved, keeping to a precise schedule, armed with strictly appropriate apparatus and instruments, each with its appointed place and exact function. . . . So far, change has not been eliminated from practice, or mystery from method, or inspiration from regular hours; but I do not vouch for the future. (19–20)

One might call Valéry's ironically presented aesthetic utopia an attempt to remain faithful to the work of art while at the same time, by changing its modus operandi, freeing it from the lie by which all art, and especially lyric poetry, is distorted under the prevailing conditions of technology. The artist is to remake himself into an instrument, to become a thing himself if he does not want to succumb to the curse of anachronism in a reified world. Valéry formulates the process of drawing in this sentence: "The artist approaches, withdraws, leans over, screws his eyes up, his whole body behaving like an instrument of the eye, becoming entirely a means for aiming, pointing, controlling, reducing to focus" (38). With this, Valéry attacks the extremely widespread conception of the work of art that ascribes it, on the model of private property, to the one who produces it. He knows better than anyone that it is only the least part of his work that "belongs" to the artist; that in actuality the process of artistic production, and with it the unfolding of the truth contained in the work of art, has the strict form of a lawfulness wrested from the subject matter itself, and that the much invoked creative freedom of the artist is of little consequence in comparison. Here he concurs with

another artist of his generation, similarly consistent and similarly discom-
fiting, Arnold Schönberg, who in his last book, *Style and Idea,* develops
the idea that great music consists of fulfilling the obligations the composer incurs with virtually the first note. In the same spirit, Valéry says:
"The truly *strong* man in any sphere is the one who most clearly realizes
that nothing is *given*, that all must be made and paid for; who is uneasy
when he fails to find obstacles, and so invents them. . . . For such a
man, form is grounded in reason" (68). Valéry's aesthetics is governed
by a metaphysics of the bourgeois. At the end of the bourgeois era, he
wants to purge art of its traditional curse of duplicity, to make it honest.
He demands that art pay the debts in which every work of art becomes
hopelessly entangled when it posits itself as real without being real. We
may question whether Valéry's and Schönberg's conception of art as a
kind of exchange process is the whole truth or whether it is under the
spell of the very state of existence that Valéry's conception prohibits
complicity with. But there is something liberating in the self-consciousness of its own bourgeois nature that bourgeois art finally achieves when
it takes itself seriously as the reality that it is not. The closed character of
the work of art, the necessity of its giving itself its own stamp, is to heal
it of the contingency which renders it unequal to the force and weight of
what is real. It is in the moment of objective obligation, and not in a
blurring of the boundary between the two domains, that the affinity of
Valéry's philosophy of art with science, and not least his kinship with
Leonardo, is to be sought.

Valéry's pointed contrast between technology and rationality on the
one hand and mere intuition, which must be overtaken and surpassed, on
the other, and his emphasis on process as opposed to the work that is
finished once and for all, can be fully understood only against the
background of his judgment on the broad developmental tendencies
within recent art. He sees in that art a retreat of the productive forces, a
surrender to sensory receptivity—in short, actually a weakening of the
human powers, of the subject as a whole, to which he relates all art. In
Germany, the words of leave-taking he devoted to the poetry and painting of the Impressionist period can be most readily understood if one
applies them to Richard Wagner and Richard Strauss, of whom they
unwittingly provide a description:

A *description* consists of phrases that can generally be put down *in any
order;* I can describe this room in a series of statements whose sequence is

almost of no importance. The eye can wander at will. What could be *truer*, more natural than this go-as-you-please, since . . . *truth itself is accident?* . . .

But if this latitude, and the habit of facility which goes with it, becomes the dominating factor, it gradually dissuades writers from employing their ability for abstraction, just as it reduces to nothing the slightest necessity for concentration on the reader's part, in order to *win him over* with *immediate effects*, rhetorical *shock tactics*. . . .

This particular creative method, which is legitimate in principle—and which has given birth to many fine works—leads, like the misuse of landscape, to a *diminution of the intellectual element in art.* (76)

And shortly afterwards, in still more basic terms:

Modern art tends almost exclusively to exploit sensory sensibility at the expense of our general or affective sensibility and our capacity for construction—for accumulating our best efforts and using the mind to transform things. It has a marvelous flair for arousing the attention, and for exploiting every means to that end—intensification, contrast, the startling, or the enigmatic. It can capture, by the subtlety of its means or the audacity of its execution, certain very valuable effects: states of extreme transience or complexity, irrational values, inarticulate sensations, resonances, correspondences, intuitions of shifting depths. . . . But these things are bought at a price. (77)

Only here does the full objective social truth content of Valéry become apparent. He posits the antithesis to the anthropological alterations that occur in a late industrial mass culture steered by totalitarian regimes or by giant corporations, a culture that reduces human beings to mere receptive apparatuses, to nodal points of conditioned reflexes, and by doing so paves the way for a situation of blind domination and a new barbarism. Art, which Valéry holds up in response to human beings as they are, has as its aim fidelity to the human being's possible image. The work of art that demands the utmost from its own logic and its own coherence as well as from the receiver's concentration is for Valéry a figure of the subject who is aware and in control of himself, a figure of the person who does not capitulate. It is no accident that he cites enthusiastically a statement of Degas opposing resignation. His work as a whole is a protest against the deadly temptation to make it easy for oneself by renouncing all happiness and all truth. It is better to be ruined attempting the impossible. The art he is preoccupied with—tightly organized, seamless, and rendered completely sensory precisely through its conscious force—is hardly capable of realization. But it embodies a resistance to the unspeakable pressure exerted on what is human by what merely exists. It acts as the representative of what we might one day be. Not to become stupid, not to be lulled to sleep, not to go along: these are the social stances sedimented in Valéry's work, a work which refuses to play the game of false humanness, of social complicity with the denigration of the human being. For him, to construct works of art means to refuse the opiate that great sensuous art has become since Wagner, Baudelaire, and Manet; to fend off the humiliation that makes works of art media and makes consumers victims of psychotechnical manipulation.

We are concerned here with the way in which Valéry, labeled an esoteric, is right, socially; with that in his work which concerns anyone and everyone, even though and precisely because he disdains to chime in with anyone. But I anticipate an objection, and I do not want to dismiss it lightly. One may ask whether after what has happened and what continues to threaten us, art itself is not utterly overvalued in Valéry's work and his philosophy; whether for that reason he does not belong after all to the nineteenth century, whose aesthetic inadequacy he perceived so keenly. Further, one may ask whether, despite the objective turn he gives to the interpretation of the work of art, he did not, like Nietzsche, impose a metaphysics of the artist. I will not attempt to decide whether Valéry, or for that matter Nietzsche, overvalued art. But in closing I would like to say something about the question of a metaphysics of the artist. Valéry's aesthetic subject, whether it be himself or Leonardo or Degas, is not a subject in the primitive sense of an artist who expresses himself. Valéry's whole conception is directed against this notion, against the enthroning of genius that has been so deeply entrenched especially in German aesthetics since Kant and Schelling. What he demands of the artist, technical self-restriction, subjection to the subject matter, is aimed not at limitation but at expansion. The artist who is the bearer of the work of art is not the individual who produces it; rather, through his work, through passive activity, he becomes the representative of the total social subject. By submitting to the requirements of the work of art, he eliminates from it everything that could be due simply to the contingency of his individuation. Also intended in this kind of representation of the total social subject, of the whole, undivided human being which Valéry's idea of the beautiful invokes, is a state of affairs that would cancel out the fate of blind isolation, a state of affairs in which the total subject would finally be realized socially. The art that achieved self-awareness as a consequence of Valéry's conception would transcend art itself and fulfill itself in the true life of human beings.

NOTES
TO
LITERATURE

II

On the Final Scene of Faust

*T*here is much in the current historical situation that speaks in favor of alexandrinism, interpretive immersion in traditional texts. Modesty resists the direct expression of metaphysical intentions; to venture such expression would be to expose oneself to gleeful misunderstanding. Objectively as well, it is not possible nowadays to ascribe meaning to what exists, and even the denial of meaning, official nihilism, has deteriorated to an affirmative message, a contribution to illusion, that tries to justify the desperation in the world as the world's essential substance: Auschwitz as a boundary situation. And so thought seeks refuge in texts. What remains of what is one's own is discovered in them. But these are not one and the same: what is discovered in the texts does not prove that something has been spared. The negative, the impossibility, is expressed in that difference, an "if only it were so," as far from the assurance that it is so as from the assurance that it is not. Interpretation does not seize upon what it finds as valid truth, and yet it knows that without the light it tracks in the texts there would be no truth. This tinges interpretation with a sorrow wholly unsuspected by the assertion of meaning and frantically denied by an insistence on what the case is. The gesture of interpretive thought resembles Lichtenberg's "neither deny nor believe"; to reduce this to mere skepticism would be to miss the point. For the authority of great texts is a secularized form of the unattainable authority that philosophy, as teaching, envisions. To regard profane texts as sacred texts—that is the answer to the fact that all transcendence has migrated into the profane sphere and survives only where it conceals itself. Bloch's old concept of "Symbolintention," symbolic intention, no doubt envisages this kind of interpretation.

In his late period Goethe found himself facing a contradiction which has now become an unreconcilable divergence, the contradiction between a language with literary integrity and communicative language. The second part of *Faust* was wrested from a deterioration of language whose course had been set at the point when a reified, facile discourse invaded expressive discourse. The latter proved so incapable of resistance because the two antagonistic media are nevertheless still one, never completely separate from one another. The elements in Goethe's late style that are commonly considered forced are the scars poetic language acquired in defending itself against communicative language, and at times they resemble the latter. For in fact Goethe committed no act of violence against language. He did not break with communication, something which ultimately became unavoidable; he did not demand of pure language an autonomy that remains forever precarious, sullied as pure language is by its consonance with the language of commerce. Rather, his restitutive nature attempts to awaken that sullied language as a literary language. This could not succeed with even a single word, no more than a diminished seventh chord in music can ever sound like that mighty chord at the beginning of Beethoven's last piano sonata after the disgrace it suffered at the hands of the vulgarity of the salons. But a run-down expression that has been eroded to the status of metaphor catches fire again when it is taken literally. This moment of catching fire holds within it the immortality of the language of the concluding scene of *Faust*.* The Pater profundus praises as "liebevoll im Sausen" ["tender in its roaring"] the "Blitz, der flammend niederschlug, / Die Atmosphäre zu verbessern, / Die Gift und Dunst im Busen trug" (lines 11876–81) ["the lightning that struck, flaming, / to improve the atmosphere / that harbored poison and fumes in its bosom"]. But since then the most pitiful conference communique justifies itself by stating its intention to improve the atmosphere when it wants to hide from an intimidated populace the fact that once again nothing has been accomplished. Even if this abominable custom is not itself already a cannibalization of a line from Goethe, someone with whom one would scarcely

---

*As there is no widely known English translation of *Faust Part Two*, I have left Adorno's quotations from it in German and provided English translations in brackets, trying to be quite literal so that the reader can follow Adorno's discussion of the specifics of the German text. *Faust Part One* is so familiar to Germans that Adorno cites lines from it without reference; I have left those citations in German, again providing English translations in brackets.—Translator's note.

expect these quotation-happy gentlemen to be acquainted, even in Goethe's day this readily accessible phrase can hardly have been a felicitous one. But he inserts it into his representation of the abyss and the waterfall, which, in an immense turnabout, transforms the expression of permanent catastrophe into an expression of blessing. "Improving the atmosphere" is the task of the dreadful emissaries of love who restore the breath of the First Day to those who are suffocating in the stifling air. They redeem the banality, which remains banality, and at the same time they sanction the pathos of the roaring natural images as a pathos of sublime purposefulness. A few lines before the end, the Mater gloriosa calls out, "Komm! hebe dich zu höhern Sphären!" (line 12094) ["Come! rise to higher spheres!"], and her slogan transforms the bourgeois mother's idle lament about the lack of a sense of reality in her child, who is all too happy to linger there, into the sense certainty of a scenery whose mountain ravines lead to a "higher atmosphere." "Weichlich" [flabby, insipid] is a pejorative word and probably was so then as well. But when the Magna peccatrix pleads "Bei den Locken, die so weichlich / Trockneten die heil'gen Glieder" (lines 12043–44) ["By the locks that so softly dried the holy limbs"], the form is filled with the literal strength of the adverbial qualifier, and receives the softness of the hair, sign of erotic love, in the aura of heavenly love. "Das Unzulängliche, hier wird's Ereignis" ["here the unattainable becomes event"], in language.

⌸

The extremes meet. People find a line by Friederike Kempner charming: instead of "Miträupchen," impossible even then, she says "Miteräupchen" in order to provide the missing syllable her trochees needed by means of a sovereignly inserted "e." In the same way, an awkward boy breaks the rules and holds onto the egg in an egg-and-spoon race in order to get it to the finish line safely. But the final scene of *Faust* uses the same device when the Pater seraphicus speaks of the waterfall that "abestürzt" [plunges down; Goethe has inserted an "e" into the word "abstürzt"] (line 11911); and in *Pandora* Goethe uses "abegewendet" [turned away; for "abgewendet"]. The philological explanation that this is the Middle High German form of the preposition does not temper the shock that the archaism, sign of a metrical predicament, might cause. What does soften that shock, however, is the immeasurable detachment of a pathos that with its very first note is already so far removed from the illusion of natural speech that no one would think of natural speech, and no one would think of laughing. The distance between the sublime and the ridiculous, which is said to be extremely short, is crucial in elevated style; only what is brought to the edge of the abyss of the ridiculous contains so much danger that the force of salvation pits itself against it and it succeeds. Essential to great literature is the good fortune that preserves it from the plunge into the abyss. The archaic quality of the inserted syllable communicates not a futile romanticizing evocation of a lost stratum of language but an estrangement of the current linguistic stratum that removes it from danger. It thereby becomes the bearer of that unsociable modernity that characterizes Goethe's late style even today. The anachronism increases the power of the passage. The passage carries the memory of something primordial, a memory which reveals the presence of passionate speech to be the presence of a world plan; as though from the very beginning it had been resolved that it would be so and not otherwise. He who wrote in this way could also, a few lines later, have the chorus of blessed boys sing: "Hände verschlinget / Freudig zum Ringverein" (lines 11926–27) ["Entwine hands joyfully to unite in a ring"] — without what later happened with the word *Ringverein* bringing disaster to the noun here. A paradoxical immunity to history is the seal of the authenticity of this scene.

▣

In the stanza of the Johannine Mulier Samaritana one reads—again for the sake of the verse, again an extreme case of making a virtue out of necessity—"Abram" instead of "Abraham" (line 12046). In the illumination of the exotic name, the familiar Old Testament figure, shrouded in innumerable associations, is abruptly transformed into the Oriental nomadic tribal chieftain. The memory that is faithful to him is seized and wrenched out of the canonized tradition. The all too promised land becomes a present-day prehistoric world. Expanded beyond the tales of the patriarchs, which have shrunk to an idyll, it acquires color and contour. The chosen people is Jewish, just as the image of beauty in the third act is Greek. If the carefully selected designation "Chorus mysticus" in the closing stanza means anything beyond the vague clichés of Sunday metaphysics, then the content, whether Goethe intended it to or not, alludes to Jewish mysticism. The Jewish inflection of the ecstasy, enigmatically built into the text, motivates the movement of the spheres of the heaven that opens out above forest, cliff, and desert waste. It simulates divine power engaged in creation. The Pater ecstaticus' lines: "Pfeile, durchdringet mich, / Lanzen, bezwinget mich, / Keulen zerschmettert mich, / Blitze, durchwettert mich!" (lines 11858–61) ["Arrows, penetrate me, / Lances, vanquish me, / Clubs, smash me, / Lightning, storm through me!"]; and certainly the Pater profundus' lines: "O Gott! beschwichtige die Gedanken, / Erleuchte mein bedürftig Herz!" (lines 11888–89) ["O, God! quiet my thoughts, / Illuminate my impoverished heart!"] are the cries of a Hassidic voice, exclamations from the Cabalistic potency of *gevurah*.* That is the "Bronn, zu dem schon weiland / Abram liess die Herde fuhren" (lines 12045–46) ["the spring to which Abraham led his herds"], and the inspiration for Mahler's composition in his eighth Symphony.

Anyone who does not want Goethe to end up among the plaster casts that stand around in the Goethe Haus in Weimar must face the question why Goethe's writing is rightly called beautiful, despite the face that the giant shadow of the historical authority of his work poses almost insuperable difficulties for anyone attempting to answer that question. The first such difficulty may well be a peculiar quality of greatness that should not be confused with monumentality but seems to defy more precise definition. Perhaps it resembles most closely the feeling of breathing freely in fresh air. It is not an unmediated sense of the infinite but rather arises where it goes beyond something finite, limited. Its relationship to the finite keeps it from evaporating into empty cosmic enthusiasm. Greatness itself becomes experienceable in what is surpasses; this is not the least of the ways in which Goethe is a kindred spirit to Hegel's Idea. In the final scene of *Faust* this greatness, which is present in pure form in the language, once again becomes the greatness of the contemplation of nature, as it was in the lyric poetry of Goethe's youth. The transcendent quality of this greatness, however, can be named concretely. The scene begins with the woodland that lurches forward, an incomparable modification of a motif from Shakespeare's *Macbeth*, taken out of its mythic context: the singing of the lines causes nature to move. Soon thereafter the Pater profundus begins:

Wie Felsenabgrund mir zu Füssen
Auf tiefem Abgrund lastend ruht,
Wie tausend Bäche strahlend fliessen

---

*In Cabala, one of the ten *sephiroth* or archetypal essences, the one representing power and severity.

Zum grausen Sturz des Schaums der Flut,
Wie strack mit eignem kräftigen Triebe
Der Stamm sich in die Lüfte trägt:
So ist es die allmächtige Liebe,
Die alles bildet, alles hegt. (lines 11866–73)

[As the rocky chasm at my feet / Rests heavily on the deep abyss, / As a thousand brooks flow, shining, / To the awesome plunge of the torrent's foam, / As the tree trunk bears itself aloft, / Straight and with its own powerful drive, / So it is almighty love / That forms and nurtures everything.]

The lines refer to the scenery, a landscape that is divided hierarchically and ascends by levels. But in what takes places there, the falling of the water, it seems as though the landscape were expressing its own creation story allegorically. The being of the landscape pauses, a figure of its becoming. It is this becoming, enclosed within the landscape, that causes the landscape, as creation, to resemble love, whose rule is celebrated in the ascent of Faust's "immortal part." When the language of natural history addresses fallen existence as love, we catch a glimpse of the reconciliation of the natural. Through remembrance of its own natural being, it rises above its submission to nature.

❖❖❖

Limitation as a precondition of greatness has its social aspect, in Goethe as in Hegel: the bourgeois as mediation of the absolute. The two clash harshly. After the emphatic lines "Wer immer strebend sich bemüht, / Den können wir erlösen" (lines 11836–37) ["He who makes an effort, striving, we can redeem"]—lines which are enclosed within quotation marks for good reasons, a maxim of inner-worldly asceticism—the angels continue: "Und hat an ihm die Liebe gar / Von oben teilgenommen, / Begegnet ihm die selige Schar / Mit herzlichem Willkommen" (lines 11938–41) ["And if indeed love has partaken of him from above, the blessed host will meet him with a hearty welcome"], as though the work's ultimate aim were merely an accidental supplement to the striving; the word "gar" [indeed] raises its forefinger didactically. In the same spirit, Gretchen is praised with petty condescension as the "gute Seele, / die sich einmal nur vergessen" (lines 12065–66) ["the good soul who forgot herself only once"]. To demonstrate his own broadmindedness, the commentator remarks that the number of nights of love is not computed in heaven, and in doing so he calls attention to the philistinism of the passage, which splits hairs in excusing the one who has had to suffer the full humiliation of masculine society while her lover, the assassin of her brother, is dealt with far more magnanimously. Rather than gloss over what is bourgeois in bourgeois fashion, one should understand it in its relationship to something that would be different. It is perhaps this relationship that defines Goethe's humaneness [*Humanität*] and that of Objective Idealism as a whole. Bourgeois reason is both universal reason and a particular reason, the reason of a transparent world order and the particular reason of a calculus that promises the rational man a secure profit. The universal reason that would supersede this particular reason is formed from it; the good universal would be realized only in and through particular situations in their finiteness and fallibility. The world beyond exchange would be one in which no one participating in an exchange would be cheated of what belonged to him. If reason were to skip over individual interests in an abstract way, without Aristotelian equity [*Billigkeit*], it would violate justice, and universality itself would reproduce particularity in the bad sense. Dwelling on — lingering with — the concrete is an inextinguishable aspect of anything that frees itself from particularity. At the same time, that movement of emancipation shows the specificity of particularity to be just as limited as the blind domination of a totality that does not respect particularity. The young Goethe celebrated "das anmuthige Beschränkte des bürgerlichen Zustands" ["the charming restrictedness of bourgeois circumstances"] in his sketch of the scene in which Gretchen first appears, and the restrictedness that was his early love penetrated into the language of the old Goethe. It no more fuses with that language than the individual fuses with the totality in bourgeois society. But the force of transcendence feeds on it as *Nüchternheit*, soberness. Language that remains self-possessed, dissonant even in the midst of the most extreme exuberance, examining and weighing itself, eludes the illusion of reconciliation that hinders reconciliation. It is only what remains calmly self-possessed and exercises restraint — as in the linguistic gesture of the more perfect angels, who say of their earthly remains, "Und wär' er von Asbest, / Er ist nicht reinlich" (lines 11956–57) ["And even if they were made of asbestos, they are not neat and tidy"] — that saturates elevation with the weight of mere existence. Elevation rises above mere existence by taking it with it instead of leaving it behind as an impotent abstract idea. Humanely, language lets the non-identical — in the protesting words of the young Hegel, the positive, the heteronomous—alone. It does not sacrifice it to the seamless unity of an idealistic principle of stylization: in being mindful of its limit, spirit becomes the spirit that moves beyond its limit. Pedantry, of which there is a touch in the whole concluding scene, is not simply an idiosyncrasy; it has its function. It endorses the obligations that circumscribe the plot as well as those the poem incurs in developing the plot. But it is only because the expression "Schuldverschreibung" [ascription of debt or guilt] retains its heavy dual meaning—a debt to be settled and the culpability of one's life circumstances—that the earthly can move in the manner required by the figure of the woodland lurching forward. The foundation formed by what is pedestrian, not fully spiritualized, is intended, through the difference between it and spirit, to vouch for the spirit's capacity for rescue. The dialectic of naming from the prologue in heaven, where Faust is "doctor" to Mephistopheles but "his servant" to the Lord, reappears here. The soberness is that of the privy councillor and a holy sobriety in one.

███

The fictitious quotation "Wer immer strebend sich bemüht," like the lines of the younger angels that follow it, refers, as we know, to Faust's wager with the devil, which has already been decided in the burial scene, where the angels carry off Faust's immortal part. There has been so much fuss about the question of whether the devil won or lost the bet. People have clung so sophistically to the subjunctive mood of Faust's words "Zum Augenblicke dürft' ich sagen" ["I could say to the moment"] to infer that Faust does not really speak the words "Verweile doch, du bist so schön" ["Linger, you are so beautiful"] in the scene in his study. All the ways that people have distinguished between the letter and the meaning of the pact, with the most pitiful generosity! As though philological fidelity were not the domain of the one who insists on signing in blood because it is a very special juice; as though a thick-headedly exalted appeal to meaning had the slightest legitimacy in a work that accords language priority over meaning as scarcely any other work in the German language does. The wager is lost. In the world in which "es mit rechten Dingen zugeht" ["things are done properly"], in which equivalents are exchanged—and the wager is itself a mythical image of exchange—Faust has played a losing hand. Only rationalistic thinking —what Hegel would call "reflektierende" or reflecting thought—would

want to twist his wrong into a right within the sphere of justice. If Faust
were supposed to win the bet, it would be absurd—it would represent
contempt for artistic economy—to put into his mouth at the moment of
his death the precise lines that, in terms of the bet, deliver him over to
the devil. Instead, law itself is suspended. A higher court ordains a stay
to the eternal equivalence of credit and debit. This is the mercy to which
the dry "gar" points: truly, that mercy which takes precedence over law,
that mercy through which the cycle of cause and effect breaks down. The
dark force of nature assists it but is not quite the same. Mercy's response
to the condition of nature, however much it may be anticipated in the
latter, nevertheless emerges as something qualitatively new and marks a
caesura in the continuity of events. Goethe's work makes this dialectic
quite clear through the old motif of the devil cheated: the devil's own
criterion, the calculating intellect which, like Shylock, insists upon ap-
pearances, denies him what he has been pledged. If the account balanced
as neatly as those who think they have to defend mercy against the devil
would have it, the writer could have spared himself the most daring
stroke in his construction: the devil, who in Goethe was already a devil
of coldness, is taken in by his own love, the negation of negation. In the
sphere of illusion, of the "farbigen Abglanz" [colored reflection], truth
itself appears as untruth; in the light of reconciliation, however, this
reversal reverses itself again. Even the natural condition of desire, which
belongs to the complex of entanglement, reveals itself to be something
that helps the entangled man escape. The metaphysics of *Faust* is not the
effortful striving to which a neo-Kantian reward beckons somewhere in
infinity but the disappearance of the natural order in a different order.

▣

Or perhaps it is not that yet either. Perhaps the wager is forgotten in
Faust's "extreme old age," along with all the crimes that Faust in his
entanglement perpetrated or permitted, even the last, monstrous crime
against Philemon and Baucis, whose hut the master of the piece of
ground newly subjected to human domination can no more tolerate than
a reason that dominates nature can tolerate anything unlike itself. Perhaps
the epic form of the work, which calls itself a tragedy, is that of form in
the process of falling under the statute of limitations. Perhaps Faust is
saved because he is no longer the person who signed the pact; perhaps the
wisdom of this play, which is a play in pieces, a "Stück in Stücken," lies
in knowing how little the human being is identical to himself, how light

and tiny this "immortal part" of him is that is carried off as though it were nothing. The power of life, as a power of continued life, is equated with forgetting. It is only in being forgotten and thereby transformed that anything survives at all. This is why *Faust Part Two* has as its prelude the restless sleep of forgetting. The man who awakens, for whom "des Lebens Pulse frisch lebendig schlagen" ["life's pulses beat fresh and lively"], and who "wieder nach der Erde blickt" ["looks back to earth again"], can do so only because he no longer knows anything about the horrors that went on before. "Dieses ist lange her" ["That was long ago"]. At the beginning of the second act as well, which shows him once more in the narrow Gothic room, "ehemals Faustens, unverändert" ["once Faust's, unchanged"], he approaches his own prehistory only as a man asleep, laid low by the phantasmagoria of what is to come, Helena. The fact that so few of the concrete details of part one are recalled in part two, that the connection becomes looser to the point where the interpreters have nothing to hold onto but the meager idea of progressive purification—that is itself the idea. But when, in an affront to logic whose radiance heals all logic's acts of violence, the memory of Gretchen's lines in the dungeon dawns on us, as if across the eons, in the invocation of the Mater gloriosa as the *Unvergleichliche,* the incomparable one, there speaks from it, in boundless joy, the feeling that must have seized the poet when, shortly before his death, he reread on the boards of a chicken coop the poem, "Wanderers Nachtlied" ["Wanderer's Nightsong"], he had inscribed on it a lifetime before. That hut too has burned down. Hope is not memory held fast but the return of what has been forgotten.

Reading Balzac

For Gretel

When the peasant comes to the city, everyting says "closed" to him. The massive doors, the windows with their blinds, the innumerable people to whom he may not speak under penalty of seeming ridiculous, even the shops with their unaffordable wares—all turn him away. A plain-spoken novella by Maupassant dwells on the humiliation of a lower-ranking officer in an unfamiliar environment who mistakes a respectable dwelling for a bordello. In the eyes of the newcomer, everything that is locked up resembles a brothel, mysterious and enticingly forbidden. Cooley distinguished sociologically between primary and secondary groups depending on the presence or absence of face-to-face relationships: the person who is thrown abruptly from the one to the other experiences this distinction in the flesh, with pain. In literature Balzac was probably the first such *paysan de Paris,* or Parisian peasant, and he maintained that demeanor even after he knew very well what was what. But at the same time, the productive forces of the bourgeoisie on the threshold of advanced capitalism were incarnated in him. His response to being locked out is that of the inventive genius: All right, I'll figure out for myself what goes on behind those closed doors, and the world will hear something then! The resentment of the provincial, who in his outraged ignorance is obsessed with the things he thinks go on even in the very best circles, where one would least expect it, becomes the driving force of exact imagination. Sometimes the dime-novel romanticism with which Balzac was commercially involved in his early days comes out; sometimes the childish mockery of sentences like this: "If one goes by the house at 37 Rue Miromesnil on a Friday around 11 in the morning and the green shutters on the second floor aren't open yet, you can be sure there was an orgy there the night before." Sometimes, however, the compensatory fantasies of the naive man are more accurate about the world than the realist Balzac is credited with being. The alienation that occasioned his writing—it is as though every sentence of his industrious pen were constructing a bridge into the unknown—is itself the secret life he was trying to discover by guesswork. The same thing that separates people from one another and keeps the writer isolated from them is what keeps the movement of society going, the movement whose rhythm Balzac's novels are imitating. The fantastic and improbable fate of Lucien de Rubempré is set in motion by the technical changes, expertly described, in printing methods and paper that made the mass production of literature possible; one of the reasons Cousin Pons, the collector, is out of fashion is that as a composer he did not keep pace with so to speak industrial advances in orchestration. Such insights on Balzac's part are worth their weight in research because they both derive from and attempt to reconstruct an understanding of the subject matter that research in its blindness tries to eliminate. Through his intellectual intuition Balzac realized that in advanced capitalism people are character masks, to use an expression Marx coined later. Reification is more terrifyingly radiant in the freshness of dawn and the glowing colors of new life than the critique of political economy at high noon. An employee of a funeral parlor in 1845 who resembles the spirit of death —in the hundred years since then no satire of Americanism, not even Evelyn Waugh's, has surpassed that. *Désillusion*, or disillusionment, which provided the name of one of his greatest novels, *Les illusions perdues*, or *Lost Illusions*, as well as a literary genre, is the experience that human beings and their social functions do not coincide. With the thunderbolt of citation Balzac brought society as totality, something classical political economy and Hegelian philosophy had formulated in theoretical terms, down from the airy realm of ideas to the sphere of sensory evidence. That totality is by no means only an extensive totality, by no means only the physiology of life as a whole in its various branches, which was to comprise Balzac's program for the *Comédie humaine*. As a functional complex, it becomes intensive as well. A dynamic rages in it: society reproduces itself only as a whole, in and through the system, and to do so it needs every last man as a customer. That perspective may seem foreshortened, too immediate, as is always the case when art presumes to conjure up in perceptible form a society that has become abstract. But the individual foul deeds through which people visibly attempt to steal from one another the surplus value that has already been appropriated invisibly make the horror graphic, something that would otherwise be possible only through conceptual mediations. In her maneuvers to acquire wealth through inheritance, the Présidente uses the shady lawyer and the concierge; equality is realized in the sense that the false totality harnesses all social classes to its guilt. There is truth even in the pulp literature at which literary taste and worldly wisdom turn up their noses: it is only on the margins that the things that go on in the pits of society, the underworld of its sphere of production, become visible—the things from which totalitarian atrocities arose in a later phase. Balzac's time favored this kind of eccentric truth, primitive accumulation,[1] an antiquated conquistadorian barbarism in the midst of the French industrial revolution of the early nineteenth century. In all probability the appropriation of heteronomous labor almost never occurred in complete accordance with the laws of the marketplace. The injustice inherent in those laws is multiplied by the injustice of every individual action, a surplus profit of guilt. Those versed in such things can find Balzac guilty of the bad psychology of the movies. There is enough good psychology in him. That concierge is not simply a monster; before she was stricken with their social disease, greed, she was what her fellow citizens call a nice person. Equally, Balzac knows how connoisseurship—the matter at hand—outstrips mere profit motive, how the forces of production outstrip the relations of production. At the same time, he also knows how bourgeois individuation, the proliferation of idiosyncratic traits, destroys individuals, the confirmed gluttons or misers. He senses that the maternal quality is the secret of friendship, and he knows instinctively how the slightest weakness suffices for the downfall of the noble person, as when Pons becomes entangled in the machinery of destruction through his gourmandise. Madame de Nucingen III using first names in front of an aristocrat to create the illusion that she is on intimate terms with her —that could come from Proust. But when Balzac really does give his characters puppet-like features, their legitimacy extends beyond the sphere of psychology. In the *tableau économique* of society, human beings behave like the marionettes in the mechanical model in the Castle of Hellbrunn. There is a good reason why many of Daumier's caricatures resemble Polichinello. In the same spirit, Balzac's stories demonstrate the social impossibility of good behavior and integrity. They sneer that anyone who is not a criminal will perish; often they shout it out. And so the light of humanness [*das Humane*] falls on the outcasts, on the whore who is capable of great passion and self-sacrifice and on the galley-slave and murderer whose actions are those of a disinterested altruist. Because Balzac's physiological suspicions tell him that the good citizens are criminals; because everyone who strolls down the street unknown and impenetrable looks as though he has committed the original sin of all of society: this is why for Balzac it is the criminals and outcasts who are the human beings. This may be why he discovered homosexuality for literature; his novella *Sarrasine* is devoted to it and his conception of Vautrin is based on it. In view of the irresistible ascendancy of the exchange principle, he may have dreamed of something like love in its undistorted form occurring in a despised and inherently hopeless love: it is the false cleric, the bandit chief who cancels the exchange of equivalents, whom he believes capable of it.

❚❘❚

Balzac had a special fondness for the Germans, for Jean Paul and Beethoven, something for which he was repaid by Richard Wagner and Schönberg. Despite his penchant for the visual, there is something musical about his work as a whole. Much of the symphonic music of the nineteenth and early twentieth centuries is reminiscent of the novel in its penchant for dramatic situations, in its passionate rise and fall, in its unruly abundance of life; conversely, Balzac's novels, archetypes of the genre, are musical in their flowing quality, in the way they spawn figures and then swallow them back up again, in setting up and transforming characters who move along as in a dream sequence. If novel-like music seems to repeat the movements of the material world in the listener's head, in the darkness, with the lights dimmed to show the contours of the material world, then the heads of Balzac's readers spin as they turn the pages waiting eagerly for the continuation, as though all the descriptions and actions were a pretense for the wild and variegated sound that floods through his work. They provide the reader with the same thing the flute, clarinet, horn, and drum lines promised the child before he really knew how to read a score. If music is the world dematerialized and reproduced in interior space, then the interior space of Balzac's novels, projected outward as a world, is the retranslation of music into the kaleidoscope. From his description of Schmucke, the musician, we can also infer what his Germanophilia was directed toward. It is the same in essence as the impact of German Romanticism in France, from the *Freischütz* and Schumann to the antirationalism of the twentieth century. But it is not only that the German obscurity in the labyrinth of Balzac's pages, as contrasted with the Latin terrorism of *clarté*, embodies an amount of utopia equal to the amount of enlightenment the Germans, conversely, repressed. In addition, Balzac may have addressed the constellation of the chthonic and *Humanität* [humanness or humaneness]. *Humanität* is mindfulness of nature in human beings. Balzac tracks it to the point at which immediacy creeps away before the functional complex of society and comes to grief. But the poetic force that gives rise to the grim scherzo of modernity in him is equally archaic. The Everyman, the transcendental subject, as it were, who sets himself up behind Balzac's prose as the creator of a society that has been magically transformed into a second nature, is a kindred spirit of the mythical "I" of classical German philosophy and the music corresponding to it, which derives everything that exists from itself. In this kind of subjectivity the human is given voice through the force of original identification with the Other which it knows to be itself, but this subjectivity is also always inhuman at the same time in that it is an act of violence that veers around and makes the Other subject to its will. Balzac attacks the world all the more the farther he moves away from it by creating it. There is an anecdote according to which Balzac turned his back on the political events of the March Revolution [of 1848] and went to his desk, saying, "Let's get back to reality"; this anecdote describes him faithfully, even if it is apocryphal. His demeanor is that of the late Beethoven, dressed in a nightshirt, muttering furiously and painting giant-sized notes from his C-sharp minor quartet on the wall of his room. As in paranoia, love and rage are intertwined. In just the same way, elemental spirits play their pranks and help the poor.

▣▤▣

The fact that the paranoid, like the philosophers, has a system did not escape Freud. Everything is connected, relationships govern everything, everything serves a secret and sinister end. But the things that are developing in the real society of which Balzac occasionally speaks, like the countesses who say "bien, bien" because they speak fluent French, are no different. A system of universal dependencies and communications is in the process of formation. The consumers serve the process of production. If they cannot pay for the goods, capital develops a crisis that wipes them out. The credit system links the fate of the one to the fate of the other, whether they know it or not. The totality threatens those who compose it with destruction by reproducing them, and while its surface is not yet completely tightly woven, it provides a glimpse of the potential for destruction. Familiar characters—the Gobsecks, Rastignacs, and

Vautrins—reappear as passersby at the most unexpected places in the *Comédie humaine,* in constellations that only delusions of reference could think up and that only the *Dictionnaire biographique des personnages fictifs de la Comédie humaine* could make order of. But the *idées fixes* that imagine the same forces at work everywhere cause short circuits in which the overall process is momentarily illuminated. This is why the subject's detachment from reality is transformed by obsession with it into an eccentric closeness.

❚❚❚

Balzac, who sympathized with the Restoration, sees symptoms in early industrialism that are ordinarily ascribed to the stage of degeneration. In the *Illusions perdues* he anticipates Karl Kraus' attack on the press; Kraus cites him. It is precisely the restorationist journalists whose situation is the worst in Balzac; the contradiction between their ideology and their a priori democratic medium forces them to cynicism. Such objective states of affairs do not sit well with Balzac's turn of mind. The conflicts within the rising new mode of production are as intense as his imagination and are perpetuated in the structure of his works. The romantic and the realistic aspects form a historical composite in Balzac's work. The financiers, pioneers of an industry not yet established, are adventurers from the genre of the epic, whose categories Balzac, born in the eighteenth century, salvages and imports into the nineteenth. Against the background of a pre-bourgeois order that is shaken but continues to survive, unleashed rationality takes on an irrationality similar to the universal nexus of guilt that that rationality remains; its first raids were the prelude to the irrationality of its late phase. The norms of *homo economicus* have not yet become standardized modes of human conduct; the hunt for profit still resembles the bloodlust of undomesticated hunters, and the totality still resembles the remorseless blind enchainment of fate. In Balzac, Adam Smith's "invisible hand" becomes the black hand on the graveyard wall. What Hegel's speculation in his *Philosophy of Right* shrank from in fear, as did the positivist Comte—the explosive tendencies of a system that suppresses naturally evolved structures—bursts into flame as chaotic nature in Balzac's enraptured contemplation. His epic is intoxicated with what the theoreticians found so intolerable that Hegel called up the state as arbiter and Comte called up sociology. Balzac needs neither, because in him the work of art itself serves as the authority that embraces the centrifugal forces of society in a sweeping gesture.

◘⢀◘

The Balzacian novel feeds on the tension between the passions of human beings and a state of the world that is already moving in the direction of not tolerating passion, which it considers a disruption of its activities. Under the prohibitions and frustrations to which, then as always, they were subjected, the passions become intensified to the point of frenzy. Unfulfilled, they become simultaneously deformed and insatiable, emotion-laden idiosyncrasies. But the instincts have not yet completely disappeared into social schemata. They fasten onto goods which are still largely unattainable, especially those subject to a natural monopoly; or, as avarice, lust for money, or promotion mania, they enter the service of an expansive capitalism which needs the additional energy of individuals until it is completely in place. The motto "enrichissez-vous" [get rich] sets Balzac's characters dancing. Down into the twentieth century, the early industrial world turns the double meaning of the word "bazaar"—the bazaar of the Arabian Nights and the department store— against those who are not yet adapted to it (by chance the name of one of Saint-Simon's most important disciples was pronounced the same way). People bustle around in front of it like agents and people hopelessly lost at the same time, agents of surplus value and Don Quixotes of a wealth from the expansion of which they hope to get something, like landed aristocrats without much work, soldiers of fortune storming the windmills of Fortuna, who knocks them down with the law of the average rate of profit. So colorful is the emergence of gray and so enchanting the disenchantment of the world; there is so much to be told about the process whose prose makes sure that soon there will be nothing left to tell. Like the lyric poets of that era, the epic poets plucked the flowers of evil in the place marked "Swamp of Capitalism" in the socialist People's Atlas. However much the romantic aspect of Balzac's work may derive, subjectively, from historical backwardness, from the precapitalist perspective of the person who looks longingly to the past as the victim of liberal society and yet would like to share in its rewards, it is still derived from social reality and from a realistic sense of form directed toward that reality. Balzac needs only to describe it with his soberly grim "This is how awful the world is," and the catastrophic protuberances turn into a halo.

◘⢀◘

What German reader of Balzac, conscientiously turning to the French original, would not despair over the countless unfamiliar terms for specific differences between objects, terms he has to look up in the dictionary if his reading is not to flounder; until finally, resigned and humiliated, he entrusts himself to the translations. The craftsmanlike precision of the French language itself, the respect for nuances of material and workmanship in which so much of culture is sedimented, may be responsible for this. But Balzac takes it to extremes. At times he presupposes familiarity with whole technical terminologies in specialized fields. This is part of a larger context in his work. The reader is often drawn into that context with the first lines of a narrative. Precision simulates extreme closeness to the matter at hand and hence physical presence. Balzac uses the suggestion of concreteness. But it is so excessive that one cannot yield to it naively, cannot credit it to the ominous richness of epic vision. Rather, that concreteness is what its ardor suggests: an evocation. If the world is to be seen *through*, it can no longer be looked *at*. One can cite no better witness to the fact that literary realism became obsolete because, as a representation of reality, it did not capture reality, than that same Brecht who later slipped into the straitjacket of realism as though it were a costume for a masked ball. He saw that the *ens realissimum* consists of processes, not immediate facts, and they cannot be depicted:

> The situation becomes so complicated because a simple "reproduction of reality" says less than ever about reality. A photograph of the Krupp factories or the AEG provides virtually no information about these establishments. True reality has slipped over into functional reality. The reification of human relations, that is, the factory, no longer delivers human relations to us.[2]

In Balzac's time that could not yet be understood. He reconstructs the world from the suspicions of the outsider. In doing so he needs, in reaction, permanent assurance that it is so and not otherwise. Concreteness is the substitute for the real experience that is not only almost inevitably lacking in the great writers of the industrial age but also incommensurable with the age's own concept. Balzac's oddness sheds light on something that characterizes nineteenth century prose as a whole after Goethe. The realism with which even those who are idealistically inclined are preoccupied is not primary but derived: realism on the basis of a loss of reality. The epic that is no longer in command of the material concreteness it attempts to protect has to exaggerate it in its demeanor, has to describe the world with exaggerated precision precisely because it has become alien, can no longer be kept in physical proximity. A pathogenic core—euphemism—is already inherent in that more modern form of concreteness, as in Stifter's technique or even in the linguistic formulas of the late Goethe, and later, in works like Zola's *Ventre de Paris,* a very modern conclusion is drawn from it, the dissolution of time and action. Analogously, the drawings of schizophrenics do not create a fantasy world out of an isolated consciousness. Rather, they scribble the details of lost objects with an extreme precision that expresses lostness itself. It is that, and no direct resemblance to objects, that is the truth of literary concretism. In the language of analytic pyschiatry this would be called a restitution phenomenon. This is why it is so silly to equate realistic stylistic principles in literature with—as the Eastern bloc cliché would have it—a healthy, non-decadent relationship to reality. That relationship would be normal, in the emphatic sense of the word, where the literary subject exorcised the social horror by breaking through the rigidified and thereby alienated facade of empirical reality.

⊞

Marx cites Balzac in a remark on the capitalist function of money in contrast to the archaic hoard:

> Exclusion of money from circulation would also exclude absolutely its self-expansion as capital, while accumulation of a hoard in the shape of commodities would be sheer tomfoolery. Thus for instance Balzac, who so thoroughly studied every shade of avarice, represents the old usurer Gobseck as in his second childhood when he begins to heap up a hoard of commodities.[3]

But the path that leads Balzac to that "profound conception of real conditions" to which Marx attests elsewhere[4] runs in a direction opposite to economic analysis. Like a child, he is fascinated by the terrifying image and the foolishness of the usurer. The emblem of the usurer is the treasure with which he surrounds himself in infantile fashion. His foolishness is something that has developed historically, a precapitalist vestige in the heart of the freebooter of civilization. It is this kind of blind physiognomy, not theoretically oriented writing, that satisfies dialectical theory and grasps the central tendency. No legitimate relationship between art and knowledge is established when art borrows theses from science, illustrates them, and anticipates science, only to have science catch up with it later. Art becomes knowledge when it devotes itself unreservedly to work on its material. With Balzac, however, this work consisted in the efforts of an imagination that never rested until its products were so like itself that they also resembled the society from which they were in retreat.

∎∎∎

Balzac is still, or already, free from the bourgeois illusion that the individual exists essentially for himself while the society, or the environment, influences him from the outside. His novels depict not only the superior power of social and especially economic interests over private psychology but also the social genesis of the characters in themselves. They are motivated first of all by their interests, interests in career and income, the hybrid product of feudal-hierarchical status and bourgeois-capitalist manipulation. In the process, the divergence between human destiny and social role becomes something unknowable. Those who by virtue of their interests function as the wheels of commerce retain certain characteristics which they lose in a later phase of development. Interests and interest-psychology do not go together. In Balzac the same people who, as captains of industry, ruin their competitors, using both economic and criminal means, ruin themselves when sex, for which their interests leave no time, overpowers them. Nucingen, elderly, brutal, and without conscience, clumsily succumbs to the very young Esther, who cheats him out of herself to the best of her ability, as a whore would, because she is the angel who vainly throws herself under the wheel of fortune in order to save her beloved.

∎∎∎

The Duke of Rhétoré tries to win Lucien Chardon, who has become an overnight success as a journalist, over to the Royalist cause with the words: "Vous vous êtes montré un homme d'esprit, soyez maintenant un homme de bon sens" ["You've shown that you are a witty man, now be a man with good sense"]. With those words he has codified the bourgeois view of reason [*Vernunft*] and understanding [*Verstand*]. That view is the opposite of Kant's teaching. Spirit, "esprit"—the "ideas"—do not guide, "regulate" the understanding; they impede it. Balzac diagnoses the health that is deathly afraid that someone might be too clever. The person who is governed by spirit instead of governing it as a means to an end, is concerned with the matter at hand as an end in itself. He is repeatedly defeated by those who are indifferent to the matter at hand, as in governing bodies; he merely delays them. They can devote their undiminished energies to tactics for accomplishing something. Contrasted with their successes, spirit becomes stupidity. Reflection that does not accommodate to given situations, demands, and necessities—lack of naiveté, that is—is too naive, and fails. Not only are *bon sens* and *esprit* not the same thing, they are antinomic. The person with *esprit* will scarcely grasp the desiderata of *bon sens:* "I have never understood the language of men." But *bon sens* is always on the *qui vive* to ward off *esprit* as a temptation to idle speculation. What the psychologist Theodor Lipps called the "narrowness of consciousness," which does not permit anyone full self-actualization in excess of the limited supply of his libidinal energies, guarantees that a person has only the one or the other, *esprit* or *bon sens*. Those who play the game without being adversely affected despise the *anima candida,* the pure spirit, as idiotic. The incapacity of human beings to rise above the sphere of their immediate interests, which is filled with the objects of pragmatic action, is not due primarily to ill will. The gaze that rises above what is closest at hand leaves it behind as something bad and hindered in its functioning. Nowadays there are many students who fear that theory will teach them too much about society: How are they then to practice the professions for which their studies are preparing them? They would get what they like to call social schizophrenia. As though consciousness had the task of making things easier for itself by eliminating contradictions whose locus is not in consciousness at all but rather in reality. As the reproduction of life, reality places legitimate demands on individuals and at the same time places itself and humankind in mortal danger through that same reproduction. Too much reason is harmful to an understanding concerned with self-preservation. Conversely, every concession to the operations of the dominant practices not only contaminates the spirit, which will not be swayed from its course, but halts its movement and stultifies it.

▄▄▄

In a letter written to Margaret Harkness when he was an old man, a letter that, ominously, has been canonized in Marxist aesthetics, Engels glorified Balzacian realism.[5] He may have taken it for more realistic than Balzac's oeuvre reads seventy years later. This might relieve the doctrine of socialist realism of some of the authority it bases on Engels' vote. More to the point, however, is the extent to which Engels himself deviates from what later became the official theory. When Engels says he prefers Balzac to "all the Zolas *passés, présents, et à venir*" [past, present, and future], he can only have been referring to those moments in which the older writer is less realistic than his scientifically minded successor; there are good reasons why Zola replaced the concept of realism with that of naturalism. Just as in the history of philosophy no positivist is positivistic enough for his successor but instead is labeled a metaphysician, so it is in the history of literary realism. But at the moment in which naturalism committed itself to a quasi-official recording of the facts, the dialectician moved to the side of what the naturalists now proscribed as metaphysics. The dialectician opposes automated enlightenment. Historical truth itself is nothing but the self-renewing metaphysics that emerges in the permanent disintegration of realism. In socialist realism as in the culture industry, it is precisely the faithfulness to the facade on the part of a method purged of Balzacian deformations that harmonizes with externally imposed intentions. Balzac's storytelling does not allow itself to be diverted for a moment by such intentions: planning is confirmed by de-structured data, but in literature, what is planned is a political point of view. What Engels wrote is directed against this, and thereby implicitly against all the art tolerated in the Eastern bloc since Stalin. For Engels, Balzac's greatness is demonstrated precisely in the depictions that run counter to his own class sympathies and political prejudices and repudiate his legitimist inclinations. The writer, like the *Weltgeist,* is one with the force of history because the force of original production that governs his prose is collective. Engels calls that the greatest triumph of Balzac's realism, the "revolutionary dialectic in his poetical justice."[6] This triumph, however, was linked to the fact that Balzac's prose does not yield to realities but rather stares them in the face until they become transparent down to their horrors. Lukács timidly pointed that out.[7] Even less is Engels concerned, as Lukács immediately affirms, with "rescuing the immortal greatness of his"—Balzac's—"realism." The very concept of realism is not a constant norm: Balzac undermined that norm for the sake of truth. Invariants are incompatible with the spirit of the dialectic even if Hegelian classicism vindicates them.

⊟

In the form of a medium of circulation, money, the capitalist process touches and patterns the characters whose lives the novel form tries to capture. In the empty space between events on the stock exchange and the events crucial to the economy—from which the stock exchange is temporarily separate, either because it discounts the movements of the economy or because it becomes autonomous and follows its own dynamics—

individual life crystallizes in the midst of total interchangeability, and at the same time, through its individuation, it handles the affairs of the overall functional complex: this is the climate surrounding the Baron Nucingen, a Rothschild figure. But the sphere of circulation, about which there were fantastic stories to be told—stocks rose and fell in those days like the floods of sound at the opera—also distorts the economics that Balzac the writer was as passionately involved with as Balzac the young *homme d'affaires*. The inadequacy of his realism ultimately derives from the fact that, for the sake of the picture he was painting, he did not penetrate the veil of money and in fact could scarcely have penetrated it even then. When paranoid fantasy runs rampant it is akin to fantasies in which one imagines that the machinations and conspiracies of financial magnates are the key to the social destiny that governs human beings. Balzac is one in a long series of writers extending from de Sade, in whose *Justine* the Balzacian fanfare "insolent comme tous les financiers"[8] ["insolent, like all financiers"] appears, to Zola and the early Heinrich Mann. What is genuinely reactionary in Balzac is not his conservative turn of mind but his complicity with the legend of rapacious capital. In sympathy with the victims of capitalism, he inflates the executors of the judgment, the finance people who present the bill, to monsters. Insofar as the industrialists appear at all, they are categorized as productive labor in Saint-Simonian fashion. Indignation over the *auri sacra fames* is part of the eternal stock in trade of bourgeois apologetics. It is a diversion: the barbaric hunters are merely divying up the booty. Nor can this illusion be explained on the basis of false consciousness on Balzac's part. The relevance of finance capital, which advanced the money for the expansion of the system, was incomparably greater in early industrialism than in later industrialism, and the practices of speculators and usurers varied analogously. The novelist can get a better hold there than in the sphere of production proper. It is precisely because in the bourgeois world one can no longer tell stories about the things that are decisive that storytelling is dying out. The deficiencies inherent in Balzacian realism already represent, in latent form, the verdict on the realistic novel.

❚❚❚

What Hegel took for the *Weltgeist*, the great movement of history, was the rise of the capitalist bourgeoisie. Balzac depicts it as a trail of destruction. In his novels the marks of trauma left on the traditionalist order by the economic rise of the bourgeoisie are the prophetic signs of the grim future that avenges on the new class the injustice that class inherited from the old class it toppled and then carried farther. This has kept the *Comédie humaine* young even as it becomes outdated. Its élan, however, its dynamic quality, is the fresh young élan of economic upswing. The boom is what gives the cycle its symphonic breath. Even its resistance to partisan politics is inspired by it. *A Merry Book Despite Death and Tears,* the subtitle that De Coster, who has many traits in common with Balzac (although he spoiled them by putting them in saccharine affirmative form) gave his chief work, could be claimed by Balzac, author of the *Contes drolatiques* or *Droll Stories.* The progress on the part of society as a whole that runs through the *Comédie humaine* does not coincide with the trajectory of an individual life. It casts a radiance on the victims of all the intrigues in a way that is no longer possible even for those who are fortunate, should they stray by chance into a narrative. The adolescent pleasure of reading Balzac is fed by the fact that an unspoken promise of justice on the part of the whole arches like a rainbow over all individual suffering. The material foundation for both the Rubempré novels is laid in the story of David Séchard's invention. Provincial swindlers cheat him of its fruits. But the invention is successful, and after all the catastrophes Séchard, a decent man, still achieves a modest affluence through an inheritance. Ulrich von Hutten, who died persecuted and syphilitic and yet cried out that living was a joy, is like a prototype of Balzac's characters, someone from the prehistoric bourgeois world whose crags and crevices the novelist, looking down from the mountain peak, recognizes.

❖

Lucien de Rubempré begins as an enthusiastic youth with high literary ambitions. Balzac may have his doubts about the quality of talent in someone who makes his debut with sonnets about flowers and an imitation of Walter Scott's bestselling novels. But he is gentle, vulnerable, everything that would later be called refined and introverted. In any case, he has enough talent to create a new kind of feuilletonistic theater criticism. He becomes a gigolo, the accomplice of the man who rescues him, a great criminal whom he later betrays. One who deals with spirit naively, without getting his hands dirty, is—in terms of the mores of the world, which he has not had anyone teach him—pampered. He refuses to separate happiness and work. Even in work and the efforts it requires, he tries not to sully himself with the things that anyone who wants to make something of himself must come to terms with. The marketplace differentiates with great precision between what is offensive to it as the intellectual's spiritual self-satisfaction and what it treasures, the social utility which offends to its core the spirit that produces it; its sacrifice is rewarded in the exchange. The person who is not prepared to make this sacrifice wants to have it good anyway; this makes him vulnerable. The configuration of purity and egoism permits the world to enter the domain of the person who is ignorant of it. Because he refused to take the bourgeois oath, the world tends to cast him down beneath the level of the bourgeoisie, to degrade the bohemian into a venal hack, a scoundrel. He goes to the dogs more easily than the others without being fully aware of it, and the world regards that as justification for increasing the punishment. The gullible Lucien slides into relationships whose implications the intoxicated man only half understands. His narcissism imagines that love and success are meant for him personally when from the outset he is employed merely as an interchangeable figure. His desire for happiness, not yet curbed and shaped by adaptation to reality, disdains the controls that could show him that the conditions for its satisfaction destroy intellectual existence—freedom. The parasitic moment in him that disfigures all spirit gains the upper hand in him unawares: from what the bourgeois call idealism it is only a step to the wage slavery of one who, even if rightly, is too good to earn his living through bourgeois labor and blindly makes himself dependent on the very thing he shrinks from. Even the boundary between what is permitted and what constitutes betrayal becomes blurred for him. The only thing that strengthens awareness of it is the activity he considers beneath him. Lucien is incapable of distinguishing between corruption and his enthusiastic love affair with Coralie. But the naive man plunges into it too openly and too suddenly for it to come out well; his shortcut is avenged as a crime, because it innocently confesses, so to speak, the things hidden along the jungle paths of bourgeois equivalence. The hangman's noose beckons to the talent that dares to jump headfirst into the stream of the world instead of developing itself in peace and quiet. Antonio, however, has become Vautrin, the cynical moralist. He enlightens the youthful failure, who had not only to lose his illusions but also to become the abominable person about whom his illusions deceived him.

⊞

One of the finds made by Balzac the man of letters is the non-identity of the writer and what is written. Since Kierkegaard, the critique of that non-identity has been one of the defining motifs of existentialism. Balzac does better than that. He does not set the writer up as the criterion of what is written. His genius is too deeply steeped in craftsmanship, and the writer knows too well that writing is not equivalent to the pure expression of an allegedly immediate self, for him to confuse, anachronistically, the writer with the Pythian oracle whose voice resounds only with inspiration from its own depths. Balzac the Catholic was as free from the mustiness of this ideological view of the writer—the same view that was later used in the campaign against the literati—as he was from sexual prejudice and any kind of Puritanism. He grants thought the luxury of leaving behind the person who thinks it. His novels prefer to take the words of Mignon, the tightrope walker's child in Goethe's *Wilhelm Meister* novels, as their guideline: "So lasst mich scheinen, bis ich werde" ["Let me appear until I become"].* The whole *Comédie humaine* is one giant phantasmagoria, and its metaphysics is the metaphysics of illusion. At the moment in which Paris becomes the *ville lumière,* the city of light, it is a city on a different star. The conditions for recognizing it as such are social. They carry spirit high above the contingency and fallibility of the person who becomes its possessor; the intellectual forces of production are also multiplied by the division of labor, something the existentialists ignore. Whatever talent Lucien has blossoms hectically, in contradiction to what he is and to his ideals. By virtue only of what infuriated solid citizens consider the irresponsibility of the literati, he becomes a true writer for a few months. The nonidentity of spirit with those who carry it is both spirit's precondition and its flaw. That nonidentity shows that spirit represents something that would be different only within what exists, which is what it detaches itself from; and by merely representing that different existence, spirit defiles it. In the division of labor, spirit both serves as the designated representative of utopia and hawks utopia in the marketplace, making it equivalent to what exists. Spirit is all too existential rather than not existential enough.

---

*Here and in the sentences that follow, Adorno plays on the various meanings of the German verb *scheinen* (to shine, to appear, to seem) and its noun *Schein* (illusion, semblance, appearance, but also shine and light). In Hegel's classic definition, beauty is "schöner Schein," beautiful semblance. —Translator's note.

◨◧◨◧◨

Valéry's Deviations

For Paul Celan

*T*wo volumes of Paul Valéry's prose have appeared in German in quick succession. Insel Verlag has published a selection from the notebooks in an excellent translation by Bernhard Boschenstein, Hans Staub, and Peter Szondi. The German title *Windstriche* reproduces the *Rhumbs* of the original in English, *Rhumbs*—the gradation marks on the compass rose, as well as the angle between one of these marks and the meridian, hence the deviation of a course from the north; what Valery has in mind is "swerves from the governing direction or 'set' of my mind . . ."[1] (v.14, p. 159). Bibliothek Suhrkamp has put out the *Pièces sur l'art* [*Pieces on Art*], abbreviating the title to *Über Kunst* [*On Art*]. The translation is by Carlo Schmid, probably the first and only front-bench politician to be familiar with Valéry's name and stature and heroically make time for such difficult and demanding texts. The two volumes lie at the opposite poles of the prose writings of the poet Valéry. The one contains ideas, flashes of insight; in a passage in the preface, Valéry, a man of order, coquettishly expresses himself embarrassed by them. The other contains official remarks made at exhibitions and similar occasions. In them Valéry occasionally displays the posture of the French Academician, something perhaps more dangerous for him than the "semblance of life" in the jottings in *Rhumbs*, whose subterranean coherence gives them more unity and form than an external architecture could have.

The late hour of their publication in Germany may prove propitious for these two books. Not only do they, like Proust, combine progressive elements with an authority of success that is rare in Germany these days. In addition, the tension in Valéry's work anticipates that of contemporary art—the tension between emancipation and integration—by thirty years. At times Valéry arrogantly disputes his qualifications as an aesthetician (v. 12, p. 112). What he has in mind, of course, is the failure of academic philosophy to deal with questions of actual artistic production; in much the same way he disputes the objective competence of literary history (v. 12, p. 163). He is much too shrewd not to arouse the suspicions of a kind of resentment whose basis he fully understood: "When a man calls another man a 'sophist,' it means that he feels intellectually inferior. If we can't attack the argument, we attack the arguer" (v. 14, p. 245). But his thought is primed by surrendering to the object without reservations and not by playing with itself. In the process, clichés disintegrate for him, although mediocre intellectuals customarily attribute the dismantling of these clichés to the vanity of someone who wants to be right at any cost. The ability to see works of art from the inside, in their logic as artifacts, things that have been produced—a union of action and reflection that neither hides behind naiveté nor hastily dissolves its concrete characteristics in a general concept—is probably the only form in which aesthetics is still possible. It proves its worth in the fact that Valéry's formulations are scarcely vulnerable to any critique but one that continues their line of thought.

In the meantime the word "aesthetics" has taken on the slightly archaic tone that Valéry's sensibility was the first to note in so much else, like virtue. As a theory that attempts to establish the laws of the beautiful once and for all—and the will to do so was not alien to Valéry, no matter how little he subscribed to it—aesthetics has become as reactionary as the solemn pathos associated with a conception of art that elevates it above empirical reality and society and into the absolute. Valéry inherited this pathos from Mallarmé, although his essay on Manet's triumphal procession in the *Pièces sur l'art* ["The Triumph of Manet," v. 12, pp. 105–14] also rises authoritatively above the phrase "l'art pour l'art" that is so simplistically ascribed to him. Valéry praises the painter and interprets him as someone whom Zola loved as much as Mallarmé did. But in the French avant-garde it has become customary to class Valéry with the reactionaries, and that will certainly be detrimental to his reception in Germany. According to Pierre Jean Jouve, Valéry belonged to the Baudelairean right-wing. What puts him there is his aristocratic classicistic cult of form with its sinister political implications. This represented one aspect of Baudelaire and in Mallarmé, according to Jouve, became divorced from the social-revolutionary impulses of *Les Fleurs du mal*. The left-wing Baudelaire, in contrast, led to Surrealism by way of

Rimbaud. The Surrealists have given Valéry a bad name. A passage from *Rhumbs,* one worthy of Nietzsche, might be applied to him, and he will have to put up with it: "Our hatred inhabits our enemy, enlarges his depths, dissects the tiniest roots of his most intimate designs. We probe into him more deeply than into ourselves—and better than he probes into himself. He forgets himself but we don't forget *him.* For we see him by way of a wound and there is no sense more potent, none that descries and magnifies more strongly all that touches it—than the sense of injury" (v. 14, p. 244). These books are not lacking in frankly reactionary material, from a bow to Mussolini as the "strong will that rules beyond the Alps" (v. 12, p. 219), to the presumptuous familiarity of his assertion that what was needed was "social conditions that allowed and maintained an aristocracy of wealth and taste, with all the courage of its own luxury" (v. 12, p. 215), or the deadly Moltkean satisfaction of "That delectable universe is not ours and, all in all, I think we should be glad of it" (v. 13, p. 188). Valéry was anti-political, like the Thomas Mann of the *Reflections of a Non-Political Man.* But he formulated his position in words that might have been written by Karl Kraus: "Politics is the art of preventing people from minding their own business" (v. 14, p. 183). It is easy enough to equate Valéry's anti-political intention with the reactionary intention of the man of independent means. But the accusation would be too hasty. Valéry describes a political meeting:

> A man climbs on to the platform. A general uproar, catcalls, angry demonstrations and so forth.
>
> He begins speaking. We expect the usual oration. But little by little the activity of thought emerges and dominates. We are shown thought in gestation: no more question of ready-made solutions, slogans, political programs, parliamentary tactics; no more flashing imagery, no more slashing repartees.
>
> Only the vast perplexity of a creative mind feeling its way uncertainly —with the future unknown, the present dimly known; with insufficient logic, undigested knowledge, defective insight, inability to grasp the object sought for, clumsy turns of phrase, conclusions always left in the balance. All that is masked by the art of the trained speaker, all that in human thought, in its raw state, reflects the chaos of the real world, comes to the fore. (v. 14, pp. 183–84)

As an aesthetician, Valéry showed the same aversion to persuasion—in his opposition to Wagner, for example. In general, "wanting to make other people share one's opinion" strikes him as "indecent" (v. 14, p.

222). His aversion to politics as a technique of domination and a form of ideology goes beyond the *engagement* that is pharisaically preached to the artist. The element in Valéry that comports itself like the "ça ne me regarde pas" of the Parisian individualist is secretly in sympathy with anarchy.

Still, Valéry's anti-political–political *parti pris* affects his artistic judgments as well. At such times he is not up to his own standards, as when he is impressed by "how . . . a painter could throw twenty characters onto his canvas or his fresco, in the greatest variety of poses; and . . . all round them was no lack of fruits, flowers, trees, and architecture . . ." (v. 12, p. 152). Since people don't have it so good nowadays, we even find statements like this: "An exclusive penchant for what is new and merely new points to a degeneration of the critical faculty, for nothing is easier than to gauge the 'novelty' of a work" (v. 14, p. 11). Or: "Art knows no compromise with hurry. Our ideals are good for ten years! The ancient and excellent reliance on the judgment of posterity has been stupidly replaced by the ridiculous superstition of *novelty*, assigning the most illusory ends to our enterprises, condemning them to the creation of what is most perishable, of what must be perishable by its nature: the sensation of newness" (v. 12, p. 220). While it may be precisely the "attraction of the new" that becomes outmoded in works of art, those which lack such charms, which do not break through the routinized consciousness of their age through that charm—a consciousness to which the questionable confidence in the judgment of posterity also belongs— will scarcely live to grow old.

But it is only in Valéry's reactionary aspects that one can see what the forward-moving aspects in him consist of. For the progressive and the regressive moments are not scattered throughout his books; rather, the progressive aspect is wrested from the regressive and transforms the latter's inertia into its own élan. As a theoretician, Valéry bridged the two extremes of Descartes and Bergson. But both for the Cartesian in him, the guardian of innate, eternal ideas, and for the one who attends in Bergsonian fashion to what is fluid and "indefinite," to what mocks conceptual fixation, Hegel—who thinks dynamically and yet in sharp outlines, without any vague or fluid transitions—must originally have been very distant. All the more emphatic is Valéry's advocacy of the dialectic, something to which he is compelled against his own education and temperament, solely by the "freedom in relation to the object" to which he tries to do justice in his thinking. His philosophical nature,

stubborn as a pounding surf, erodes from below what the two philosophical archenemies have in common: the illusion of immediacy as an
assured first principle. In a thought experiment one can imagine finding
in Hegel's *Phenomenology,* or perhaps in his *Philosophy of Right*—the
Hegel who was forgotten in France from the time of Cousin until the
recent wave of interest in things German—Valéry criticized the notion
of taking one's own consciousness as having this kind of immediacy and
using it as a point of departure. He implicitly opposed the purity of the
person who cannot let go of himself:

> A man who judged everything solely in the light of his own experience;
> who refused to argue about things he had not seen and experienced; who
> spoke strictly for himself; who allowed himself only direct, provisional
> but well-founded opinions; who whenever a thought occurred to him
> made a point of noting either that he had formed it himself or that he had
> read it somewhere or heard it from others and that in the former case it
> was due to chance, to an unknown source, while in the latter it was a mere
> echo—and that he thinks nothing, understands nothing whatever except
> by way of chance and echoes—such a man would be the most honest man
> in the world, the most veracious, most detached. But his very purity
> would make him incommunicado; his truth reduce him to nonentity. (v.
> 14, pp. 184–85)

One cannot live autarchically in the immediate certainty of the *ego
cogitans,* nor will the belief in nature as immediacy hold up: "There's no
such thing as nature. Or, rather, what one takes for nature in its 'given'
state is always a more or less bygone invention. There is a stimulating
force in the notion of regaining contact with reality in the virgin state.
We fancy that such virginities exist. But trees, the sea, the sun itself—
and above all the human eye—all are 'artificial,' in the last analysis" (v.
14, p. 186). In the *Pièces sur l'art* this is broadened to become a
denunciation of the forest-and-meadow aesthetics of the simple things, a
notion the philistine cherishes as his legacy from Winckelmann: "The
will to simplicity in art is fatal every time it becomes self-sufficient and
deludes us into saving ourselves some trouble" (v. 12, p. 138). For
Valéry as for Hegel, what is immediate and simple is not something
primary but the result of a mediation. Valéry explains this in connection
with an anecdote of Chinese beauty:

> One of the finest horsemen of all time, having grown old and poor,
> obtained a post of groom, under the Second Empire, at Saumur. There

his favorite pupil, a young squadron leader and a brilliant rider, came to see him one day. "I'll do a little riding for you," Baucher told him. They put him on his horse; he set off across the field at a *walk*, came back. . . . Dazzled, the other watched him advancing, the perfect Centaur. "You see," his master told him. "No showing off. I've reached the top of my style: *a faultless walking pace.*" (v. 12, p. 138)

Just as Valéry recognizes the immediate as mediated, so too he is open to the immediate as the telos of mediation. That for him is culture. For Valéry, the art of the Renaissance was "not something whose existence had to be tolerated," not "an exceptional element of existence, but a natural and almost essential condition the absence of which would create a real privation" (v. 12, p. 225). From this it is not far to Hegel's definition of art as a manifestation of truth. The affinity extends even into logic. Analyses like the following would not cut a bad figure in Hegel's logic of essence: "Every statement has several meanings, the most remarkable of which, beyond all doubt, is the cause of its being made at all. Thus Quia nominor Leo does not really mean 'For I am named Lion' but rather 'I am an example in the Latin Grammar' " (v. 14, p. 258). Conversely, in sentences like "the worse the artist the more one sees the man himself, his particularity and his arbitrariness," Hegel was plagiarizing Valéry prophetically. Sentences like these anticipated, early on, the dynamics of the idea of progress to whose late period the subjectivist Valéry still belonged, at least aesthetically. For him the bearers of that idea are Manet, Baudelaire, and Wagner; in them the sensual charm and refinement common to both Impressionism and Symbolism were made principles and brought to their highest peak. Valéry was one of the first to record the resulting losses in the forces of objectivation and coherence. Stamped by Symbolism himself, he was immune to the *laudatio temporis acti*, and yet he could gauge the price in consonance works paid for their permeation by subjectivity. Post-Valéryan modern art drew the conclusions from this independently of him. The emancipation of painting and sculpture from resemblance to the object and of music from tonality is essentially motivated by the drive to recreate in the work, immanently, some of the objectivity it loses when it stops at a subjective reaction to something pregiven, whatever form it takes. The more the work of art divests itself critically of all the determinants not immanent in its own form, the more it approaches a second-order objectivity. To this extent, the radicalization of art has regained what Valéry saw in retrospect as deficient in the progress his own period made. Moreover, in a society that is perpetually unfree, the emancipation of the subject, which is its duty and its happiness, both remains illusion and contributes to the general illusion. For the aesthetic subject, the authority of everything traditional has been irretrievably lost. The subject must depend upon itself, may rely only on what it can develop from within; for it, the critical path is truly the only one open. It can hope for no other objectivity. Thrown back upon itself, this subject is of necessity what is closest and most immediate to itself artistically. Socially, however, it remains derivative, a mere agent of the law of value. The more deeply it expresses its own truth as something it alone can attain, something to which it alone can give substance, the more it becomes entangled in untruth. Valéry's socially naive lament for the past bears faithful witness to this antinomy. Similarly, in its hermetic insulation from the horrors of communication, the aesthetic self-reliance he champions in his ideas about the authentic works of the past is in accordance with tendencies in those to whom Valéry is anathema and whom he himself would unhesitatingly have condemned as decadent. Now that Mallarmé's theory of the dice throw has taken on contemporary relevance with tachism and experiments in aleatory music, one context into which the oeuvre of Mallarmé's pupil Valéry fits has become apparent. After Valéry, the tension in art between contingency and the law of construction was intensified to the breaking point; similarly, deviation was a constituent of his own anachronistic insistence on concepts like order, regularity, and permanence. For him, deviation is the guarantee of truth. Valéry expresses sharp opposition to the commonsense view of knowledge: "Unless it's new and strange, every visualization of the world of things is false. For if something is *real* it is bound to lose its reality in the process of becoming familiar. Philosophic contemplation means reverting from the familiar to the strange, and, in the strange, encountering the real" (v. 14, pp. 39–40). In a society whose totality has sealed itself up as ideology, only what does not resemble the facade can be true. The conservative artist's critical awareness that the banal is a lie later becomes Brecht's alienation effect. Neither in the artist's ideas nor in artistic practice can the universal be so perfectly reconciled with the particular as traditional art and aesthetics envisioned. Mindful of what has been forgotten on the path of progress, of what has eluded the great tendency whose advocate he is as an advocate of the aesthetic domination of nature, Valéry the reactionary has to come down on the side of difference, of what does not come out even. Hence the nautical name he gave his notebooks. No interpretation could put that more precisely than his own formulation, "an accident that is my substance" (*Rhumbs*, p. 662).

Proust, Valéry's declared antithesis, for whom classical rationality and orderly structure were suspect from the start, would have agreed with that: what Valéry is forced into in spite of himself is the formal law of Proust's work as a whole. But in Valéry, Proust's enthusiastic confidence in the truth content of the incommensurable, of involuntary memory, is broken and melancholy: "Flashes of insight are always unexpected. Every unexpected idea rates as an insight, for a few moments" (v. 14, p. 254). The obviousness of things that come involuntarily, the temporal core of truth as that which is always new, truth that manifests itself suddenly— all that has an aspect of illusoriness and fragility. This is the reason for the pain that abrupt and irrefutable insights caused both Valéry and Proust. Valéry, successor to Baudelaire, who glorified the lies of the beloved, makes of Baudelaire's spleen a sorrowful physiognomy such as Proust might have drawn of Albertine. "Human beings silently entreat each other to say what they do not think. 'Tell us what we'd like to hear! Say something nice,' our eyes implore" (v. 14, p. 31). La Rochefoufjcauldian enlightenment and neoromantic sensibility merge in this observation. Like Proust, Valéry repudiated the rigid division between thought and intuition, a division to which reified consciousness clings contentedly: "unless we read into 'inspiration' a power so flexible, so adjustable, so sagacious, so shrewd that there is really no reason why we shouldn't call it Intelligence and Knowledge" (v. 14, p. 200). At times the agreement between Proust and Valéry extends even to the philosophical thesis: "The past is not as we think it. It is not at all something that *was;* it is only what remains of what was. Relics and memories. The rest has no existence at all" (v. 14, p. 167). Reflection on the classical concept of the enduring, a concept Valéry does not question, leads to a negation of the *monumentum aere perennius*. In Valéry's philosophy of history a fissure opens up in the structure of the *vérités éternelles*. The common denominator for Proust and Valéry, however, is none other than Bergson, whose eulogy Valéry delivered under the Nazi occupation.

Nowhere in Valéry can one see more clearly the compulsion to transcend, through antithesis, the kind of position all traditional philosophy clings to jealously than in his relationship to music. He called himself unmusical, if not anti-musical: "After a short time music gets on my nerves" (v. 14, p. 8). The man who praised the "powerful inspiration"

(v. 3, p. 213) of a mediocre composer like Honegger described the opera-like characteristics of Racine, "whose tragedies Lully went so studiously to hear, and of whose lines and movements the beautiful forms and the pure developments of Gluck seem to be the immediate translations" (v. 7, p. 164), not realizing there were hardly "developments" in Gluck and that the primitiveness of Gluck's formal structures would arouse his scorn if he encountered it in painting. Nevertheless, immediately thereafter he gives a description of bad habits in the recitation of verse that could apply word for word to bad musical interpretation: "The verse is broken up, or obscured; or, at other times, only its awkwardnesses seem to be retained: the actor stresses and exaggerates the frame and supports of the alexandrine, those conventional signs which to my mind are very useful but which are crude procedures if diction does not envelop and clothe them with its grace" (v. 7, pp. 164–65). So close was Valéry to music, and so far from it. At first he accepted the schema that places the visual, as the statically rational, in simple opposition to the flowing and chaotic character of aconceptual temporal art. He ascribes to painting, as opposed to poetry and music, an object-like positivistic moment. Hence his reservations about the magical effects of the image. Valéry the Symbolist sided with the Impressionists and not with Puvis de Chavannes: "Painting cannot, without a certain risk, set out to picture our dreams. I do not think *L'Embarquement pour Cythère* is the best Watteau. I find Turner's fairy visions disenchanting at times" (v. 12, p. 146). It is not when art desperately protects its magical legacy but only when it renounces it through disillusionment that it can survive and make the transition to language, as which Valéry read it. This is the point to which his interpretation of Manet leads. Like Baudelaire, the "Naturalists," with whom, in this context, he classes Manet, "have found (or rather . . . have introduced) *poetry*, and sometimes the highest poetry, in things or themes which until then had been considered base or insignificant" (v. 12, p. 109). But he was not as intransigently opposed to music as he was to false metamorphoses into music. At the very beginning of *Rhumbs*, in a remarkable parallel to Kierkegaard, he talks about the "philosophic ear" (v. 14, p. 169). Valéry himself had such an ear. As a lyric poet, the man who claimed to have no musical sense could not deceive himself about the fact that "the paths of poetry and music intersect" (v. 14, p. 211). "It was the age of symbolism: we were, each according to his disposition and poetic allegiance, quite bent on increasing, as best we could, the amount of music that the French language can allow in discourse" (v. 3, p. 214). But Valéry does not adhere to the synaesthetic program of Verlaine's "Art Poétique"; instead, he analyzes his own contradictory experience. His quip, "Adding music to a good poem is like using a stained-glass window to light a painted picture" (v. 14, p. 214), is maliciously aimed at music.[2] It falls short. Otherwise the quality of songs could scarcely be so dependent on that of the poems; rather than reproducing them, the songs settle into the empty spaces in the poems and help them out in their fallibility. On the other hand, the estrangement wrought in a picture by light coming through stained glass is not a bad image for the transfiguration of good poetry in a good song. And Valéry also acknowledges something Goethe did not want to say— his antimusical stance is a defense against a temptation to which he then succumbs after all: "My 'unfairness' toward music may perhaps be due to a feeling that something as powerful as that is capable of animating us to the point of absurdity" (v. 14, p. 219), capable of creating contexts of meaning beyond the rational: "Moreover, and above all, do not be in a hurry to reach the meaning" (v. 7, p. 165). Accordingly, Valéry's postulate of a pure poetry that transcends the sense of language contains the criteria for a musician who knows what he is doing: "How shameful to set up as a writer without knowing the true nature of language, metaphors, vocables, shifts of ideas and tone; without a conception of how the work should be *constructed* in length or the conditions of its ending; hardly knowing the *why* and not at all the *how!* Well might the Pythia blush! . . ." (v. 14, p. 101). The yearning for meaning to vanish into verse is inherent in music, which knows intentions only in the process of their disappearance. Valéry notes the correlate to this in language: "Although the tone and rhythm are present to help the sense, they intervene only for a moment as immediate necessities and as aids to the meaning which they are transmitting and which at once absorbs them without an echo . . ." (v. 7, p. 163). What testifies to the contradictory unity of the two media is the fact that while in lyric poetry musical structures transcend language and its intentions, music comes to resemble prose in structure, the very prose from any traces of which Valéry wants to protect poetry. The aesthetics of the anti-musical sometimes sounds like an aesthetics of music: "All parts of a work should 'pull their weight' " (v. 14, p. 105). This is exactly how musical terminology employs the notion of thematic work. Valéry's unconscious accord with music often works to the credit of compositions he never heard. "When a work is very short the effect of the tiniest detail is of the same order of magnitude as the work's general effect" (v. 14, p. 106)—that is the physiognomy of Anton von Webern. For the optical-crystalline Valéry, every art is ultimately transformed into the music he feared; not only is all art language for him, as in Benjamin's early work, but there are "aspects, forms, momentary states of the visible world which can *sing*" (v. 12, p. 141). The poet's gaze, sucking in colors and forms, discovers that song.

Valéry's touchy attitude toward music, however, is relevant not only for a general differentiation of the arts from one another but also for their unity. A problematic Valéry was concerned with has recently become of central interest in composing: the relationship between chance, on the one hand, and integral construction, which carries the idea of the work's autonomy, its independence of any specific receiver, to its ultimate conclusion, on the other. In the idea of the integral work of art, seamlessly enclosed within itself and bound solely by its immanent logic—an idea that follows from the overall tendency of the arts in the West to progressive domination of nature, or, concretely, to complete control over their material—something is missing. Art accommodates to the advances of a civilizing rationality and owes the historical unfolding of its productive forces to it, but at the same time it intends a protest against that development, a remembrance of what cannot be accommodated within it and is eliminated by it—the non-identical, to which the word "deviation" alludes. Hence art does not fuse perfectly with total rationality, because by its very nature it is deviation; only as deviation does it have a right to exist in the rational world and the power to assert itself. If art were simply equivalent to rationality, it would disappear in it and die off. It cannot, however, evade rationality unless it wants to settle helplessly into special preserves, impotent in the face of the inexorable domination of nature and the social ramifications of that domination and, as something merely tolerated by it, genuinely in thrall to that domination for the first time. The aesthetic metaphor for this kind of paradox is chance, that which is non-identical to *ratio*, the incommensurable as a moment within identity, a moment of rational lawfulness of a specific type—statistical lawfulness, something to which Valéry's thoughts turn frequently. As chance, the form of subjectivity, alienated from itself, gains the ascendancy in the objective work of art, whose objectivity can never be an objectivity in itself but must be mediated through the subject despite the fact that it can no longer tolerate any immediate intervention by the subject. At the same time, chance proclaims the impotence of a subject that has become too negligible to be authorized to speak directly about itself in the work of art. Chance negates law for the sake of aesthetic freedom and yet in its heteronomy remains the opposite of freedom. Valéry confirms that, as though he were criticizing the contemporary dream of a music that would be totally determined and completely independent of the subject: "In all the arts—and that is precisely why they are arts—the sense of having become so out of necessity, something a work brought to successful completion must plausibly convey to us, can be evoked only through an act of free creation. The joining and ultimate harmonization of traits that are independent of one another and must be woven together is achieved not through a recipe or an automatic mechanism but by miracle or ultimately by effort—by miracle in conjunction with efforts borne by a will" (*Pièces sur l'art*, p. 1248). Chance is steered in accordance with this will, as it is in recent art, and subjected to the rationality of the whole. But chance also marks the limits of rationality in the material that rationality processes; except that the material has already been sucked so dry by rationality that its abstractness once more becomes equivalent to mere lawfulness, to the formal unity of the concept that chance opposes: the non-identical as identical. The estrangement from meaning that chance imports into every work imitates the estrangement of the age; through its unvarnished acknowledgment of the totality's estrangement from meaning, chance lodges a protest against it. Valéry experienced all this. Like Mallarmé, he sympathized with chance without reservation or apology, splendidly unconcerned about the contradiction with his primary inclination, despite the fact that his whole pathos stems from the notion that the way the mind gains possession of itself is through the process of the work's gaining possession of the mind. The constellation of these two moments is outlined in the essay in *Pièces sur l'art* on the dignity of artistic techniques that involve fire: "But all the fire worker's admirable vigilance and all the foresight learned from experience, from his knowledge of the properties of heat, of its critical stages, of the temperatures of fusion and reactions, still leave immense scope for the noble element of uncertainty. *They can never abolish chance.* Risk remains the dominating and, as it were, the sanctifying element of his great art" (v. 12, p. 171). Valéry sets as much store by necessity as by what escapes necessity, and in chance he hopes to find the neutral point between the two. It is this moment in chance, the moment that is alien to meaning, a true threshold value in *temps espace*, that he associates with the Bergsonian *temps durée*, involuntary memory as the sole form of survival. For in the anarchy of history this memory is itself contingent.

For Valéry this defines the dignity of chance. He writes of a ceramics exhibition: "Nothing more closely resembles our present resources of learning, our historical capital, than this collection of objects *accidentally* preserved. All our knowledge is, in the same way, a residue. Our documents are leavings which one age lets fall to the next, in haphazard disorder" (v. 12, p. 167). This salvaging, however, does not diminish Valéry's distrust of the unmediated contingency of the process of artistic production, of what is too easy. The emphasis he puts on the resistance of materials, which brings chance into the work of art, stems from that same distrust of the contingency of mere subjectivity. "That explains why true artists resent the risk and vexation of too great a facility in any art where the material fails in itself to offer any positive resistance" (v. 12, p. 169). While chance, as something that eludes the artist's control, may be incompatible with the already somewhat antiquated notion of the "act of free creation," that incompatibility defines the question of how art is still possible.

Valéry's contradictions have a socio-historical side. Just as, following neo-Romantic custom, his essays on the Italian painting of the Renaissance, especially Veronese, pay homage to authority as such, to the grand airs and sovereign control that seem to have splintered into formlessness in bourgeois individualism, so Valéry may have suspected itinerant musicians of being frivolous people whose fleeting spectacle is no more stable, binding, reliably settled in space and immanent within order than the itinerants themselves. Not the least of Valéry's ideals is that of an art that has divested itself of its vagabondage and its social odium, no matter how well sublimated it may be. In fact, however, this element of vagabondage, this lack of subjection to the control of a settled order, is the only thing that allows art to survive in the midst of civilization. But the purity of a thought that does not let itself be constrained by the ideology to which it has sworn allegiance does not stop even with this motif. As the child of a rational age, Valéry does not acknowledge the neat distinction between production and reflection in art. He is much too self-reflective to deceive himself about the fact that even artists who disdain economic considerations remain tied to the precarious status of the mind in the dominant society, with which they must comply even while opposing it. Artists today are intellectuals, whether they accept that fact or not, and as such they are what social theory calls "third persons": they live on profit that has been diverted to them. While they perform no "socially useful work" and contribute nothing to the material reproduction of life, it is they alone who represent theory and all consciousness that points beyond the blind coercion of material circumstances. They are defenseless against the distrust both of the status quo, which they live on without serving it dependably, and its enemies, for whom they are nothing but impotent agents of power. Hence, as society's painful nerve, they draw the hatred of the whole world down upon themselves. But if one is to defend them, it cannot be by praising the mind abstractly but only by expressing the negative element in them as well. Only when the ideological husk of their own existence falls away, only in a process of merciless self-reflection that would be the self-reflection of society as well, would they attain their social truth. Valéry contributes to this process. He incorporates into thought the flaw that mars all thought: "Without its parasites—thieves, singers, dancers, mystics, heroes, poets, philosophers, businessmen—humanity would be a community of animals, or not even a community, but a species: the earth would lack salt" (v. 14, p. 187). The same list of "third persons" could appear in Marx, someone whose name would hardly have crossed Valéry's lips. Nor is Valéry unfamiliar with the connection between mind and mental production on the one hand and what the language of political economy calls the "sphere of circulation" on the other. "If the essence of tradesmanship is to buy with the intention of selling, then the artist or author who observes, travels, reads, and exists solely, or almost solely, with the object of producing—and putting his impressions on the market—is a tradesman. 'He is not acquiring anything for its own sake,' you say. But perhaps 'acquiring for its own sake' means nothing" (v. 14, p. 192). This man who firmly insists on the purity of the work for its own sake also understands how much the purity of an autonomous aesthetic owes to something heteronomous, the market. While petty artists drivel on about being creators and precisely by praising that status in ideological terms assure themselves of universal agreement in the marketplace, Valéry acknowledges the paradoxical relationship of the autonomous work to its commodity character. The autonomous work becomes something objective only when the producer does not stand in direct relationship to his experiences but instead objectifies them. Truth which has become estranged from itself becomes the acknowledged model of the absolute work. What in its own terms is originality and genius is in social terms a natural monopoly. One of those witty remarks that, as Nietzsche says, produce a just noticeable smile alludes to this: " 'What!' a man of genius may have asked himself. 'Am I really such a freak? Can it be that what seems to me so natural, a casual image, a self-evident observation, an effortless phrase, a fleeting recreation of my inner eye, my secret ear, my leisure hours, all these chance connections of thoughts or words—can it be that they make me a monstrosity? How strange is my "strangeness"! Am I no better than a curio? And if so, supposing there existed a hundred thousand men like me, would that be enough to make me pass unnoticed, without any change having taken place within me? Suppose there were a million like me. I should come to rank as a commonplace ignoramus, and my value decline to its millionth part' " (v. 14, p. 224). Such reflections culminate in an amazing identification of mind, self-alienation, and commodity character: "The more a consciousness is 'conscious,' the more foreign to it seems the man who has it and equally foreign its opinions, actions, characteristics, and sentiments. For this reason it tends to regard all that is most personal and private in it as 'accidental' and extraneous" (v. 14, p. 43). A pointed self-destructiveness is unmistakable here. As in Nietzsche, there are anti-intellectual motifs alongside daring attempts to rescue what is most vulnerable in the mind. We hear voices from the pre-fascist era: "The intellectual's job is to juggle with all things under their signs, names, or symbols without the counterpoise of real action. That is why the intellectual's remarks are startling, his politics precarious, his pleasures superficial. Such men are social stimulants, having the utility and dangers of stimulants in general" (v. 14, p. 188). But when it comes to the area of Valéry's specific experience, artistic production, he has no room for this kind of humbug. Intuition, the trademark of the anti-intellectual, fares badly with him. He polarizes it into the two extremes of consciousness and chance and mockingly pins the yellow star of the "third person" on the very thing that finds official favor: "For poets it is, or should be, an intolerable image: that represents them as getting their best creations from imaginary beings. Mere mouthpieces—what notion could be more humiliating? Personally I have no use for it. I invoke no inspiration except that element of chance, which is common to every mind; then comes an unremitting toil, which wars against this element of chance" (v. 14, p. 241).

What is especially apparent in such formulations but in fact defines the rhythm of Valéry's thought in general is what the official history of philosophy would call the opposition of rationalist and irrationalist motifs. The status of those motifs, however, is the opposite in France of what it is in Germany. In Germany it is customary to class rationalism with progress, and irrationalism, as a legacy of Romanticism, with reaction. For Valéry, however, the traditional moment is identical to the Cartesian rationalist moment, and the irrationalist moment is Cartesianism's self-criticism. The rational-conservative moment in Valéry is the dictatorial civilizing moment, the autonomous ego's avowed power to control the unconscious. "Morning brings a sloughing off of our dreams, dispelling all that has taken advantage of our negligence and absence to proliferate, clutter us up; natural products, dirt, mistakes, stupidities, terrors, obsessions. The beasts go back to their dens. The Master is back from a journey; the witches' sabbath is put to rout. Absence and presence" (v. 14, p. 171). Now as ever, such domination is justified in Cartesian terms, on the basis of *clara et distincta perceptio*. Even Valéry's doubts about definitive·answers, doubts that are the catalyst for his irrational deviations, are gauged in terms of such definitiveness: "But our answers are very seldom correct; most are feeble or quite off the mark. So well do we feel this that in the end we turn against our questions—which is all wrong, since they should be our point of departure. What we ought to do is to draw up within ourselves a question antecedent to all others, which inquires of each in turn what value, if any, it may have" (v. 14, p. 226). Cartesianism overturns itself through the driving force in its own methodology—doubt:

> Now and again I picture to myself a man who, while in possession of all our knowledge of specific operations and procedures, would nevertheless be wholly ignorant of all notions and words that do not call up clean-cut images and do not give rise to acts which are uniform and capable of being repeated. This man has never heard talk of "mind," of "thought," of "substance," of "freedom," of "will," of "space" or "time," of "forces," of "life," of "instincts," of "memory," of "causation," of "gods"; nor of "morality" nor of "origins." In brief, he knows all the things we know and is ignorant of the things we do not know—only his ignorance goes further: *he doesn't even know their names*. Then, under these conditions, I make him come to grips with the problems of life and the feelings they give rise to and, having now built up my imaginary man, I set him moving and launch him into the thick of circumstances. (v. 14, p. 45)

Insistence on the requirement of absolute certainty ends in openness, in what by Descartes' criteria is uncertain. The *sum cogitans* is shown the contingency of its mere existence, something Descartes had not reflected on and which would have cut the ground from under the feet of his *Meditations*. The epistemological consequences of this are made explicit;

what exists is not identical with its concept: "Small unexplained facts always contain grounds for upsetting all explanations of 'big' facts" (v. 14, p. 35). Without presuming to decide it, Valéry reduces the debate about rationalism to a formula of almost mathematical elegance: "What has not been 'fixed' is nothing. What's been fixed is dead" (v. 14, p. 239). If there is anything at all that may still lay claim to the name of philosophy, it is such antitheses. By leaving them unreconciled, thought expresses its own limits: the non-identity of the object with its concept, which must both demand that identity and understand its impossibility.

The rationalism debate too has a historico-philosophical dimension in Valéry, a dialectic of enlightenment. Valéry was aware of something central in enlightenment, the emergence of a purely instrumental thought, the triumph of subjective over objective reason through the advance of rationality as such: "What is more, our ideas, even the basic ones, are coming to lose the status of essences and acquiring that of implements" (v. 14, p. 189). He does not shrink from the conclusion that reason, unleashed, turns against itself: "Science has done away with the satisfying ʹcertitudes of 'good sense' and 'common sense' " (v. 14, p. 189). The horrors of actual practice have since outdone the shudder that came over him then: "The revolt of common sense is the instinctive recoil of man confronted by the inhuman; for common sense takes stock only of the human, of man's ancestors and yardsticks; of man's powers and interrelations. But research and the very powers that he possesses lead away from the human. Humanity will survive as best it can—perhaps there's a fine future in store for humanity" (v. 14, p. 190). Neither the interconnection between an unleashed subjective rationality and the subject's self-alienation nor the connection between this tendency and the tendency to totalitarianism escape Valéry:

> A too precise idea of Man, a too clear perception of his mechanism, a too total lack of superstitions about his nature, a too peremptory refusal to look on Man as a thing-in-itself and as an *end*, a too statistical view of human beings, a too clear prevision of their reactions, of the inevitable shifts and reversals of some of their feelings within a few weeks or years, a too strong sense of order and of the ideal form of government—such qualities, perhaps, are out of place at the *highest* level. Suppose intelligence were in command, what then?" (v. 14, pp. 246–47)

Valéry talks about the new ideal of the state in metaphors, like Karl Kraus: "The State is a huge, appalling, unwieldy creature; a Cyclops of prodigious strength and awkwardness, the monstrous spawn of Might and Right whose contradictions have given birth to it. It owes its life solely to a crowd of little men who keep its inert hands and feet in clumsy movement, and its big glass eye sees nothing but cents and millions. Friends of all, and each man's enemy—there you have the State!" (v. 14, p. 246).

So complex an issue is Valéry's conservatism. For all his aversion to the administered world, he refuses to hide behind invectives condemning decadence and perversions. What befalls reason, human beings as its bearers, and the subject, is the very principle of reason: "The thinking mind is brutal—no concessions. What, indeed, is more brutal than a thought?" (v. 14, p. 256), or even: "What's vilest in the world if not the Mind? It is the *body* that recoils from filth and crime. Like the fly, the Mind settles on everything. Nausea, disgust, regrets, remorse are not its properties; they are merely so many curious phenomena for it to study. Danger draws it like a flame and if the flesh were not so powerful would lead it to burn its wings, urged on by a fierce and fatuous lust for knowledge" (v. 14, p. 39). In Valéry pure mind confesses its own untruth. Its complicity with the abominable, however, is nothing but a legacy of violence, the violence that for centuries it has allowed to be perpetrated on everything that exists in subjugating it to the principle of its own self-preservation. In Valéry the mind has become tempered enough to look its own secret in the eye.

For one who is willing to risk so much, not even art is taboo. As something permeated with mind, art is entangled in progress and science, for better or for worse. "In all the arts there is a physical component which can no longer be considered or treated as it used to be, which cannot remain unaffected by our modern knowledge and power" (v. 13, p. 225). Valéry's pride does not establish a kingdom of its own on some Elba of irrationality: "For the last twenty years neither matter nor space nor time has been what it was from time immemorial. We must expect great innovations to transform the entire technique of the arts, thereby affecting artistic invention itself and perhaps even bringing about an amazing change in our very notion of art" (v. 13, p. 225). Valéry, archenemy of naturalism, does not spare the Romantics:

> Their minds sought refuge in a·version of the Middle Ages they had fashioned for themselves; they shunned the chemist for the alchemist. They were happy only with legend or history—that is, with the exact opposite of physics. They escaped from organized life into passion and

emotion, and on these they founded a culture (and even a type of drama).
. . . In short, the idol of Progress was countered by the idol of damning
Progress; which made *two commonplaces*. (v. 10, pp. 160–61)

In the almost Weberian gesture with which the artist takes the side of the
rationality of art, of course, the reactionary element surfaces, in the form
of a complicity with developments whose bearer has been and continues
to be the culture industry. In fact, the mind and that which does not
resemble mind have been linked in art from the beginning and have
become increasingly closely intertwined: "Now the passage of time—or,
if you like, the demon of unexpected combinations (a demon who derives
the most surprising consequences from the present, and out of these
composes the future)—amused itself by making a quite admirable mud-
dle out of two exactly opposite notions" (v. 10, p. 161). But when Valéry
defines those "concepts" as "the miraculous and the scientific" (v. 10, p.
161) and expresses his hopes that "these two old enemies [will conspire]
to involve our lives in an endless career of transformations and surprises"
(v. 10, pp. 161–62), his confidence resembles too closely the poets'
enthusiasm for the visionary possibilities that film was expected to offer.
The dominance of the mechanical mass media often keeps even Valéry
from asking whether advances in the rational domination of nature are
not perverted to ideology when they distill magic in the form of art.
Valéry too pays tribute to an age in which the positivist "given"—and
his meditations show more than just a trace of the cult of that "given"—
converges effortlessly with the enchantment of the world. The superior
power of the status quo becomes a magical aura for the world.

Valéry is not blind to the culture industry's crimes or its social basis:
"The manufacture of machines to work miracles provides a living for
thousands of people. But the artist has had no share in producing these
wonders. They are the work of science and capital. The bourgeois has
invested his money in phantoms and is speculating on the downfall of
common sense" (v. 10, p. 162). But his critique remains ambiguous. It
does not armor him against a banality that he elsewhere takes as the index
of untruth: "In short, nearly all the dreams of humanity, as found in the
fables of various types—flying, deep-sea diving, apparitions, speech
caught and transmitted, detached from its time and source, and many
strange things that no one ever dreamed of—have now emerged from
the impossible, from the mind" (v. 10, p. 162). He forgets to add that,
as in fairy tales, the fulfillment of its wishes has never yet proved to be a

blessing for a humankind that remains under the spell of renunciation despite all its downpayments on utopia. According to Valéry, "Louis XIV, at the height of his power, hadn't the hundredth part of the authority over Nature, the means of amusement, of cultivating his mind, or of providing it with sensations, which are today at the disposal of so many men of moderate station" (v. 10, p. 163). Such comparisons are risky. It is hardly possible to compare happiness across different eras. But one would like to believe that the pleasures of the Roi Soleil somewhat surpassed those enjoyed in front of the television screen. In 1928, when Valéry set down these ideas, it may not yet have been possible for Europeans to see where the consumer culture was heading. Certainly the course the world has taken since then has refuted Valéry's glorification of "the young man today" who can fly where he likes, sleep "every night in a palace" (v. 10, p. 163), take on a hundred different ways of life, and transform himself into a happy man at every moment. For the hundred forms of life no longer hide the skeleton of their standardized unity. Nor are they at all the native realm of the person on whom they are forced; his happiness is merely a subjective caricature of that realm, and often not even that. The unity of art and science was not to be had as cheaply as Valéry sardonically imagines. To be sure, he regarded the technical utopias of the futurists and the constructivists, rather than the *juste milieu* of radio and cinema, as models of rational art. "A fine book is above all a perfect machine for reading, whose specifications can be defined quite precisely through the laws and methods of physiological optics; at the same time it is an object of art, a thing" (*Pièces sur l'art*, p. 1249). Klee christened a famous painting of his "Zwitschermaschine," a twittering machine.

Valéry's estimate of what recent developments would mean for traditional cultural objects was all the more unerring: "It must be confessed that nowadays it is only from a sense of duty that we can admire a picture in which we are compelled to consider the complexity of the program, the rigor of the conditions an artist has imposed on himself" (v. 12, p. 151). For "all works die" (v. 12, p. 238). Instead of bewailing the decline of traditional works, Valéry uses his own experience to convey the inevitability of that decline. There was enough of the *fin de siècle* in him to keep him from shedding crocodile tears over a loss of the center brought about by modernity: "All this, as I have said, could only have happened by the example of certain men who were of the first rank. Only they could open up the way; no less ability is needed to inaugurate a decadence than to lead things on to the heights" (v. 12, p. 154). That decline, the decline of the works themselves as well as of their reception, is objectively dictated by the shrinking of historical consciousness, of the sense of continuity. Valéry was probably the first to give an account of this, even before Huxley's *Brave New World:*

> Suppose that the enormous transformation which we are living through and which is changing us, continues to develop, finally altering whatever customs are left and making a very different adaptation of our needs to our means; the new era will soon produce men who are no longer attached to the past by any habit of mind. For them history will be nothing but strange, almost incomprehensible tales; there will be nothing in their time that was ever seen before—nothing from the past will survive into their present. (v. 10, pp. 163–64)

Valéry admits that culture has deserved this gathering barbarism. Culture reveals its guilt by beginning to seem comical:

> One of the surest and cruelest effects of progress, then, is to add a further pain to death, a pain increasing of itself as the revolution in customs and ideas becomes more marked and rapid. It is not enough to perish; one has to become unintelligible, almost ridiculous; and even a Racine or a Bossuet must take his place alongside those bizarre figures, striped and tattooed, exposed to passing smiles, and somewhat frightening, standing in rows in the galleries and gradually blending with the stuffed specimens of the animal kingdom. . . . (v. 10, p. 164)

The fate that befalls culture reveals it to be something it never went beyond—mere natural history. Valéry verifies Kafka's statement that progress has not yet begun.

This sheds light on Valéry's theory of time. It refers directly back to Baudelaire, to the cult of death as *le Nouveau,* the new, the unknown pure and simple, the sole refuge of spleen, which has lost the past and for which progress bears the stigma of eternal sameness. In a Kierkegaardian paradox, utopia cloaks itself in the X: "We take refuge in the unknown. We hide in it from what we know. On the unknown hope stakes its hopes. Thought would die out with the end of indetermination. Hope is a mental activity that promotes ignorance, transforms a solid wall into a cloud; there is no skeptic, no Pyrrhonian so destructive of logic, reason, probability, hard facts, as is that incorrigible demon, Hope" (v. 14, p. 179). But Valéry subjects even this murky point to analysis. He defines it as a moment, a unique fulfillment, as the differential that rises a little bit above the lost past and the hopeless future. Valéry's passion for Impressionism is focused on the immortalizing of the moment through artistic techniques that elevate presence of mind to the highest virtue of the spirit: "Genius is an instant flash. Love is born of a glance and a glance is enough to kindle lifelong hatred. If we are worth anything it is only because we have been, or have the power to be, 'beside ourselves' for a moment" (v. 14, p. 180). The extreme opposite of this idea is the bourgeois concept of the abstract labor-time in terms of which commodities are exchanged. Idiosyncratically, Valéry opposes the emergence of an age without time:

> To think that time is money is the vilest of ideas. Time serves for ripening, classifying, setting in order, perfecting. Time creates a wine, and its excellence—I am thinking of wines that mature slowly and should be drunk at a certain age; just as for a certain type of woman there's an age which must be waited for and not allowed to pass, for loving her. Some great nations lack a delicate perception of the complexity of wines, of the subtle balance of their virtues, of the age at which they should be drunk, when they are "just right"—and it is these nations which have adopted and foisted on the world that inhuman equation, time = money. They are equally insensitive to women and the fine shades of femininity. (v. 14, p. 180).

Seldom has anything more forceful been said in defense of a condemned Europe. Time consciousness is constituted between the two poles of duration and the *hic et nunc;* what threatens us no longer knows either— duration has been junked, and the Now becomes interchangeable. Valéry, grandson of Baudelaire's *vieux capitaine,* failing heroically, throws himself into the breach: "The mind abhors infinite recurrence, and now the waves, which will perish, greet it all day long . . ." (*Rhumbs,* p. 663). For this kind of mind, the sunset becomes a Baudelairean allegory of the mind's own sunset: "There is a feeling of decapitation in the depths that this duration inhabits. Slowly the head of this day falls. The disk drowns" (*Rhumbs,* p. 664).

The mind, condemned to death, sympathizes with the material element, the element within mind that is not itself mind. In this second-order materialism, Valéry joins Walter Benjamin, whose aesthetics probably learned more from Valéry than anyone else. For Valéry, material things are an antidote to a self-destructive mind that he, like Nietzsche, suspects of being an "amplifier," falsifying experience by intensifying it. In one daring meditation, material things, bread and wine, become the preconditions for Christianity, the religion of *logos:*

> In countries where bread and wine are rare or lacking, the religion consecrating them seems out of place. It is like a foreigner who can thrive only on outlandish foods imported from far lands. In lands where rice, yams, bananas, mead, sour milk, and plain water are staples, bread and wine pass for exotic products and the ritual act of taking from the table what is simplest, and treating it as what is most august, ceases to be an act performed on the level of everyday life, an act whose effect is to provide supernatural sustenance in the guise of the same things that sustain and prolong life on the material plane. (v. 14, p. 181)

Here Valéry touches on a moment of inexorable immanent dissolution, something that enthusiasm for binding ties is quick to drown out: the fact that the substance of Christianity, like that of the other great religions, cannot be isolated from material aspects of life that have vanished in the course of history. If Christianity declares itself free of everything material, everything defined in time and space, it becomes pure spirit, and truly delivers itself over to demythologization. Then it not only negates its own authority but finally dissolves into the human by way of pure symbolism and loses its substantiality. The shrinkage of that substantiality at the hands of liberal theology was something dialectical theology has warned it about, without, however, being able to stop the process. The fact that Valéry the aesthetician says nothing about any of that merely intensifies the force of thought-figures like that of bread and wine. Valéry honors the material stratum as the only one in which the artistic spirit gains mastery of itself. The more deeply this spirit, in the process of production, immerses itself in the material on which it labors, the more it molds its own form to that of the material that resists it, the higher it rises: "A poet: a man who is given ideas by the difficulty inherent in his art; not the man for whom it dries them up" (v. 14, p. 199). It is precisely the intellectual artist who has lost the naiveté to tolerate anything in art that does not become externalized: the pathos of objectivation converges with sympathy with the material. With a gesture that says, "That's it exactly," Valéry takes the side of the poem's graphic image as opposed to its meaning: "The writer's mind sees itself in the mirror provided by the printing press" (*Pièces sur l'art*, p. 1249). In doing so, Valéry the anti-idealist is by no means glorifying material things as the vehicle of the spirit, à la Fichte, and thus debasing them once more. Instead, he mournfully grants them the victory that spirit merely usurps. So ephemeral is that victory that all artifacts become victims both of the destructive power of materials and of their own inadequacy: "Books have the same enemies as man: fire, moisture, animals, the weather—and what's inside them" (v. 14, p. 95). Such mourning, however, secretly makes common cause with the frailty of artifacts. Spirit becomes spirit only when it comes to recognize its own quasi-natural character:

> Some have the merit of seeing clearly what all others see confusedly. Some have the merit of glimpsing confusedly what no one sees as yet. A combination of these gifts is exceptional. The first are finally caught up with by the rest of men. The second are swallowed up by the first or else utterly and irrevocably wiped out, leaving no trace behind. The former are lost to view, dissolved into the mass. The latter disappear into the former—or else into time, pure and simple. Such is the lot of thinkers. (v. 14, p. 220)

To think their lot, rather than mercilessly depriving themselves of food and drink, would constitute the thinkers' freedom as human beings. In his reflections on ceramics, Valéry expresses this extreme idea epigrammatically, in the form of a joke: "And there is a kind of poetry that might be designed to be read in the rounds of dishes" (v. 12, p. 165).

For Valéry's aesthetic experience, the subject's strength and spontaneity prove themselves not in the subject's self-revelation but, in Hegelian fashion, in its self-alienation. The more fundamentally the work detaches itself from the subject, the more the subject has accomplished in it. "A work endures insofar as it is capable of looking quite different from the work the author thought he was bequeathing to the future" (v. 14, p. 114). Valéry has cutting criticisms for something too weak to objectify itself—for mere intentions, for what poets think in connection with their works or put into their works without it becoming emancipated from the author and eloquent and cogent in itself. "Once a work is published its author's interpretation of it has no more validity than anyone else's" (v. 14, p. 109). Valéry, in whom the poetic and the philosophical faculties fostered one another as in hardly anyone else, hated "philosopher-poets" who confuse "a seascape painter with a ship's captain" (v. 14, p. 214). "To philosophize in verse was, and still is, to try to play a game of chess according to the rules of checkers" (v. 14, p. 235). The counterpoint to

Valéry's self-reflections on works of art is provided by something extremely hard to grasp for someone who approaches works of art from the outside: the fact that they do not belong to their author, are not essentially likenesses of him. Instead, with the first movement of conception, the author is bound to that conception and to his material. He becomes an organ for the accomplishment of the work's desires. "For every work is the work of lots of other things besides an 'author' " (v. 14, p. 201). The force of artistic production is one of self-extinction: "Even in prose we are continually obliged to write things we did not want to write but which are wanted by what we *did* want to write" (v. 14, p. 102). In the end, the accepted notion of the creative artist is corrected through antithesis:

> The work modifies its author. With each of the efforts drawing it from him he undergoes a change. When completed, it reacts on him once more; for example, he becomes the man who was capable of bringing it to birth. He refashions himself, as it were, into a creator of the finished product— a mythical being. (v. 14, p. 230)

The implication here is that the aesthetic subject is not the individual producer in his contingency but instead a latent social subject for whom the individual artist acts as an agent. Hence Valéry's contempt for theories of inspiration: for him the work is not something bestowed upon the subject as private property but something that makes demands upon him, something that deprives him of happiness and incites him to unlimited efforts. Valéry pictures a great artist saying of his work: "the sudden impact of the finished work, the shock of discovery, the message of the newborn whole, the contained emotion—all these are not for me. They're for people unacquainted with the inside story of this book of mine, who have not lived with it, who guess nothing of the fumblings, setbacks, moments of despair, and risks that went to its making, and who, seeing only the result, picture it as a magnificent conception brought off at the first attempt." (v. 14, p. 231). As midwife to this kind of objectivity, the artist is the opposite of what the bourgeois religion of art characterizes him as being: "In the long run every poet's value will equal his value as a critic (of himself)" (v. 14, p. 17). Implicitly, this delivers the verdict on aesthetic relativism. Art's objectivity, which is marked out in advance by the form of the problem and not by the author's intention, produces cogent criteria in each case. Those criteria, however, cannot be reduced to abstract rules or a priori categories: "the object of painting is indeterminate" (v. 14, p. 5). Valéry's artist is a miner without light, but the shafts and tunnels of his mine prescribe his movements for him in the darkness: for Valéry, the artist as critic of himself is one who criticizes "without stint" (v. 3, p. 214). Because the process of production becomes a process of reflection on what the self-alienating work wants, both from its producer and from its recipient, thinking about art—and in Valéry the fusion of such thought with the artistic process constitutes a permanent challenge to normal consciousness—becomes legitimate. The work unfolds in words and thoughts. Commentary and criticism are essential to it: "All the arts live by words. Each work of art demands its response; and the urge that drives man to create—like the creations that result from this strange instinct—is inseparable from a form of 'literature,' whether written or not, whether immediate or premeditated" (v. 12, p. 134). As a philosopher of history, Valéry recognizes the unity in two things commonly considered divergent—aesthetic irrationality and aesthetic theory:

> Here I must note that those artists who have sought to create from their own resources the strongest influence on our senses, almost to the point of abuse of intensity, contrast, resonance, and tone, combining the acutest stimuli, speculating on the all-pervading power of the inmost sensibility, on the *irrational* connection of the upper regions of consciousness with the "vague" and the "emotional"—which are our absolute masters—were also the most "intellectual," the most theoretical, the most obsessed with aesthetics of all. Delacroix, Wagner, Baudelaire—all great theorists, bent on dominating other minds by sensuous means. (v. 12, p. 136)

The organon of this unity is artistic technique, which deploys both spontaneous impulses and heteronomous material: "It is only by means of the 'craft' in itself, and according to its own laws, that the artist can develop his aims and ideas" (v. 12, p. 184). The heavy emphasis the work carries with Valéry, his repudiation of poetry as experience, ultimately also condemns the consumer's ideological need to be given something by art. Valéry's humanism denounces the vulgar demand that art be human: "Some think that the duration of works depends on their 'humanness,' their endeavor to be *true to life*. Yet what could be more enduring than certain works of fantasy? The untrue and the wonderful are more *human* than the 'real' man" (v. 14, p. 16). The objectified work of art's detachment from human immediacy leads Valéry to an important insight, again one he shares with Benjamin. It appears in a metaphysical context in Benjamin's critique of Goethe's *Elective Affinities:* the idea that art is not capable of representing the moral at all, and is barely capable of representing the psychological. For Valéry, talking about all that makes as much sense as discussing the Venus de Milo's liver (v. 14, p. 215). The objectivation of the work of art takes place at the expense of the depiction of the living. Works of art acquire life only when they renounce their likeness to the human: "The expression of true feelings is always commonplace, and the more sincere one is, the more commonplace one is. For, to avoid banality, we need to choose our words" (v. 14, p. 20). Valéry calls "literary superstition" "all beliefs having the common trait that they overlook the *verbal* condition of literature. This applies to the existence and the so-called psychology of 'characters' in books—living beings without entrails" (v. 14, p. 124). In return, however, these imaginary creatures have a life with a structure of its own, with a development, a flowering, and a withering away: "Pleasure first: then lessons in technique; and, lastly, documentary values" (v. 14, p. 239). The morphology of this kind of life terminates in a historico-philosophical definition of the classical that could easily outweigh everything ever thought about this concept, the most outworn concept in aesthetics: "Those works, perhaps, are 'classical' which can grow cold without dying or decomposing. It would be interesting to trace the will to lastingness implicit in the notions of perfection and flawless form, and to bring to light the part it played in the rules, laws, or canons of the arts in the ages we style 'classical' " (v. 14, p. 11). This, however, explodes Valéry's own classicism. For classical works survive by virtue of their authority, their fame, and that is overshadowed by blind chance: "Today's fame gilds the works of the past with the same intelligence that a fire or a bookworm in a library employs in the destruction of whatever comes its way" (v. 14, p. 205). The fatal loss of authority on the part of so much traditional art today has fundamentally confirmed Valéry's suspicions. Conversely, all art, even the most advanced, has taken on a conservative cast, the bearing of hibernation. Even the artist who goes to extremes, and perhaps he most of all, works under highly uncertain auspices, preparing a stockpile which only a reconciled humankind would have at its disposal. His actions do not have the contemporary relevance he thinks they do; they may awaken sometime in better days. Valéry was aware of this: "Poetry is survival. In an age when language is being simplified, forms are being altered, and the public is insensitive to them —an age of specialization—poetry is a legacy of the past. By which I mean that no one would invent poetry today" (v. 14, p. 98).

But despite all that, Valéry's objectivist aesthetics does not become stubbornly dogmatic. His reflections catch up with the fetishistic traits of their Baudelairean origins and go beyond them: even the dehumanization of the work of art is reduced to the subject, to its entanglement in nature and its mortality. The objectivated work of art wants permanence, the utopia of survival, however impotent and itself mortal that utopia may be; in this sense Valéry is carrying out Nietzsche's program of a philosophy that is simultaneously antimetaphysical and aesthetic. For the sake of such a philosophy, Valéry engages in anthropological speculations:

> But there are other reactions which quite to the contrary arouse desires, needs, and changes of state that tend to preserve, recapture, or reproduce the initial sensations. If a man is hungry, his hunger will make him do whatever must be done to annul it as quickly as possible; but if he finds the food delectable, his delight will *strive in him* to endure, to perpetuate itself, or to be reborn. Hunger impels us to cut the sensation short; pleasure to develop another; and these two tendencies will become so independent of one another that the man soon learns to indulge in delicacies and to eat when he is not hungry. What I have said about hunger can easily be extended to the need for love; and indeed to all kinds of sensation, to every mode of sensibility in which conscious action can interfere to restore, prolong, or increase what reflex action in itself seems made to annul. Sight, touch, smell, hearing, movement, speech may from time to time cause us to dwell on the impressions they induce—to sustain or renew them. (v. 13, pp. 80–81)

A theodicy of art emerges from this: "Taken together, all those reactions I have singled out as tending to perpetuate themselves might be said to constitute the *aesthetic order*. To justify the word *infinite* and give it a precise meaning, we need only recall that in the aesthetic order *satisfaction* revives *need*, a *response* renews *demand, presence* generates *absence,* and *possession* gives rise to *desire*" (v. 10, p. 81). "Denn alle Lust will Ewigkeit" ["All pleasure wants eternity" (Nietzsche)]. The motive that impelled Proust to construct life out of helpless, involuntary memory was none other than this. A desperate, *Jugendstil*-like element, the gesture of meaning projecting itself out of what has been abandoned by meaning, is unmistakable here. Aesthetic consciousness, which presupposes, explicitly in Baudelaire and implicitly in Valéry, the collapse of religions, cannot simply take categories like eternity from the theological sphere and use them in secular form in art as though their status and truth content were unaffected by the transposition. Valéry's critique of the artistic self's resemblance to God should not have passed over in silence the idea of the work's permanence, an idea about whose reality Valéry had doubts in any case. Since then, modern art has crossed boundaries that Valéry's generation respected, boundaries within which Valéry's aesthetics has grown outdated.

Among the ideals of Valéry's self-reflected, refracted classicism are the somewhat stuffy attributes of ripeness and perfection (v. 14, pp. 210–11). In fact, however, the exemplary works are by no means those which are complete and perfect but rather those in which the conflict between the goal of perfection and its unattainability has left the deepest marks. Valéry sees something like this in archaic works: "Long epic poems, when they are things of beauty, are beautiful in spite of their length, and then only in parts. . . . There are no 'pure' poets at the outset of a literature, any more than there are 'pure' metals for primitive artificers" (v. 14, p. 213). Like Nietzsche, Valéry is aware of the degree to which order, the canon of classicalness, is wrested from the chaotic by force; "the terrestrial world," he said, "gave [the ancients] the impression of being very little regulated" (v. 14, p. 116). Accordingly, " 'impure' is not a reproach" (v. 14, p. 213). "It is impossible to construct a poem containing only poetry. If a piece contains nothing else, it is not constructed; not a *poem*" (v. 14, p. 103). This works to the credit of modernity. "What surprises one about the extravagances of the literary revolutionaries of yesterday is always their timidity" (v. 14, p. 198). And in fact, today the works of the generation of Schönberg and Picasso reveal themselves to be permeated with elements that work against any pure consistency and thoroughgoing construction; they are permeated with residues of what they have rejected. But that does not diminish their quality. The authenticity of such products might well have its substance precisely in the conflict between what has been and what has not yet been; the New rubs up against that substance and increases its potency. Works from the decade prior to the First World War have more of this tension than do the more harmonious works that came after the Second World War, and it permits them to survive; the loss of tension in so much of what came later might be a function of its own consistency. Despite this defense of what is not stylistically unified, however, permanence, the bourgeois residue in his thought, was for Valéry a truth conceived on the model of possession, equivalent to order. As the sole power human beings are given "over events," in comparison to which their direct actions accomplish nothing, "imposing order" is for him, as for all classicists, "godlike" (v. 12, p. 117). He supports his classicism with the powerful argument that the customary distinction between classical and romantic styles is not adequate to grasp a successful work of art.[3] "The difference between the romantic and the classical writer is a very simple one; it is the difference between the man who does not know his trade and the man who does. The romantic always becomes a classicist once he has learned his craft. That is why our Romantics ended up as Parnassians" (v. 14, p. 120). For him, the order that confers permanence is called form. Through Valéry's critique of all content, even an intellectual content that is the philosophy the work intends, form moves to the center of his aesthetics. But its concept remains a weak one. "One is led to the *form* adopted by a desire to leave the smallest possible share to the reader—and by the same token to leave oneself the least possible scope for arbitrariness and uncertainty" (v. 14, p. 105). True as it is that every artistic form mastered exercises a constraint on the recipient, a constraint that is experienced as the authentic element in the work of art, that alone does not guarantee its quality. It is Valéry himself who insists that the aesthetic concept of form involves no consideration of the receiver or the producer. But he does not face the issue squarely, perhaps because if he did the metaphysics of art would be threatened. "Form," he said, concurring with a stale formalism, "is *per se* bound up with recurrence" (v. 14, p. 105). As though even in his time the most authentic works of art had not sought their formal law in the exclusion of the external and regressive formal techniques of repetition; as though he did not write a few pages later: "The mind cannot endure reiteration" (v. 14, p. 111). An academic concept of form is the only one he can effectively contrast with an alleged craving for innovation. "Therefore fetish-worship of 'the new' is incompatible with a concern for form" (v. 14, p. 105). Form that revolts against that parody of form, the academic exercise, can hardly be distinguished from obsession with the New. But Valéry shows himself to be in league with neoclassicism in that he justifies externally established forms, without regard to the immanence of form in the internal laws of the individual work. The person who does not want to owe anything to anything but genius is seduced by a masochistic pleasure in types of form that exercise a heteronomous and unlegitimated authority. He is smitten with the charms of an ambiguous contingency masked as law, charms which would quickly be consumed, leaving the ashes of boredom. Many things in the *Rhumbs* could stand in Stravinsky's musical poetics: "Rhyme has the great advantage of infuriating the simple

people who naively think there is something under the sun more important than a convention. They have an innocent belief that an idea may be
'deeper,' more durable than any convention" (v. 14, p. 102). Both
objectively and in terms of its literary genesis, Valéry's aesthetic objectivism is carried by a subject that knows itself to be irrevocably alienated
from the substantiality of forms and nevertheless retains a need for them.
The subject points to them as a means of discipline, a difficulty art must
provide for itself in order to become perfect—as though artistic practice
had not made itself all too comfortable using such techniques. Valéry is
led astray by the arbitrariness of a subjectivity that is no longer essentially
bound to those forms, nor capable of constituting form from within
itself, through the labor and efforts Valéry never tires of demanding,
that is, through a self-immersion unconcerned with models and past
social agreements. In this frame of mind Valéry praises—with a touch
of provocative irony—the poetic form that more than any other arouses
the suspicion of being mere mechanical clatter:

> Sometimes I am the kind of man who, if he met the inventor of the sonnet
> in the underworld, would say to him with great respect (if there is any
> left, in the other world): "My dear colleague, I salute you most humbly.
> I do not know the worth of your verses, which I have not read, but I
> would wager that they are worthless, for the odds always are that verses
> are bad; but however bad they are, however flat, insipid, shallow, stupid,
> and naively made they may be, I still hold you in my heart above all other
> poets on earth and in Hades! . . . You invented a *form*, and the greatest
> poets have adapted themselves to that form." (v. 7, p. 160)

One may well ask how compatible thinking about the invention of a
form is with the form's dignity, which aroused the thought in the first
place. That is the line that separates Valéry from certain German experiences with which in other respects his speculations converge. In order
for art to remain the supreme value for him, he must keep his eyes shut
by force. Ultimately, for him art is not an unfolding of truth, as it was
for Hegel, but rather, to use Hegel's language, a pleasant chiming of
bells. The worldly and civilizing element in it is considerable enough in
comparison with imprisonment in a kingdom of the mind that the
prisoner takes literally and absolutizes. Still, it prevents Valéry from
fully grasping the work of art as a force-field constituted by subject and
object. Valéry sensed even this. In contrast to a tolerance for things that
are not completely serious, he affirms the incompatibility of intellectual

works that are at the same time mutually dependent upon one another: "I can't imagine one of [the important artists] singly; nevertheless, each of them burnt himself out in a effort to make the others nonexistent" (v. 14, p. 241). In this way Valéry dismantles a cliché that has come down from classical philosophy, one that now serves only as a pretext for the bourgeois culture that worships freedom where there ought to be necessity because necessity rules where there ought to be freedom: *"De gustibus . . .* but there has to be arguing about tastes" (v. 14, p. 185). In no way does Valéry rely on the category of taste, which is sancrosanct in France: "If you always have 'taste' it means you have never risked delving very deeply into yourself. If you never have it, it means you have taken that risk, but gained nothing by it" (v. 14, p. 105). Valéry would scarcely have walked out of the Paris premiere of Mahler's Second Symphony in protest, as the *musicien français* Debussy did. And yet for him the work of art contains an element of the informal; it is in some sense not binding. His supreme aesthetic category, the law of form, is based on choice, decision, and recollection. He balked at the fact that precisely through an excess of objectivity not fused with the subject—the objectivity to which his objectivism is oriented—objectivity itself is degraded to the status of an illusion, to a mere subjective operation. And thereby to ideological ornamentation. Despite all his polemics against communication and the context of reception, Valéry's work of art willingly accommodates to the charmed circle of society, a circle Gallic thought, always mindful, as Cocteau put it, of how far one can go in going too far, hesitates to leave. "A poem should be a festival or banquet of the Intellect. It cannot be anything else. A festival, that is to say, a game, but a solemn, controlled, significant game; an image of what one is normally not, of the state in which efforts are rhythms and thus redeemed. We celebrate something by enacting it or representing it in its purest, loveliest state" (v. 14, p. 96). We should not let the intellectualization of the idea of celebration blind us to the fact that the celebratory work of art remains committed to the affirmation of what is. The aesthetic conformism of Valéry's doctrine of form is a social conformism as well.

Even Valéry's neoclassicism, however, is not without its leavening. As we know, in terms of artistic strategy, the whole neoclassical movement in France was a counter-attack against Wagner. The order called for was to resist the intoxication, the obscure mingling of the arts, the German proclivity for the superlative (v. 14, p. 202). Valéry subscribed to this platform as a poet as well, in his plan for the musical drama *Amphion*, which was finally set to music by Honegger after Debussy proved uncooperative. Not only the Greek material but the idea is neoclassicist. It is based on Valéry's sharp distinction between the arts, something that negates Wagnerian music drama from the start. In his own development Valéry experienced it as the distinction between architecture, his first love, and music; but he did not let the matter rest with that distinction, nor with copies of seventeenth- and eighteenth-century styles. In his medium, language, which for him was something musical and not a medium of conceptual signification, he kept faith with architecture. What inspired him was the fact that the two kinds of art are related in that they neither imitate nor designate anything tangible. He addresses this *coincidentia oppositorum*:

> *Composition*—which is the relation of the particular details to the whole —is much more felt and required in works of music and architecture than in the arts whose object is the reproduction of visible things; for these arts borrow their materials and their models from the outside world, the world of ready-made objects and fixed destinies, and the result is a sort of impurity, an allusion to that foreign world . . . an ambiguous and fortuitous impression. (v. 3, p. 216)

It is this that defines his idea of form: the return of the architectonic within the musical. "Even in the slightest of compositions one must think of duration, that is, of *memory*, which is to say *form*, just as the builders of steeples and towers must think of structure" (v. 3, p. 215). The artist, for whom reflection on art and art itself are one and the same, draws the impulse for his music drama from that idea. His model is the ancient history of music in its opposition to architecture, the two mediating one another in their dramatic unity. Whether the project succeeded or not, however, is unimportant: once Valéry had become involved in the adventure of this kind of mediation, categories like the clean separation of the arts, the optically oriented primacy of order, and ultimately neoclassicism, had to fight for their lives. Valéry greets with enthusiasm E. T. A. Hoffmann's description of someone possessed by music who "imagines he hears a *sound*, of extraordinary intensity, and purity, which he calls the *Euphon*, and which opens up the infinite and separate universe of hearing. . . . Similarly, in the plastic arts, the *seeing man* suddenly feels himself become the *singing mind*; and this state of song engenders a creative longing which tends to prolong and perpetuate that momentary grace" (v. 12, pp. 148–49). He hits on the idea "of working out the music to this dance. For any given work of sculpture one could find a corresponding piece of music, created to the rhythms of the sculptor's actions" (v. 12, p. 180).

The Baudelairean-neoromantic motif of synaesthesia is sublimated here. Sounds and fragrances no longer blend in the evening air; instead, separate entities are synthesized by virtue of their rigid separateness. That too would be incompatible with a dogmatic conception of form. Valéry's devouring consciousness, a consciousness that does not stop at any fixed definition, explodes that notion by interpreting art as a language in its own right. Art is imitation, but not of something material; rather, it is mimetic behavior. In the name of such imitation, even the aesthetic category that seems to be purely subjective, the category of expression, becomes something objective: it becomes the imitation of the language of things themselves. It is bound up with the work ridding itself of any likeness to objects: "Poetry is an attempt to reproduce or restore by means of articulated language those things or that thing which cries, tears, caresses, kisses, sighs, and so forth struggle obscurely to express; and which objects seem to try to express with all in them that has the appearance of life or (presumably) design" (v. 14, p. 97). Musical terminology has something closely related to this in the performance indication *espressivo,* which depends neither on what is expressed nor on the subject expressing it. As a metaphysics of mimesis, Valéry's aesthetics gropes toward its most extreme formulation at the end of the essay on the dignity of the arts of fire: "The arts of fire might thus be the most venerable of all, deriving directly as they do from the transcendent operations of some demiurge" (v. 12, p. 172). Art is an imitation not of what has been created but of the act of creation itself. This speculative idea is at the root of Valéry's provocative, decidedly alexandrine view that the process of artistic production is also the true subject matter of art: "Why, after all, should the making of a work of art not be considered a work of art in itself?" (v. 12, p. 180). Like almost no other theory, this one destroys the illusion of the work of art as an existing entity. Precisely as an objective entity, the work of art is transformed into a becoming, whereas the vulgar notion conceives it as static and attributes its dynamic moment to the artist's presumed act of creation, while for Valéry the artist is extinguished in that supreme imitation. This paradox can be explained by the fact that Valéry's objectively oriented aesthetics, which accepts the work as a mimesis neither of something external nor of something internal, the author's soul, is touched less by the "direct pleasure" that works of art give him "than by the ideas they suggest to [him] of how they were made" (v. 12, p. 178). To follow Valéry's abyssal passage about the prehistoric person who, "must have been the first to run his fingers absentmindedly over a rough vase, and feel inspired thereby to model another, *made to be caressed*" (v. 12, p. 172), art might be the imitation of creative love itself. As imitation of a creative act rather than of solid objects, art comes to stand in contrast to nature: "We feel certain desires that nature is unable to satisfy, and we have certain powers that she has not" (v. 13, p. 187). Thus Baudelaire's *paradis artificiels* come into their own, mimesis of something that precedes objectness, through an artistic freedom exempt from the spell of objects. This theory of imitation connects the ideal of *l'art pour l'art* with the notion that art's resemblance—no longer a resemblance to any thing —is a function of its immanent form. "It is useless to *look* for likeness above all else: it ought, on the contrary, to result from the convergence of observation and action as they build up in the total form a continually increasing quantity of observed relations between the parts. It is in the nature of good work that it can always be pushed further toward precision without any change of intention or of points of reference" (v. 12, pp. 181–82). For Valéry, works of art become the more similar to one another the more thoroughly their own form is developed and brought to completion: "likeness" is only "in relation with the more general principle and aim of the art" (v. 12, p. 182). It is not named and it appears in disguised form, but his image is the act of creation, and the work of art ranks the higher the more it resembles that act, the more, one might say pleonastically, it resembles itself. "Was aber schön ist, selig scheint es in ihm selbst" ["What is beautiful seems blessed in itself" (Eduard Mörike)]—that is utopia in its aesthetic form. Utopia, pure possibility, is the aim of the movement of Valéry's thought. "In my thoughts I try to come to terms with all this magical power of the sea by telling myself that it never ceases to show me what is possible" (*Pièces sur l'art*, p. 1335). It is only through blind obsession with itself and not by means of a clear-sighted intention directed toward something that would be more than itself, that the work of art becomes more than it is. Its resemblance to itself turns it into language. Only in this resemblance to language does all art have its unity. Its idea is as different from propositional language as aesthetic resemblance is from resemblance to things. The very incommensurability of languages points to this level: "There are doctrines which cannot survive translation into a language other than the original; once translated, they lose the magic, the discretion, the consecration by use and wont that have been theirs since the time when they were crystallized in words reserved to them and veiled in mystery" (v. 14, p. 43). In the conception of nonobjective resemblance, the neoromantic cult of nuance comes into its own theoretically: "The beautiful demands perhaps the slavish imitation of what is indefinable in things" (v. 14, p. 240) reads the finest sentence in *Rhumbs*. The indefinable is the inimitable, and aesthetic mimesis becomes a mimesis of the absolute by imitating this inimitability in the particular. This is the locus of its utopian promise: "Pay attention to this subtle continuous sound; it is silence. Listen to what one hears when one no longer perceives anything" (*Rhumbs*, p. 656).

Valéry's utopia passes into Proust's: "There is a woman selling flowers under the big porch of the public building just across the road; flowers that transmit messages, thoughts of love, to every passer-by. What will never happen, what can never be, has a fragrance of its own, scents the air" (v. 14, p. 173). This utopia is the object of the thinker's yearning for a form of thought freed of its own coerciveness. "How splendid it would be to think in a form one had invented for oneself!" (v. 14, p. 228). Thought's unlimited and wearisome labor has as its aim the disappearance of that toil in fulfillment. Intellectual exertion has as its aim the abolition of the force of self-imposed laws (v. 12, p. 136). Valéry's drive for self-mastery is insatiable, and his theory of art wants to extend autonomy to the point where only contingency opposes it: "It isn't 'novelty' or 'genius' that appeals to me, but full possession of oneself" (v. 14, p. 224). But this ideal transcends its own subjectivism. "A man bent on his work says to himself: 'I want to be stronger, cleverer, luckier than— Myself' " (v. 14, p. 20). The subject's unlimited power of disposition over itself signifies its sublation into something objective. The work, which imitates the language of things as the likeness of the act of creation, requires the authority of the producer, whom the work then subjugates in turn. Thus for Valéry the work becomes a punishment as well: " 'And for thy chastisement thou shalt make very, very beautiful things.' This is what a God (definitely *not* Jehovah) *really* said to Man after the Fall" (v. 14, p. 229). But Valéry does not want to make common cause with punishment. It undermines, he says, once again speaking in Nietzschean tones, "morality, since it provides a calculated compensation for each crime. It reduces the horror of the crime to the horror of its penalty; in a word, it absolves. Thus it treats crime as something measurable, marketable—one can haggle over the price to pay" (v. 14, p. 50). Valéry, the thinker, understands that as calculation thinking itself is defiled: " 'What has most value should cost nothing.' And also: 'We pride ourselves most on that for which we are least responsible' " (v. 14, p. 100). Thus, in thinking, thought's very principle, domination itself, is revoked. The man for whom everything hangs on his power as an artist denounces works of art for exercising power:

> Nothing could be remoter from Corot than the ambition of such violent and tormented minds, anxious to reach and as it were possess (in the diabolic sense) that tender and hidden region of the soul by which it can be held and controlled entire, through the indirect path of the visceral and organic depths of being. They wish to enslave; Corot to win us over to what he feels. He has no thought of bringing us into bondage. All he hopes for is to make us his friends, the companions of his contemplation of a fine day, from dawn until night. (v. 12, pp. 136–37)

The idea of art's implacable efforts has reconciliation as its end.

Short Commentaries on Proust

*I*n arguing against short commentaries on individual passages from
Remembrance of Things Past, one might say that with Proust's bewilder-
ingly rich and intricate creation the reader is more in need of an orienting
overview than of something that entangles him still more deeply in
details—from which the path to the whole is in any case difficult and
laborious. This objection does not seem to me to do justice to the matter.
We are no longer lacking in grand surveys of Proust. In Proust, however, the relationship of the whole to the detail is not that of an overall
architectonic plan to the specifics that fill it in: it is against precisely that,
against the brutal untruth of a subsuming form forced on from above,
that Proust revolted. Just as the temperament of his work challenges
customary notions about the general and the particular and gives aesthetic
force to the dictum from Hegel's *Logic* that the particular is the general
and vice versa, with each mediated through the other, so the whole,
resistant to abstract outlines, crystallizes out of intertwined individual
presentations. Each of them conceals within itself constellations of what
ultimately emerges as the idea of the novel. Great musicians of Proust's
era, like Alban Berg, knew that living totality is achieved only through
rank vegetal proliferation. The productive force that aims at unity is
identical to the passive capacity to lose oneself in details without restraint
or reservation. In the inner formal composition of Proust's work, however—and it was not only on account of its long, obscure sentences that
Proust's work struck the Frenchmen of his time as so German—there
dwells, Proust's primarily optical gifts notwithstanding and with no
cheap analogy to composition intended, a musical impulse. It is evi-

denced most emphatically in the paradox that Proust's great theme, the rescue of the transient, is fulfilled through its own transience, time. The *durée* the work investigates is concentrated in countless moments, often isolated from one another. At one point Proust extols the medieval masters who introduced ornaments into their cathedrals so hidden that they must have known that no human being would ever set eyes on them. Such unity is not one arranged for the human eye but rather an invisible unity in the midst of dispersion, and it would be evident only to a divine observer. Proust should be read with the idea of those cathedrals in mind, dwelling on the concrete without grasping prematurely at something that yields itself not directly but only through its thousand facets. This is why I do not want merely to point out the ostensible high points of his work, nor to advance an interpretation of the whole that would at best simply repeat the statements of intention which the author himself inserted into his work. Instead, I hope through immersion in fragments to illuminate something of the work's substance, which derives its unforgettable quality solely from the coloring of the here and now. I believe I will be more faithful to Proust's own intention by proceeding in this way than by trying to distill it and present it in abstract form.

On Swann's Way, *vol. I, pp. 57–60* *

In his *Introduction to Metaphysics*, Henri Bergson, Proust's kinsman in more than spirit, compares the classificatory concepts of causal-mechanistic science to ready-made clothing that hangs loosely on the bodies of objects, while the intuitions he extols are as precisely tailored to the matter at hand as the creations of *haute couture*. While Proust was equally capable of expressing a scientific or metaphysical relationship in a simile drawn from the sphere of worldliness, it is also true that he himself followed Bergson's rule, whether he was acquainted with it or not. To be sure, he did not use intuition alone. In his work its powers are counterbalanced by those of French rationality, of a fitting quantity of sophisticated human understanding. It is the tension and conjunction of these two elements that make up the Proustian atmosphere. But Bergson's allergic reaction to ready-made thought, to the pre-given and established

---

* References are to *Remembrance of Things Past*, translated by C. K. Moncrieff and Frederick A. Blossom, 2 vols. (New York: Random House, 1927–32).

cliché, is certainly characteristic of Proust: his sense of tact cannot stomach the things everyone says; this sensitivity is his organ for untruth and thus for truth. Although Proust adds his voice to the old chorus about social hypocrisy and insincerity, but like that chorus never expressly criticizes their social basis, he nevertheless became a critic of society, against his will and hence all the more authentically. He had a far-reaching respect for society's norms and its contents; as a novelist, however, he suspended its system of categories and thereby pierced its claim to self-evidence, the illusion that it is a part of nature. Only someone who senses his immense energy of opposition to opinion, from which every sentence of Proust, the Platonist, has been polemically wrung, will understand him, secure against mistaking him for the spoiled narcissist that he of course also was. It is this resistance, a second alienation of the alienated world as a means to its restitution, that gives this refined man his freshness. It makes him as unsuitable for a literary model as only Kafka can be, for any imitation of Proust's mode of proceeding would presuppose that this resistance had already been effected, would exempt itself from it, and hence would fail from the outset to achieve what Proust did. The anecdote about the old monk who appears in a dream on the first night after his death to a friend in his order and whispers, "It's all completely different," could serve as the motto for Proust's "search for lost time" [as the French title reads literally] — a body of research into the way it really was, as opposed to the way everyone says it was: the whole novel is an appeal at law filed by life against life. The episode about Marcel's disagreement with his revered Uncle Adolf ultimately reveals the complete disparity between subjective motives and objective events. But despite Marcel's break with Uncle Adolf, the demimondaine who occasions the disaster through no fault of her own is not lost to the novel. As Odette Swann, she becomes one of its central figures and manages to achieve the highest social honors, just as the son of the same uncle's valet, Morel, brings about the fall of the powerful Baron de Charlus thousands of pages later. Proust's work captures one of the strangest of experiences, an experience that seems to elude all generalization and for that reason is the prototype of true universality in Proust's work: that the people who are decisive in our lives appear in them as though appointed and dispensed by an unknown author, as though we had awaited them in this very place and no other; and that, perhaps divided up into several figures, they cross our paths again and again. This experience probably boils down to the fact that as it came to its end liberal society, which still mistakenly thought of itself as an open society, became a closed one in Bergson's terms, a system of preestablished disharmony.

On Swann's Way, *vol. I, pp.* 133–37
On The Guermantes' Way, *vol. II, pp.* 724
and 785

Of the rigidified notions that prevailing consciousness guards like possessions and that Proust's obstinacy, the obstinacy of a child who cannot be talked out of something, destroys, perhaps the most important is the notion of the unity and wholeness of the person. There is scarcely any point on which his work contains such a wholesome antidote to the false idols of today as this one. The supremacy of time provides the aesthetic demonstration of Ernst Mach's thesis, derived from Hume, that the ego cannot be salvaged; but whereas Mach and Hume rejected the ego only as the unifying principle of cognition, Proust presents the full empirical self with the bill for its non-identity. The spirit in which that occurs, however, is not only akin to that of positivism but also opposed to it. Proust carries out concretely what poetics usually only sets up as a formal requirement—the development of the characters. In the process it becomes clear that the characters are not characters: a frailty appears in what is stable, a frailty ratified but by no means produced by death. This process of dissolution, however, is not so much psychological as it is a fugitive series of images. In them Proust's psychological work attacks psychology itself. What changes in people, what becomes alien to the point of unrecognizability and returns as in a musical repeat, are the images into which we transpose them. Proust knows that there are no human beings in themselves beyond this world of images; that the individual is an abstraction, that its being-for-itself has as little reality as its mere being-for-us, which the vulgar prejudice considers an illusion. From this point of view, the infinitely complex structure of Proust's novel is an attempt to reconstruct, through a totality that includes psychology, personal relationships, and the psychology of intelligible character, or the transformation of images, a reality which no view oriented toward mere psychological or sociological data for the sake of isolating them can grasp. In this too Proust's work represents the end of the nineteenth century, the last panorama. Proust sees the ultimate truth, however, in the images of human beings, which are above those human beings, beyond their essence and beyond their appearance, which itself forms part of their essence. The process by which the novel unfolds is the description of the path traveled by these images. That path has stations, like the three passages about Oriane Guermantes: the first confrontation of her image with empirical reality in the church at Combray, then her rediscovery and modification while the narrator's family is living in the Duchess' house in Paris, in her immediate proximity, and finally the fixing of her image in the photograph the narrator sees at the home of his friend Saint-Loup.

On The Guermantes' Way, *vol. II*, *pp. 741–42*

One of the formulations that can be used to characterize Proust could itself have been drawn from his novel, which reflects on itself like a hall of mirrors. It is the notion that Proust, born in 1871, already saw the world with the eyes of someone thirty or fifty years younger; hence that at a new stage in the novel form he also represents a new mode of experience. This places his work, which plays with so many models from the French tradition—the memoirs of Saint-Simon and Balzac's *Comédie humaine*, for instance—in direct proximity to a movement that was antagonistic to tradition, a movement whose beginnings Proust lived just long enough to experience: Surrealism. This affinity sums up Proust's modernness. The contemporary becomes mythical for him as it does for Joyce. In the guise of metaphors, disruptive Surrealist "actions" like Dali's appearing at a soirée in a diving suit would be completely appropriate in a description like that of the Princesse de Guermantes' grand soirée in *Cities of the Plain*. But Proust's mythologizing tendency is not out to reduce the contemporary to the archaic, to what remains identical to itself; certainly it is not the product of a craving for psychological archetypes. Rather, it is surrealist in that it coaxes mythical images out of modernity at the points where it is most modern; in this, it is akin to the philosophy of Walter Benjamin, Proust's first great translator. In *The Guermantes' Way*, a theater party is described. The auditorium with its elegantly dressed audience is transformed into a kind of Ionian seascape and even comes to resemble the underwater realm of maritime nature deities. But the narrator himself talks about how "figures of sea monsters," mythical images, take form only in accordance with the laws of optics and the angle of refraction—thus in obedience to a natural-scientific necessity external to consciousness. The things we see around us look back at us ambiguously and enigmatically, because we no longer perceive what we see as in any way like us: Proust speaks of "minerals and people to whom we have no relationship." The social alienation of human beings from one another in liberal bourgeois society as it displayed and delighted in itself in the theater; the disenchantment of the world, which gave human beings things and made human beings mere things: all this bestows another meaning on the inscrutable. Proust reminds us that it is an illusory one when he says that in such moments we doubt our sanity. Nevertheless, it is truth. Alienation becomes complete, and social relationships reveal themselves to be a blind second nature, like the mythical landscape into whose allegorical image what is unattainable and unapproachable congeals. The beauty that things take on in such descriptions is the hopeless beauty of their semblance. In representing history they express history's bondage to nature.

On The Guermantes' Way, *vol. II,*
pp. 742–43

The description of the theater as a prehistoric Mediterranean landscape introduces several pages about the Princess de Guermantes-Bavière, who can then be introduced as the Great Goddess. The things Proust says about her and the effect she has on those present provide an example of the passages scattered throughout his work that lead unsympathetic readers to complain about his snobbery, passages that challenge the stupid notion of a mediocre Progress, which asks why one should be interested in an aristocracy that by Proust's day had already been deprived of its actual function and that is not at all statistically representative. Even André Gide, who in a sense belonged, socially speaking, to that group by birth more than Proust did, seems to have been irritated by Proust's princesses, and André Maurois, many details of whose book point beyond the sphere of communications from which it derives, mentions snobbery as a danger that Proust overcame. Instead, it would be more appropriate to deal with Proust in accordance with Hugo von Hofmansthal's remark that he would rather give a good explanation for a weakness he had been reproached with than deny it. For it is obvious that

Proust himself was impressed with his Swann because, as the narrator never tires of repeating, Swann actually belonged to the Jockey Club and was received in high society even though he was the son of a stockbroker. It is so obvious that it must have been important to Proust to call attention to his own provocative inclination. The best way to track down its meaning, however, is to follow the provocation. Snobbery, as the concept dominates Proust's novel, is the erotic cathexis of social matters. Hence it violates a social taboo, which is revenged on the person who broaches the delicate issue. If the pimp, the antithesis of the snob, acknowledges the intertwining of sex and gain through his profession, an intertwining that bourgeois society covers up, then conversely the snob demonstrates something equally universal, the deflection of love from the immediacy of the person to social relationships. The pimp socializes sex; the snob sexualizes society. Precisely because society does not actually tolerate love but rather subordinates it to the realm of its ends, it keeps a fanatical eye out to make sure that love has nothing to do with it, that it is nature, pure immediacy. The snob disdains the socially accepted love match that has an ulterior purpose but falls in love with the hierarchical order itself, which drives love out of him and which simply cannot tolerate being loved. The snob lets the cat out of the bag, the cat the Proustian oeuvre then bells. Like Carl Sternheim forty years ago, Proust, the critic of snobbery, is automatically charged—and with good reason —with having succumbed to that vice, a vice, incidentally, he called harmless. But only someone who has succumbed to social relationships in his own way instead of denying them with the resentment of one who has been excluded can reflect them back. What Proust came to see in these allegedly superfluous lives of luxury, however, vindicates his infatuation. For the enraptured snob the social order is transfigured into a fairytale image, just as the beloved was once transfigured for the true lover. Proust's snobbery is absolved by what the instincts of a homogenized middle-class society secretly hold against him: the fact that the Archangels and Powers he adores no longer have swords and have themselves become defenseless imitations of their liquidated past. Like every love, snobbery wants to escape from the entanglement of bourgeois relationships into a world that no longer uses the greatest good of the greatest number to gloss over the fact that it satisfies human needs only by accident. Proust's regression is utopian. He is defeated by it, as is love, but in his defeat he denounces the society that decrees that it shall not be. The impossibility of love that Proust depicts in his socialites, and especially in the Baron de

Charlus, who is actually the central figure of the novel, and who ultimately retains the friendship only of a pimp, has since then spread like a deadly chill over all of society, where a functionalized totality stifles love wherever it still stirs. In this respect Proust was prophetic, a quality he once attributed to the Jews. He humbly courted the favor of arch-reactionaries like Gaston Calmette and Léon Daudet, but one of those who sometimes wore a monocle was named Karl Marx.

On Within a Budding Grove, *vol. I,*
pp. 568–70

The Baron de Charlus is the brother of the Duke of Guermantes. The scene in which he first appears testifies to Proust's relationship to French *décadence,* which he both embodies and detaches himself from, in that his work calls it by name historically. A famous novel of that period is called *A Rebours, Against the Grain:* Proust brushed experience against the grain. But "it's all completely different" would remain stamped with the impotence of the exotic if its force were not also that of "this is how it is." I would like to call attention to Proust's remark that many people sigh to indicate that it is too hot for them without really feeling that way. This remark is as eccentric as it is obvious. False generality disintegrates under Proust's ravenous gaze, but in return what is usually considered coincidental acquires an oblique, irrational universality. Everyone who brings to the reading of Proust the necessary prerequisites for it will feel at many points that this is what it was like for him too, exactly what it was like. Proust shares with the great tradition in the novel the category of the contingent as developed by the young Lukács. He depicts a life bereft of meaning, a life the subject can no longer shape into a cosmos. For Proust's perseverance, however, which surpasses that of the nineteenth-century novelists, contingency is not completely bereft of meaning. It carries with it a semblance of necessity, as though some reference to meaning had been interspersed throughout existence, chaotic, mocking, haunting in its dissociated fragments. This constellation of a necessity in something that is wholly contingent, a necessity that can be perceived only negatively—this too anticipating Kafka—carries Proust's fanatically individuated work far beyond his own individuation: at its center he reveals the universality through which it is mediated. Such universality, however, is that of the negative. Like the Naturalists, his antitheses, before him, Proust is correct in his most out-of-the-way observations, but his correctness is that of disillusionment, and it refuses all consolation. He gives where he takes: where he is correct, there is pain. His medium is paranoia, to which Proust was close in his instinctual structure and which is also present in the physiognomy of his Charlus. The one who has burnt his bridges behind him gives sense and meaning to the meaningless, but it is precisely his madness that captures what the world has done to itself and to us.

On The Captive, *vol. II, pp. 425–27*

Like the second part of the first volume, the fifth volume of Proust's novel is a depiction of jealousy. The narrator has brought Albertine to live with him; he distrusts everything she says and does and keeps her under a control from which she finally escapes through flight; afterwards she has a fatal accident. The author never tires of asserting that even while he is plumbing the depths of his sufferings over Albertine he no longer loves her. Love and jealousy are not so closely linked as the popular notion would have it. Jealousy always presumes a relationship of possession that makes the loved one into a thing and thus offends against the spontaneity in which the idea of love is rooted. But Proust's jealousy is not merely an impotent attempt to hold onto the fugitive, whom he loves for her fleetingness, because of the fact that she can never be completely captured. Rather, this jealousy wants to restore love, as Proust wanted to restore, or reproduce, life. But it can do so only at the price of the loved one's individuation. If she is not to be damaged by her own falseness, the beloved must be transformed back into nature, into a generic creature, a member of a species. In forfeiting her own psychological individuality she acquires that other and better individuality that is the object of love, that of the image that every human being embodies and that is an alien to him as, the Cabalah claims, the mystical name is to the one who bears it. This takes place in sleep. In sleep Albertine lays aside what makes her a character in the order of the world. Dissolving into the amorphous, she takes on the form of her immortal part, to which love is directed: beauty without gaze or image. It is as though the description of Albertine's sleep were an exegesis of Baudelaire's line about the woman whom night makes beautiful. This beauty provides what existence withholds, security; but it is security in something that has been lost. Poor, frail, confused love finds a refuge in the place where the beloved comes to resemble death. In the era of its decay, love has not been more fervently celebrated since the second act of Wagner's *Tristan and Isolde* than in the description of Albertine's sleep, which with sublime irony proves the narrator wrong in denying his love.

On The Captive, *vol. II, pp. 508–10*

One can no longer speak directly of the ultimate things. The impotent word that calls them by name weakens them. Both naiveté and a defiant casualness in expressing metaphysical ideas reveal their lack of grounding. But Proust's spirit was completely metaphysical in the midst of a world that forbids the language of metaphysics: this tension is the moving spirit behind his whole work. Only once, in *The Captive*, does he open a crack, so hastily that the eye has no time to accustom itself to such light. Even the word he uses cannot be taken at its word. Here, in his depiction of Bergotte's death, there is actually a sentence whose tone, at least in the German version, echoes Kafka. It reads: "So that the idea that Bergotte was not wholly and permanently dead is by no means improbable" (510). [The German translation by Eva Rechel-Mertens to which Adorno refers reads: "Der Gedanke, Bergotte sei nicht für alle Zeiten tot, ist demnach nicht völlig unglaubhaft."] The idea that leads to this statement is the idea that the moral force of the writer whose epitaph Proust is writing belongs to an order other than the order of nature, and for this reason it holds out the promise that the order of nature is not the ultimate order. This experience is comparable to the experience of great works of art: the sense that their substance could not possibly *not* be true, that their success and their authenticity themselves point to the reality of what they vouch for. One feels impelled to put the role of art in Proust's work, his trust in the objective force of its success, into conjunction with that thought, that last, pale, secularized, and nevertheless inextinguishable shadow of the ontological proof of God. The man whose death is the only thing in Proust's work associated with hope is not only witness to "kindliness and conscientiousness" but himself a great writer. Proust's model for him was Anatole France. The thought of eternal life is inspired by the Voltairean skeptic: enlightenment, the process of demythologization, is to veer around and carry beyond its own context a nature mindful of itself. Proust's work is authentic because its intention, which aims at salvation, is free of apology, of any attempt to justify anything that exists, to promise any permanence. On the principle of *non confundar* he places his hopes on unreserved surrender to the natural context; for him once again, the rest, in all its hidden meaning, is silence. Hence time, the power of transience itself, becomes the highest being that Proust's work, it too a *roman philosophique* like those of Voltaire and France in its thousand refractions, acknowledges. Proust keeps a greater distance from any kind of positiveness, and the substance of his work is proportionately closer to the theological than Bergson's doctrine. The idea of immortality is tolerated only in what is itself, as Proust well knew, transient—in works of art as the last metaphors for revelation in the authentic language. Thus in a later passage, on the night after his first feuilleton has appeared in *Le Figaro*, Proust dreams of Bergotte as though he were still alive—as though the printed word were lodging a protest against death, until the writer, awakening, realizes the vanity of even this comfort. No interpretation is adequate to this passage, not, as the cliché would have it, because it is above thought in its artistic dignity, but because it has made its home on the border where thought too finds its limit.

▣▦▣

Words from Abroad

For Gertrud von Holzhausen

After the radio broadcast of "Short Commentaries on Proust," I received letters of protest about my allegedly excessive use of foreign words for the first time since my youth. I looked through the text of the talk and found no unusual number of foreign words in it, although people may have held some French expressions that arose in connection with the French subject matter against me. Thus I can hardly explain the outraged correspondence except through the contrast between literary texts and their interpretation. With great narrative prose, interpretation easily takes on the coloration of the foreign word. The syntax may sound more foreign than the vocabulary. Attempts at formulation that swim against the stream of the usual linguistic splashing in order to capture the intended matter precisely, and that take pains to fit complex conceptual relationships into the framework of syntax, arouse rage because they require effort. The person who is naive about language will ascribe the strangeness of such writing to the foreign words, which he holds responsible for everything he doesn't understand even when he is quite familiar with the words. Ultimately, what is going on is largely a defense against ideas, which are imputed to the words; the blame is misdirected. I once tested this in America when I gave a disconcerting lecture to an emigré association to which I belonged, a lecture from which I had carefully eliminated every foreign word. Nevertheless, the lecture met with precisely the same opposition I am now encountering in Germany. I have had this kind of experience since my childhood, when old Dreibus, a neighbor who lived on my street, attacked me in a rage as I was conversing harmlessly with a comrade in the streetcar on my way to school: "You goddamned little devil! Shut up with your High German and learn to speak German right." I had scarcely recovered from the fright Herr Dreibus gave me when he was brought home in a pushcart not long afterwards, completely intoxicated, and it was probably not much later that he died. He was the first to teach me what *Rancune* [from the French, meaning rancor or spite] was, a word that has no proper native equivalent in German, unless one were to confuse it with the word *Ressentiment* [resentment], a word currently enjoying an unfortunate popularity in Germany but which was likewise imported rather than invented by Nietzsche. In short, it is a case of sour grapes: outrage over foreign words is to be explained in terms of the psychic state of the one who is angry, for whom some grapes are hanging too high up.

I don't want to make myself sound better than I was. When my friend Erich and I took some delight in using foreign words at the Gymnasium, we were acting as though we were already the privileged possessors of the grapes. It would be difficult to determine now whether this behavior preceded the *rancune* or not; certainly the two went together very well. Using *Zelotentum* [zealotry] or *Paränese* [paraenesis] was so enjoyable because we sensed that some of the gentlemen to whom we were entrusted for our education during World War I were not quite sure what those words meant. Of course they could warn us with red marks to avoid unnecessary foreign words, but otherwise they could do nothing more to us than they did when Erich chose "Dear Habakuk" as the salutation for his essay "My Summer Vacation: Letter to a Friend," while I, more cautious and more staid but equally unwilling to divulge the name of my real friend to the head teacher, used the precocious phrase "Dear friend" in my essay. I will not deny that I sometimes followed the bad example of an elderly great-aunt. As a child, according to the family history, she had looked up the French word for "kneading trough" in her French dictionary and then asked her poor tutor for it; when he had no answer she responded scornfully, "Tsk tsk! *La huche.*" Despite this sinister legacy, however, we considered ourselves the avengers of Hanno Buddenbrooks, and felt that with our esoteric foreign words we were shooting arrows at our indispensable patriots [in the classroom on the home front] from our secret kingdom which could neither be reached from the Wester Forest [i.e., Westerwald's German dictionary] nor "eingedeutscht," "Germanized," as they liked to say, in any other way. And our instincts were not so wrong. Foreign words constituted little cells of resistance to the nationalism of World War I. The pressure to think along prescribed lines forced resistance into deviant and harmless paths, but in times of crisis gestures that are in themselves irrelevant often acquire disproportionate symbolic significance. But the fact that we happened upon foreign words in particular was hardly due to political considerations. Rather, since language is erotically charged in its words, at least for the kind of person who is capable of expression, love drives us to foreign words. In reality, it is that love that sets off the indignation over their use. The early craving for foreign words is like the craving for foreign and if possible exotic girls; what lures us is a kind of exogamy of language, which would like to escape from the sphere of what is always the same, the spell of what one is and knows anyway. At that time foreign words made us blush, like saying the name of a secret love. National groups who want one-dish meals even in language find this response hateful. It is from this stratum that the affective tension that gives foreign words their fecund and dangerous quality arises, the quality that their friends are seduced by and their enemies sense more readily than do people who are indifferent to them.

This tension, however, seems peculiar to the Germans, just as one of the stereotypical, although hardly sincerely intended accusations directed by German nationalism against the German spirit is that it lets itself be impressed in too servile a way by things from abroad. Language too bears witness to the fact that civilization as Latinization only half succeeded in Germany. In the French language, where the Gallic and the Roman elements interpenetrated so early and so thoroughly, there seems to be no consciousness of foreign borrowings at all; in England, where the Saxon and the Norman linguistic layers were superimposed on one another, there may be a tendency to linguistic doubling, in which the Saxon elements represent the archaic or concrete aspect and the Latin represent the civilizatory or modern aspect, but the latter are too widespread and too much the marks of a historical victory to be experienced as foreign by anyone but an intransigent romantic. In Germany, however, where the Latinate civilizatory components did not fuse with the older popular language but instead were set off from it through the formation of educated elites and by courtly custom, the foreign words stick out, unassimilated, and are available to the writer who chooses them with care; Benjamin spoke of the author inserting the silver rib of the foreign word into the body of language. What seems inorganic here is in actuality only historical evidence, evidence of the failure of that unification. Such disparateness means not only suffering in language, and what

Hebbel called the "schism of creation," but suffering in reality as well. From this perspective Nazism may be regarded as a violent, belated, and therefore deadly attempt to force a bourgeois integration of Germany that had not taken place. No language, not even the old vernacular language, is organic and natural—something restorationist doctrines would like to make it; but every victory of the advanced, civilizatory linguistic element contains as a precipitate something of the injustice done to the older and weaker element. Karl Kraus sensed this when he wrote an elegy for a sound that had been eliminated in the process of rationalization. The Western languages have tempered that injustice in something like the way British imperialism dealt politically with its subject peoples. Compensation as consideration for those who have been subjugated may well be the general definition of culture in the emphatic sense; in Germany, however, this equilibrium was never achieved, precisely because the Roman, rational principle never achieved uncontested dominance. The foreign words in the German language call attention to that: to the fact that no *pax romana* was concluded, that what was untamed survived, and to the fact that when Humanism took the reins it was experienced not as the substance of human beings, as intended, but as something unreconciled, something imposed upon them. To this extent German is both less and more than the Western languages; it is less by virtue of the brittle and unfinished quality that provides the individual writer with so little that is firm, a quality that stands out crassly in the older New High German texts and is still evident in the relationship of foreign words to their context; and it is more because the language is not completely trapped within the net of socialization and communication. It can be used for expression because it does not guarantee expression in advance. It is consistent with this state of affairs that in the more culturally encapsulated domains of the German language like Viennese, where prebourgeois courtly and elite features were mediated with the popular language by the Church and the Enlightenment, the foreign words (with which the Viennese dialect teems) lose the extraterritorial and aggressive quality that characterizes them elsewhere in the German language. One need only hear a Viennese *Portier* [doorman] talk about a "rekommendierter Brief" [registered letter] to become aware of the difference, a linguistic atmosphere in which what is foreign is foreign and familiar at the same time, as in the conversation the two counts in Hoffmannsthal's *Der Schwierige* have about the lead character, the "difficult man": the one complains that "he has us saying too many words that end in *-ieren*,"* to which the other responds, "Yes, he could have restrained himself [*sich menagieren*] a bit."

No such reconciliation has been achieved in German, nor can any be brought about by the writer's individual will. He can, however, take advantage of the tension between the foreign word and the language by incorporating that tension into his own reflections and his own technique. With the foreign word he can effect a beneficial interruption of the conformist moment of language, the muddy stream in which the specific expressive intention drowns. The hard, contoured quality of the foreign word, the very thing that makes it stand out from the continuum of the language, can be used to bring out what is intended but obscured by the bad generality of language use. Further, the discrepancy between the foreign word and the language can be made to serve the expression of truth. Language participates in reification, the separation of subject matter and thought. The customary ring of naturalness deceives us about that. It creates the illusion that what is said is immediately equivalent to what is meant. By acknowledging itself as a token, the foreign word reminds us bluntly that all real language has something of the token in it. It makes itself language's scapegoat, the bearer of the dissonance that language has to give form to and not merely prettify. Not the least of what we resist in the foreign word is that it illuminates something true of all words: that language imprisons those who speak it, that as a medium of their own it has essentially failed. This can be demonstrated with certain neologisms, German expressions invented to replace foreign words for the sake of the illusory ideal of indigenousness. They always sound more foreign and more forced than the genuine foreign words themselves. In comparison with the latter, they take on a deceitful quality, a claim to an equivalence of speech and object that is refuted by the conceptual nature of all speech. Foreign words demonstrate the impossibility of an ontology of language: they confront even concepts that try to pass themselves off as origin itself with their mediatedness, their moment of being subjectively constructed, their arbitrariness. Terminology, the quintessence of foreign words in the individual disciplines, and especially in philosophy, is not only thing-like rigidification but also its opposite: critique of concepts' claim to exist in themselves when in fact language has inscribed in them something posited, something that could be other-

---

*In German, *-ieren* is the suffix used to create new infinitives from foreign roots. —Translator's note.

wise. Terminology destroys the illusion of naturalness in language, which is historical, and because of that, restorationist ontological philosophy, which would like to impute absolute Being to its words, is particularly inclined to eliminate foreign words. Every foreign word contains the explosive material of enlightenment, contains in its controlled use the knowledge that what is immediate cannot be said in unmediated form but only expressed in and through reflection and mediation. Nowhere do foreign words in German prove their worth more than in contrast to the jargon of authenticity, terms like *Auftrag, Begegnung, Aussage, Anliegen* [mission, encounter, message, concern], and the like. They all want to conceal the fact that they are terminology. They have a human sound, like the Wurlitzer organs in which the vibrato of the voice is inserted technologically. But foreign words unmask these terms: only what is translated back into foreign words from the jargon of authenticity means what it means. Foreign words teach us that language can no longer cure us of specialization by imitating nature; it can do so only by assuming the burden of specialization. Among German writers Gottfried Benn was probably the first to use this element of foreign words, the scientific element, as a literary technique.

But it is against precisely this that the most telling objection to foreign words is directed. Privilege entrenches itself in science as a specialization, a separate branch, a division of labor; the privilege of education continues to entrench itself in foreign words. But the less substance the concept of education or culture comes to have, the more foreign words —many of which once belonged to modernism and were its linguistic advocates—take on an archaic, at times helpless quality, as though they were spoken into the void. Brecht, who aimed at the moment in language through which it, as something general, resists the privilege of the particular, clearly tended to avoid foreign words; not without, however, a secret affectation of the archaic, the desire to write High German like a dialect. Benjamin sometimes adopted this implicit hostility to foreign words when he called philosophical terminology a pimp language. And in fact the official philosophical language, which treats any and all terminological inventions and definitions as if they were pure descriptions of states of affairs, is no better than the puristic neologisms of a metaphysically consecrated New German, which, incidentally, is derived directly from that scholastic abuse. Foreign words can still be accused of excluding those who did not have the opportunity to learn them early in life. As components of a language of initiates they have a rasping tone to them, for all their enlightened quality; it is precisely the combination of that rasping tone with the note of enlightenment that constitutes their nature. The Nazis also tolerated foreign words, whether with the military in mind or in order to present themselves as genteel folk. There is virtually no convincing argument against the social critique of foreign words other than its own implications. For if language is subjected to the criterion of intelligibility "for everyone," then foreign words, which are usually only blamed for what people resent in the ideas, are certainly not the only guilty parties and hardly the most important. Purges in the style of the people's democracies could not rest content with foreign words but would have to do away with the better part of language itself. Consistently, Brecht once provoked me in conversation by asserting that the literature of the future should be composed in pidgin English. At this point in the discussion Benjamin refused to follow him and went over to my side. The barbaric futurism of such proclamations—which Brecht himself probably did not intend very seriously, by the way—is an alarming confirmation in the domain of language of the positivist enlightenment's tendency to regress when left to its own devices. Truth, which is only a truth for something else when it becomes a mere means to an end, shrivels up like pidgin or Basic English and then becomes truly fit for giving commands—which is what the impulse behind the new type of antagonism to foreign words was initially directed against. Similarly, derisively gave Europeans once orders to their colored servants in the same debased speech they wished their servants would use. A critique of foreign words that mistakenly considers itself progressive serves a communicative ideal that is in actuality an ideal of manipulation; today the word that is designed to be understood becomes, precisely through this process of calculation, a means to degrade those to whom it is addressed to mere objects of manipulation and to harness them for purposes that are not their own, not objectively binding. In the meantime, what was once called agitation can no longer be distinguished from propaganda, and the word aims squarely at transfiguring advertising by appealing to higher ends independent of individual interests. The universal system of communication, which on the face of it brings human beings together and which allegedly exists for their sake, is forced upon them. Only the word that takes pains to name its object precisely, without having an eye to its effect, has an opportunity to champion the cause of human beings by doing so, something they are cheated of as long as every cause is presented as being theirs here and now. Foreign words no longer have the function of protesting nationalism, which in the era of the great power blocs no longer coincides with the individual languages of individual nations. But foreign words are the twice-alienated remnants of a culture that disintegrated along with classical liberal society but once had as its aim humanness or humaneness [*das Humane*], to be demonstrated in the unselfish expression of the matter at hand rather than in the service of human beings as potential customers. As such, they can help a form of cognition that is unyielding and penetrating to survive, a cognition that threatens to disappear with the regression of consciousness and the decline of education. Certainly foreign words should not become naive in the process; they should not present themselves as still confident that they will be heard. Rather, they should express the solitude of intransigent consciousness in their reserve and shock with their obstinacy: in any case shock may now be the only way to reach human beings through language. Like Greeks in Imperial Rome, foreign words, used correctly and responsibly, should lend support to the lost cause of a flexibility, elegance, and refinement of formulation that has been lost and that people do not want to be reminded of. Foreign words should confront people with something that would be possible only if educational privilege ceased to exist, even in its most recent incarnation, the leveling of all people to a schooled half-culture. In this way foreign words could preserve something of the utopia of language, a language without earth, without subjection to the spell of historical existence, a utopia that lives on unawarely in the childlike use of language. Hopelessly, like death's-heads, foreign words await their resurrection in a better order of things.

But arbitrary and unconsidered use will not make them fit for this; what they once seemed to promise in unmediated form is gone forever. Their legitimacy vis-à-vis the positivism of a colloquial language that is generally intelligible and thereby alienated from its own substance can be demonstrated only where they are superior to linguistic positivism by its own criterion, that of precision. Only the foreign word that renders the meaning better, more faithfully, more uncompromisingly than the available German synonyms will allow a spark to flow in the constellation into which it is introduced. The efforts of the writer who freely ponders where a foreign word should be used, and where it should not, do honor not only to the word but also to the red ink on the school composition. An abstract defense of foreign words would have no force. Not for illustration but for legitimation, their defense requires the analysis of passages into which foreign words have been introduced deliberately and consideredly. I have chosen the examples for this analysis from a text of my own, not because I consider the text exemplary but because I am more aware of the decisive considerations and can explain them better than those of other authors. I will refer intentionally to the "Short Commentaries on Proust" that brought the protests.

I will select a series of passages and tell you what considerations led me to use the more esoteric foreign words or kept me from using the more or less corresponding German expressions. On p. 176, for instance, it is said of Proust that as a novelist he "suspendiert" [suspended] the categorical system of the bourgeois society to which he himself belonged by virtue of his origins, way of life, and attitudes. One might propose "ausser Kraft gesetzt" [literally, put out of force, rescinded] as an alternative to "suspendiert." But that would be much stronger than "suspendiert" and would imply a harsh critique where in fact something is cautiously left hanging. "Ausser Aktion setzen" [to put out of action] would come closer to this but would itself contain a foreign word and would not imply the notion of something hovering or suspended. But above all, with "suspendiert" one thinks of a judgment that has been stayed but not revoked. This leads one into the sphere of Proust's novel as a trial about happiness that goes through innumerable courts of appeal —an aspect that none of the German alternatives would capture.

On p. 176 I speak of the "Disparatheit" [disparity] between subjective motives and objective events, and the cluster of foreign words is admittedly not pretty. I tried to avoid the most unfamiliar of them, "Disparatheit," which is patched together out of Latin and German and hence particularly objectionable. But the only alternative available was "völlige Auseinanderweisen" [complete separation from one another], and not only did making a substantive out of a verbal expression seem uglier to me than the expression that would have been directly appropriate, but the "Auseinanderweisen" also failed to render the idea accurately. For the phenomenon in Proust's novel that I wanted to call attention to was conceived as something given, a condition, not something active. What finally led me to the choice of the word was reflection on my text as a whole, where compound words ending in *-weisen* were more frequent than I would have liked. I had to sacrifice the ones that least corresponded to what was intended.

Further: it is said that Proust's novel bears witness to the experience that the people who are decisive in our lives appear in them as though "designiert" [appointed, designated] by an unknown author (p. 176).

The literal translation of "designiert" would be "bezeichnet" [indicated, represented]. But that would miss the meaning. It would assert only that the people in question were characterized as by an unknown author, but not that they were selected for us, put in relation to our lives as if by plan. The illusion of a hidden intent behind the chance that leads people who become important to us to cross our paths would not emerge at all, and the passage would become truly unintelligible. But if one said "geplant" [planned] instead of "designiert," a moment of rationality and definitiveness would enter the description of the phenomenon and would give a crude specificity to the vague and obscure quality inherent in the matter. In addition, today the jurisdiction of the word "geplant" falls within a conceptual domain that would introduce a completely false note, that of the administered world, into Proust's liberal sphere.

A sentence on p. 177 asserts that in Proust death ultimately "ratifiziert" [ratifies] the frailty of what is stable and solid in a person. "Bestätigen" [confirm] would be too weak for that; it would remain within the sphere of mere cognition, of the verification of a hypothesis. What I wanted to express, however, was that death, like a verdict, appropriates the decay that is life itself. At the same time, the moment of definitiveness that lends weight to Proust's romanticism of disillusionment is much clearer in "ratifiziert" than in the blander word "bestätigen."

The case of "imagines" [the plural of the Latin *imago*; images] (p. 177) is instructive. "Bilder" [pictures, images] is much too general an expression to capture the transposition from the world of experience to the intelligible world effected by Proust's way of regarding human beings. "Urbilder" [primordial images or archetypes], however, would call to mind the Platonic notion of ideas identical with themselves, whereas the very substance of Proust's world of images lies in what is most transitory. The strangeness of this subject matter—perhaps Proust's innermost secret—could be evoked only by the alien quality of a term that is derived from psychoanalysis but is given a new function by its context.

The choice of the word "Soirée" in place of "Abendgesellschaft" [literally, evening party] (p. 178) brings up a matter that is important in all translation but has not received adequate attention, at least not theoretical attention. The issue concerns the weight of words in different languages, their status in their context, which varies independently of the meaning of the individual words. The equivalent in English of the

German word "schon" is "already." But "already" is much heavier; it carries a greater load than "schon." If there is no special emphasis on an unexpectedly early point in time, "hier bin ich schon" will generally be translated not "I am already here" but "Here I am"; in Anglo-Saxon countries Germans can easily recognize one another by the too frequent use of "already." Such distinctions should not be ignored in less formal expressions either, in nouns with concrete content. "Abendgesellschaft" is heavier than "Soirée." It lacks the self-evident quality that the French word has in French, just as social forms in general are not so self-evident in German, not so much second nature as they are in France. There is something forced and artificial about the word "Abendgesellschaft," as though it were an imitation of a soirée and not the real thing; this is why the foreign word is to be preferred. If one said simply "Gesellschaft" [social gathering], the weight relationships would be approximately correct, but something essential to the content of the French word, its reference to evening, would be lost, as would the reference to the somewhat official nature of the event.

The foreign word is better whenever its literal translation is not literal, for whatever reason. "Sexus" [sex], at a somewhat later point (p. 180) means "Geschlecht" [sex, race, genus]. But the German word, *Geschlecht*, covers a substantially greater range of meaning than the Latin word, *Sexus*; it includes what is called the "gens" in Latin, the clan or tribe. And above all, it has much more pathos than the foreign word, less sensual, one might say. *Geschlechtliche* love is not the same as *sexuelle* love; it provides room for a certain erotic element to which the expression *sexuell* presents a certain contrast. In attempting to clarify the concept of the sexual and to distinguish it from the more general and less offensive concept of love, Freud calls attention to its "indecent," prohibited aspect. One does not necessarily think of that aspect in connection with the German word *Geschlecht*, but one does with the foreign word. It is precisely this illicit quality, however, that is crucial in the passage in question.

There is a paradoxical problem behind the expression "society-Leute" [literally, society people], which I chose for an influential group of figures in Proust's novel (p. 181). For the word "society" has a double meaning in German as well as in English: it means both society as a whole, the object of sociology, for example, and "high society," as it is called, those who are accepted, the aristocracy and the upper bourgeoisie. The cumbersome "Leute aus der Gesellschaft" [people from the society] would at best not have been completely clear; it would have suggested people from a group that had just assembled. "Gesellschaftsleute" would have been completely impossible. Moreover, in comparison with "society," the German word "Gesellschaft" has the same artificial quality that "Abendgesellschaft" has in comparison to "soirée." Compared with "society column," the name of a column in a women's magazine, "Aus der Gesellschaft" ["From Society"], reads like an imitation over which one has foolishly taken great pains. To emphasize the nuance I was concerned with, I had to use "society," following colloquial German. Although the English expression is in itself just as ambiguous as the German, in German the word "society" takes on a specificity lacking in the native word; to say nothing of an aura perceptible to anyone who understands the kind of chattering Proust has his Odette do.

The expression "kontingent" [contingent] (p. 181), which without a doubt is not naturalized in German and is incomprehensible to many people in the radio audience, is derived from philosophy. Its use brings up the problem of terminology. "Kontingent" means "accidental"; it refers, however, not to an individual chance event or even the general contingency abstracted from it but rather to chance as an essential feature of life. The expression is used this way in my text as well: "Proust shares with the great tradition in the novel the category of the contingent." To say instead "the category of the accidental" would be imprecise; one might think that there was something accidental about the novel as a whole, or its manner of presentation. But by virtue of the philosophical tradition inherent in it the word "kontingent" means something I added as clarification in the next sentence: "a life bereft of meaning, a life the subject can no longer shape into a cosmos." No literal translation is adequate to that. One can debate whether philosophical terms have any legitimacy outside what goes by the abominable name of "Fachphilosophie," technical philosophy, a name that contradicts the thing itself. But if one rejects this notion of technical philosophy and conceives of philosophy as a mode of consciousness that does not let the boundaries of a specific discipline be forced upon it, one gains the freedom to use words originating in the domain of philosophy in places where conventional usage does not expect philosophy. Here, certainly, the use of the foreign word, which is truly scarcely understood any more due to its foreign derivation, takes on a desperate and provocative quality, a quality that must be freely chosen if one does not want to be a naive victim of his own academic discipline.

The word "Spontaneität" [spontaneity] (p. 212) is also derived from the philosophical tradition, the Kantian tradition in particular. There is so much compressed into it that no translation could accomplish what that word does without extensive paraphrase; often, however, a literary text requires a single word and precludes explication because it would disturb the distribution of emphasis in the text. This was what determined my choice. Even though a person without philosophical training may not be aware of everything contained in the term "Spontaneität," I have not been able to completely shake off the conviction that such terms preserve a certain power of suggestion; that they convey something of the richness objectively contained in them even to the person for whom their meaning is not completely clear. On the one hand, and first of all, "Spontaneität" means the capacity for action, production, generation. On the other hand, however, it means that this capacity is involuntary, not identical to the conscious will of the individual. It is immediately evident that this duality in the concept of "spontaneity" does not appear in any German word. The subject of the passage in question is jealousy, which turns love into a relationship of possession and thereby makes the beloved a thing. For this reason, it is said, jealousy violates the "spontaneity" of love. To say instead that it violates the "Unwillkürlichkeit" [involuntariness] of love would be nonsensical, and even "Unmittelbarkeit" [immediacy], which in itself is closer to what is meant, would not be adequate, because, as no one knew better than Proust, all love contains mediated elements. So it had to be "Spontaneität." If someone is praised for behaving spontaneously in a situation, that describes his behavior more graphically than any of the circumlocutions I looked for.

It is generally the need for conciseness that prompts the choice of foreign words. Compactness and conciseness as the ideal of presentation, the omission of things that are self-evident, silence about what is already logically contained in the thought and should therefore not be repeated verbally—all that is incompatible with circumlocutions or extensive paraphrases of words, which would often be necessary if one wanted to avoid foreign words and yet not sacrifice any of their meaning. I have spoken of "Authentizität" [authenticity] (p. 183) in connection with Proust and at other times as well. Not only is the word an uncommon one in German; the meaning it takes on in the context in which I set it is not at all assured. It is supposed to be the characteristic of works that gives them an objectively binding quality, a quality that extends beyond the contingency of mere subjective expression, the quality of being socially grounded. If I had said simply "Autorität" [authority], using a foreign word that has at least been adopted into German, I would have indicated the force such works exercise but not the justification of that force by a truth that ultimately refers back to the social process. I would have missed the distinction I was concerned with, the distinction between what is grounded through its content and what has usurped its place through violence. Of course a word that is currently very popular in Germany was available: "Gültigkeit" [validity]. Here, however, we must bear in mind that words have not only a contextual but also a historical status. The word "gültig" has currently been thoroughly compromised by expressions like "gültige Aussage" [valid statement]. A certain kind of robustness is evident in it, an unctuous-slick affirmative quality that plays a pernicious role in contemporary ideology. I could not have let myself get involved with that at any cost. One cannot attack the jargon of authenticity and then speak of "valid works," a concept in which notions of old and invariable truth, and ultimately of public recognition as well, resonate. Certainly one cannot expect all these complex considerations and critical reflections—to communicate which would completely disrupt the equilibrium of a text directed toward its subject matter—to be condensed into the "Authentizität." But in the hesitation the word gives rise to, all the concepts it calls to mind and nevertheless avoids flash by. This delay may convey more than a more colloquial expression that is thereby less appropriate to what is intended. It is not too far-fetched to hope that the intention will be carried out, because the word "Authentizität" is not an isolated spot of ink on the page; the context throws a much refracted light on that magic word. With a certain amount of literary ability and good fortune, one can put into a foreign word things that a seemingly less esoteric word would never be capable of, because it drags along too many of its own associations to be capable of being completely gripped by the will to expression.

In my attempt to vindicate foreign words, I could not suppress the criticisms they are currently vulnerable to; nor could I take a standpoint as rigid as that of their opponents tends to be. Even the writer who imagines that he is going right to the subject matter itself and not to the way it is communicated cannot willfully ignore the historical changes language undergoes in the process of its communicative use. He has to do his formulating from the inside and the outside at the same time, as it were. This contradiction affects his relationship to foreign words as well. Even when they sound objectively right to him, he has to sense what is happening to them in contemporary society. Often they turn into empty shells, like the word "Authentizität" when looked at purely in itself. What language is in itself is not independent of what it is for others. But blindness to that dependency, which the writer who is serious about language needs, can turn into the stupidity of the person who imagines himself safely in possession of pure means when precisely because of their purity those means are no longer good for anything. The problem of foreign words is truly a problem, and that is not merely a manner of speaking. What I tried to show in my discussion of the word "Authentizität," a word I am not comfortable with and yet cannot do without, holds for the use of foreign words in general. It is not a linguistic *Weltanschauung*, not an abstract pro or con, that decides on that use but a process of countless interwoven impulses, promptings, and reflections. The limited consciousness of the individual writer has little control over the extent to which this process is successful. But the process cannot be avoided: it repeats, if inadequately, the social process undergone by foreign words, and in fact by language itself, a process in which the writer can intervene to make changes only by recognizing it as an objective one.

◻◻◻◻

Ernst Bloch's Spuren:
On the revised edition of 1959

The title *Spuren* [traces or tracks] puts childhood experiences of reading Indian stories to work in the service of philosophical theory. A broken twig, an imprint on the ground speak to the expert eye of youth, which does not confine itself to the things everyone sees but engages in speculation instead. There's something here, something hidden here in the midst of normal, everyday life: "Something's going on" (15).* What it is, no one quite knows, and at one point Bloch says, speaking with the Gnostic school, that perhaps it does not even exist yet and is only in the process of becoming. But *il y a quelque chose qui cloche*—something's wrong—and the more mysterious the source of the track, the more insistent the feeling that this is what it is. This is the point on which speculation focuses. As if mocking phenomenology with its self-possession and scientific circumspection, speculative thought seeks out aconceptual phenomena and experiments with interpretation, feeling its way. Indefatigable, the philosophical moth flies at the plane of glass in front of the light. The enigmas of what Bloch once called the form of the unconstruable question are to crystallize into the answers they happen to suggest at the moment. The traces come from the unutterable domain of childhood, which once said all there was to say. Many friends are quoted in the book. Most likely they are friends from adolescence, Ludwigshafen relations of Brecht's Augsburg pals, of George Pflanzelt and Müllereisert. In the same way, half-grown boys smoke their first pipe as

---

*Ernst Bloch, *Spuren* (Berlin: Neue erweiterte Ausgabe, 1959). Page numbers in parentheses refer to this edition.

though it were the pipe of perpetual peace: "Wonderful is the coming of evening, and beautiful is the talk of men together." But these are men from Brecht's city of Mahagonny in Dream-America, along with Old Shatterhand and Winnetou from Leonhard Frank's Würzburg gang of thieves, a smell that is more pungent between the covers of a book than it ever was by the fishy river or in the smoke-filled bar. The grown man, however, remembering all this, wants to turn the cards he played then into a winning game, but without betraying the image of them to his all too grown-up reason; almost any interpretation first assimilates the rationalistic interpretation and then undermines it. The experiences are no more esoteric than whatever it was about the ringing of the Christmas bells that seized us and can never be completely eradicated: the feeling that what exists here and now cannot be all there is. Something has been promised, and it seems, even if that is an illusion, guaranteed as only in great works of art—with which Bloch's book, impatient with culture, does not want to have much to do. Under the compulsion of artistic form, all happiness is too little and is in fact not happiness at all: "Here too something is growing more luxuriantly than the familiar breadths of our subject (and the world) allow; excessive fear and 'unfounded' joy have concealed their causes. They are hidden within the human being and not yet loose in the world; joy least of all, and yet it is the most important thing" (169). Bloch's philosophy wants to tear the promise of joy away from cozy petit-bourgeois security with the grappling iron of the literary pirate, rejecting what it wants in the here and now and projecting what is closest to hand onto something that is supreme, something that has not existed. Happiness, divided à la Goethe into the happiness of what is close at hand and the happiness of what is highest, is forced back together until it reaches the breaking point; the happiness close at hand is happiness only when it signifies happiness in the highest, and the highest is present only in what is close to hand. The expansive gesture wants to transcend the limits set for it by its origins in what is close at hand—in immediate individual experience, chance psychological phenomena, mere subjective mood. The arrogance of the initiate takes no interest in what the state of permanent amazement says about the one who experiences it. It turns its attention instead to what the amazement reveals, indifferent to the question of how the poor fallible individual subject reached that state: "The thing-in-itself is objective imagination" (89). The individual's fallibility, however, is incorporated into this construction. The inadequacy of finite consciousness makes infinite consciousness, which it is to participate in, something uncertain and enigmatic; but at the same time it confirms it as something compelling and definite, on the grounds that its uncertainness is nothing but subjective inadequacy.

Thinking that follows trails is narrative thinking, like the apocryphal model of the adventure story about the journey to a utopian goal, a model for which Bloch would like to create a radiant image. Bloch is led to narrative as much by his overall conception as by his natural inclinations. To read Blochian narrative as mere parable would be to misunderstand it. The parable's lack of ambiguity would deprive narrative of its color, a color whose optics place it outside the spectrum, like the trumpet-red in one of Leo Perutz's ingenious thrillers. Instead, the narrative tries, through adventure and extraordinary events, to construct a truth that is not already in our possession. The reader is seldom provided with compelling interpretations. It is as though the audience for one of Wilhelm Hauff's fairy tales were sitting around listening to someone from some south-German Orient, where there is a city called Backnang and an expression that goes "ha no." First one thing and then another is brought out—progressively, however, with a conceptual motion that says nothing about Hegel but knows full well what it is doing. Across the gap between something concrete that actually only stands for the concrete and a thought that transcends the contingency and blindness of the concrete but in return forgets the most important thing, there echoes the sound of someone who emphatically has something special to tell us, something other than the same old thing. The narrative tone presents the paradox of a naive philosophy; childhood, indestructible in the midst of reflection, transforms even what is most mediated into something unmediated, which is then reported. This affinity with the concrete, beginning with material strata devoid of meaning, puts Bloch's philosophy in contact with the lower depths, with things ostracized by culture and openly shabby; only in these things does his philosophy, a late product of the anti-mythological Enlightenment, hope to find salvation. As a whole, one might define it as the philosophy of someone cast out into the great cities like the "poor B. B." [in Brecht's poem "Vom armen B. B."], someone who tells belatedly of things never told before. The impossibility of narration itself, which condemns the descendants of the epic to kitsch, becomes the expression of something impossible, something that is to be narrated and defined as a possibility. At the moment we sit down to listen to a story, we concede the narrator something, not knowing whether or not he will fulfill our expectations. In the same way, one must take this philosophy on faith as an oral rather than a written philosophy. The gesture of oral delivery prevents the responsible production of text, and Bloch's texts become eloquent only when one does not read them as such. The torrent of narrative thought, with everything it carries with it, overflows argument and captures us alive; this is a philosophy in which, in a certain sense, no thinking goes on at all—eminently clever, but not at all brilliant in the scholastic sense. The things that reverberate in the narrative voice do not become material for reflection but instead come to resemble that voice. This is true even of the things, and in fact precisely of the things, which the voice does not penetrate, stylize, and melt down. To ask where the stories came from or what the narrator is trying to do would be ridiculous in view of Bloch's intention to achieve a second-order anonymity, to vanish into truth: "If this story is nothing, say the tellers of fairy tales in Africa, then it belongs to the one who told it; if it is something, it belongs to us all" (158). Accordingly, critique of this philosophy cannot criticize its flaws as though they were the faults of an individual, which can be corrected; instead, it must spell out the wounds of Bloch's philosophy as Kafka's delinquent [in his story "In the Penal Colony"] spells out his.

But this narrative voice is not at all authentic in the clichéd sense of "genuine." Bloch's ear, extremely refined even in the midst of his turbulent prose, notes how little something truly different would be captured by that philistine concept of pure identity with the self. "A soft, feelingful story in the dusky must of the nineteenth century, with all the romantic colportage the motif of parting requires. Its pulse is most appropriately colored in the tones of half-sincere feeling; parting itself is sentimental. But sentimental with a depth to it; it vibrates indiscernibly between illusion and depth" (90). This vibrato survives in the great popular artists of an age that no longer tolerates popular art. The voice of Alexander Girardi was exaggerated in this way, plaintive and insincere like someone having hysterics; what was authentic about it was its inauthenticity, its untamed quality, and the echo of its own impossibility. Masses in particular find themselves enraptured, not always to their advantage, by the kind of exaggerated expression whose excessiveness reminds the mediocre mind of the things that really count. Thus a servant girl created a variation of Scheffel's "Das ist im Leben hässlich eingerichtet" ["Things are badly organized in life," a line from J. V. von Scheffel's *The Trumpeter of Säckingen*]: "entsetzlich eingerichtet" ["organized horribly"]. Bloch blasts away like Scheffel's trumpeter. Naive philosophy chooses the disguise of the blusterer, the pianist at the piano bar, poor and unrecognized, who tells the astonished patrons buying his beer that he is really Paderewski. One of those historico-philosophical insights for which Bloch is famous sets this atmosphere ablaze: "Even the young music-maker Beethoven, who suddenly knew, or asserted, that he was a genius like no other, was perpetrating a scurrilous fraud when he considered himself to be Ludwig van Beethoven, who he had not yet become. He used this effrontery, for which there was no basis, to become Beethoven, and in the same way nothing great would ever have come into being without the boldness, even the brazenness of this kind of anticipation" (47).

Like the pianist in the piano bar, philosophy as colportage has seen better days. Ever since it began bragging that it had got hold of the Philosopher's Stone and was in on a mystery that would necessarily forever remain a mystery to the *hoi polloi,* it has contained an element of charlatanism. Bloch absolves it. He competes with the barker at the unforgotten annual fair, he screeches like an orchestrion in an empty restaurant waiting for its customers. He disdains the impoverished cleverness that tries to hide all that and invites in the kind of cleverness that high idealistic philosophy excluded. As a corrective, his oral exaggeration confesses that it itself doesn't know what it is saying, that its truth is untruth when judged by the criterion of what exists. The narrator's victorious tone is inseparable from the substance of his philosophy, the rescuing of illusion. Bloch's utopia settles into the empty space between the latter and what merely exists. Perhaps what he aims at, an experience that has not yet been honored by experience, can be conceived only in an extreme form. The theoretical defense of illusion is also Bloch's own defense. In this he bears a profound likeness to the music of Mahler.

What remains of the total music of German Idealism is a kind of noise that intoxicates Bloch, who is musical and a Wagnerian. Words become heated up as if they were to start to glow again in the disenchanted world, as if the promise hidden in them had become the motor of thought. From time to time Bloch gets tangled up with "all that is powerful," and waxes enthusiastic about "open and collective battle" that "is to force things to go our way." This strikes a note dissonant to his antimythological tenor, the appeal he is trying to win for Icarus. But the impulse in him that opposes the law of eternal invariance of fate and myth, the impulse that opposes entanglement in the natural order, feeds on nature, on the power of a drive that philosophers have seldom allowed to speak so freely. Bloch's phrase about the breakthrough of transcendence is not spiritualistic. He does not want to spiritualize nature. Rather, the spirit of utopia would like to bring about the moment when nature, pacified, would itself be free of domination, would no longer need domination and would create a space for something other than nature.

In the *Spuren*, which are developed out of the experience of individual consciousness, the rescuing of illusion has its center in what Bloch's book *The Spirit of Utopia* called *Selbstbegegnung*, encounter with the self. The subject, the human being, is not yet himself at all; he appears as something unreal, something that has not yet emerged from potentiality, but also as a reflection of what he could be. Nietzsche's idea of the human being as something that has to be overcome is modified to become nonviolent: "for the human being is something that still has to be invented" (32). Most of the tales in the volume are about the human being's non-identity with himself, with a knowing look at wayfarers, fairy tale lads, confidence men and all those who are led astray by the dream of a better life. "One meets less self-interest here than vanity, insatiable *amour-propre*, and folly. If *amour-propre* takes aristocratic forms, it does not do so in order to step on those below, like the *parvenu* or even the servant become master. Nor is the aristocracy actually affirmed; the self-styled *seigneur* is not class-conscious" (44). Instead, utopia rattles the cage of identity, in which it senses the injustice of being precisely this person and only this person. At the level on which this book was written thirty years ago, Bloch deliberately and directly juxtaposes two aspects of this non-identity. The first is the materialist: that in a society of universal exchange human beings are not themselves but agents of the law of value; for in previous history, which Bloch would not hesitate to call prehistory, humankind has been object, not subject. "But no one is what he intends to be, and certainly not what he represents. And everyone is not too little but rather from the outset too much for what they became" (33). The other aspect is the mystical: that the empirical "I," the psychological "I," and even the person's character is not the Self intended for each man, the secret Name with which alone the notion of rescue is concerned. Bloch's favorite figure for the mystical self is the house in which one would be at home, inside, no longer estranged. Security is not to be had, there is no ontologically embellished *Befindlichkeit* [state-of-mind (Heidegger)] in which one can live; instead, Bloch notes the way it should be but is not. Bloch's traces are in complicity with happiness, but this alliance does not barricade itself up in the positiveness of happiness. Instead, it holds positiveness open as something promised, and all positive, actually existing happiness remains under suspicion of a breach of faith. Such dualism is an easy target for criticism. The direct contrast between the metaphysical self and the social self that is to be produced takes no account of the fact that all the defining characteristics of that absolute self stem from the sphere of human immanence, from the social sphere; Bloch, the Hegelian, could easily be convicted of interrupting the dialectic at a central point with a theological *coup de main*. But to leap to this hasty conclusion would be to invade the issue of whether a dialectic that does not negate itself at a certain point is even possible; even the Hegelian dialectic had its encapsulated "maxim," the identity thesis. In any case, Bloch's *coup de main* renders him capable of an intellectual modus operandi that does not otherwise tend to thrive in the climate of the dialectic, whether idealist or materialist: nothing that exists is idolized for its necessity; speculation attacks necessity itself as an image of myth.

The fact that narration and commentary revolve around illusion in the *Spuren* stems from the fact that the boundary between finite and infinite, between phenomenal and noumenal, the intellect with its limitations and faith with its lack of logic, is not respected. Behind every word stands the will to break through the blockade that common sense has been placing between consciousness and the thing-in-itself since Kant. Bloch ascribes the very fact that this boundary is sanctioned to ideology, as an expression of bourgeois society's restriction of itself to the reified world it has established, a world that exists for it, the world of commodities. This was the point where Bloch's and Benjamin's theories coincided. By tearing up the boundary posts out of a pure emancipatory impulse, Bloch gets rid of the rigidified "ontological difference" between essence and mere existence that is customary in philosophy here in Germany. He takes up motifs from German Idealism and ultimately from Aristotle and makes existence itself a force, a potentiality that is impelled toward the absolute. Bloch's fondness for colportage has its systematic roots, if one may use such a term, in its complicity with the lower strata, both in the sense of what is materially unformed and in the sense of those who have to bear the social burden. The upper stratum, however—culture, form, what Bloch calls "polis"—he considers hopelessly entangled in domination, oppression, myth. The latter are genuinely superstructure: only what has been cast out contains the potential for something that would be beyond all that. This is why he hunts around in kitsch for the transcendence that is blocked by the immanence of culture. But the least of the reasons why his thinking operates as a corrective to contemporary thought is that it does not put on airs when it comes to facticity. He refrains from the contemporary German custom of classifying being as a branch of philosophy and thereby condemning philosophy to the irrelevance of a resurrected formalism. Nor, however, does he collaborate in the degradation of thought to a mere agency of reconstructive ordering. The lower stratum is neither dissolved nor covered up and immediately left behind, as in classificatory thought: instead, it is swept along like the thematic elements in certain music. The sphere of music takes up more space in Bloch's thought than in almost any other thinker, even Schopenhauer or Nietzsche. Its sounds reverberate in his thought like a railway station orchestra in dreams; Bloch's ear has no more patience with technical musical logic than with aesthetic refinement. Nor is there any transition, any "mediation" between infantile pleasure in the merry-go-round and its metaphysical rescue: "And especially when the ship with music arrives, we find hidden in kitsch — non-petit-bourgeois kitsch — something of the jubilation of the (possible) resurrection of the dead" (165). Each such audacious extrapolation implicitly presupposes Hegel's critique of Kant: that to set limits is always already to transcend them; that to qualify itself as finite, reason must already be in command of the infinite, in whose name it sets this limit. The main stream of the philosophical tradition distinguishes between thought and the unconditioned, but one who does not want to swim with the current does not want to refrain from knowledge of the unconditioned — for the sake of its realization. He does not knuckle under and resign himself. The "Es ist gelungen" ["It has been accomplished"] of the final scene of *Faust*, the Kantian idea of perpetual peace as a real possibility, sees the critical element in philosophy as postponement and denial. This mode of thought conceives fulfillment not as a task or an idea but in terms of the model of bodily pleasure, $\dot{\eta}\delta o\nu\dot{\eta}$. In this respect it is anti-idealist and materialist. Its materialism forbids the construction of a seamless Hegelian identity, however mediated, of subject and object, a construction that requires that all objectivity ultimately be assimilated into the subject and reduced to mere "spirit." While Bloch, heretically, denies the boundary, he continues to insist, against Hegel's speculative idealism, on the unreconciled distinction between immanence and transcendence; he is as little inclined to mediation in his overall scheme as in his individual interpretations.

The "here" is defined in terms of historical materialism, and the "beyond" is defined through its refractions, through the traces of it one might find here. Without glossing over the distinction, Bloch philosophizes in a manner that is utopian and dualistic at the same time. Because he conceives utopia not in terms of the metaphysical construction of the absolute but in terms of the drastic theological conception—something the starving consciousness of the living feels cheated of when offered the consolation of the idea, Bloch can grasp utopia only as something illusionary. It is neither true nor not true: "Even an obvious mirage at least imitates or anticipates, impiously and deceitfully, a gleam that must somehow be embedded in life's inherent tendencies, in life's mere but nevertheless real 'possibilities.' For in itself a mirage is infertile; without palm trees there would not be even a fata morgana in the distances of time and space" (240).

The initial experiences Bloch presents are plausible enough: "Most people turn toward the wall when going to sleep, although in doing so they turn their backs to the dark room that is in the process of becoming unfamiliar. It is as though the wall suddenly began to exercise an attraction and paralyzed the room, as though sleep discovered something in the wall that is normally reserved only for the better death. It is as though in addition to disturbances and strangers sleep too instructed us in dying; to be sure, the scene seems to look different in that case, it displays a dialectical semblance of one's homeland. And in fact a dying man who was saved at the last moment explained this in the following way: 'I turned toward the wall and felt that what was out there, in the room, was nothing, no longer concerned me; what I was concerned with was to be found in the wall' " (163). But Bloch himself calls the secret of the wall a dialectical illusion. He does not let himself be lured into taking that insight literally. It is only that for him semblance is, psychologically, not subjective but objective illusion. Its plausibility is intended as a guarantee that, as in Benjamin and Proust as well, the most specific experiences, those which are completely submerged in particularity, are transformed into universality. What inspires the narrative profile of Bloch's philosophy is his suspicion that this kind of transformation eludes dialectical mediations. As much as its didactic content is admittedly indebted to dialectics, this profile is undialectical. The narratives deal with what exists, even if only in the future; the form ignores the process of becoming that the content proclaims, trying only to emulate its tempo, so to speak. But the possibility of creating what has been promised remains as uncertain as in dialectical materialism. Bloch is a theologian and a socialist, but not a religious socialist. What haunts immanence in the form of the displaced meaning or "spark" of a messianic end of history is credited as meaning neither to immanence nor to its rational reorganization. Positive religious content is neither to justify mere existence nor to rule it transcendentally. Bloch is a mystic in his paradoxical unity of theology and atheism. The mystical mediations in which the transmission of the spark takes place, however, presuppose dogmatic doctrinal content which they then destroy through interpretation, whether it be the Jewish doctrine of the Torah as a sacred text or christological doctrines. Without a claim to a revealed core, mysticism presents itself as mere cultural nostalgia. Bloch's philosophy of illusion, for which that kind of authority is irrevocably lost, is no more intimidated by that than were the mystical offshoots of the great classical religions in their final, enlightened phases; he does not deduce religion from a philosophy of religion. Speculative thought itself reflects on the dilemma this creates for it. But it prefers to simply put up with the dilemma, to acknowledge itself as illusion, rather than to resign itself to positivism or positive faith. The vulnerability that it takes pains to draw attention to is a consequence of its content. If that content were to be constructed and presented in pure form, the illusion that is its vital element would be artificially concealed.

It is easy to calculate in advance that what is unconditioned cannot be known by something conditioned: Bloch's philosophy itself is not immune to the apocryphal element it arrogantly intends to explode. What is narrated is consumed in the process of narration; when an idea that has not been thought catches fire there is a short circuit. For this reason, and not from a lack of conceptual power, the interpretations of Bloch's stories are largely inferior to the stories themselves, like an antinomian sermon on the text "Behold, I will give you stones instead of bread." The higher the sermon tries to reach, the more its straining increases the feeling of futility. The mingling of the spheres, which is as characteristic of this philosophy as the dichotomy between the spheres, adds an obscure element to it, an element that challenges all established notions of something existing purely in-itself, all Platonism. Even though Bloch would have it that the most extreme and the most trivial are one and the same, there is often a gap between them, and what is most extreme becomes trivial: "Is it good? I asked. For the child things taste best at other people's houses. They soon see what is not right there either. And if things were so good at home they wouldn't be so happy to leave. They often sense early on that things could be different in both places" (9). This is the gnostic doctrine of the inadequacy of Creation in the form of a platitude. Bloch's sovereign attitude is not disturbed by involuntary humor: "In any case it is not always what is expected that knocks at the door" (161). This philosophy is not satisfied with culture, but at times it fails to measure up to culture and falls flat on its face. For just as there is nothing between heaven and earth that cannot be seized upon psychoanalytically as a symbol for something sexual, so there is nothing that cannot be used as symbolic intention, nothing that is not suitable for a Blochian trace, and this everything borders on being nothing. The *Spuren* are most suspect when they tend to the occult: once forays into intelligible worlds become established as a principle there is no antidote to the dreams of a spirit-seer. Bloch tells numerous superstitious stories about superstition; while he quickly underlines the sorry quality of backroom spirit-world gossip, he makes no theoretical distinction between his metaphysical intentions and a metaphysics reduced to the level of facts. Still, something speaks in Bloch's favor, even where kitsch threatens to swallow up its savior. For it is one thing to believe in ghosts and another to tell ghost stories. One is almost tempted to concede true pleasure in these stories only to the person who does not believe in them but rather gets involved in them precisely in order to enjoy his freedom from myth. Both the reflection of myth in the narrative and Bloch's philosophy as a whole are aimed at this freedom. In ghost stories one does not believe in, what remains is amazement at the inadequacy of the unemancipated world, something Bloch never tires of relaying. The stories are a means of expression: the expression of alienation.

Giving primacy to expression rather than signification, concerned not only that words interpret concepts but also that concepts reveal the' meanings of words, Bloch's philosophy is the philosophy of Expressionism. It holds to Expressionism in its idea of breaking through the encrusted surface of life. Human immediacy wants to express itself directly: like the Expressionist subject, Bloch's philosophical subject protests the reification of the world. Bloch cannot, as art does, rest content with forming something which can then be filled with subjective content. Rather, he thinks beyond subjectivity and renders its immediacy transparent as something which is itself socially mediated, alienated. In making this kind of transition, however, he does not, as Lukács, the friend of his youth, does, extinguish the subjective moment in the fiction that a state of reconciliation has already been attained. This protects him from second-order reification. His historico-philosophical impulse maintains the perspective of subjective experience even where he has transcended it in the Hegelian sense. The intention of his philosophy is objective, but its speech remains unabatedly expressionist. As thought, it cannot remain a pure verbal expression of immediacy. Nor can it cancel out subjectivity as the basis of knowledge and the organon of language, for there is no objective order of being that could encompass the subject substantively, without contradiction, no objective order whose language would be identical to the subject's own. Bloch's thought does not spare itself the bitter knowledge that at the present time the philosophical step beyond the subject is a regression into the pre-subjective and works to the advantage of a collective order in which subjectivity is not superseded but merely suppressed by a heteronomous force. Bloch's perennial expressionism is a shrill response to the fact that reification persists and that where its abolition has been asserted it has hardened to mere ideology. The breaks in his speech are an echo of a historical moment that compels a philosophy of the subject-object to admit the continuing breach between subject and object.

Bloch's philosophy shares its most intimate theme with literary Expressionism. There is a sentence by Georg Heym that reads: "One might say that my writing is the best proof of a metaphysical country whose black peninsulas extend far into our fleeting days"—probably the same country whose topography was charted in Rimbaud's work. In Bloch the claim to this kind of proof is intended to be taken literally; that land is to be hauled in by means of ideas. Because of this, Bloch's philosophy is metaphysics of a different kind than traditional metaphysics. It cannot be reduced to questions of being, of the true essence of things, of God, freedom, and immortality, even though those questions reverberate through it everywhere. Rather, it wants to describe, or, to use Schelling's term, "construct" that other space: metaphysics as the phenomenology of the imaginary. Transcendence, having migrated to the profane sphere, is conceived as a "space." The reason it is so difficult to distinguish it from spiritistic colportage from the fourth dimension is that, devoid of any aspect of existence, it becomes a symbol, Bloch's transcendence becomes an idea. And Bloch's philosophy thereby turns back into the very idealism whose confines it was intended to escape. "This space, it seems to me, is always around us, even when we only suck on its edges and no longer know how dark the night is" (183).

Bloch's "motifs of disappearance" are intended to escort us into this space. Dying becomes a gateway, as in many moments in Bach. "Even the nothingness that unbelievers preach is unimaginable, fundamentally more obscure, in fact, than a something that would remain" (196). Bloch's obsession with the imaginary as something existing gives rise to this remarkable quality of stasis in the midst of dynamism, the paradox of the expressionist as an epic poet. It also gives rise to the excess of blind, unprocessed material. At times Bloch's work reads more like Schelling than Hegel, more like a pseudomorph of the dialectic than dialectics itself. The dialectic would hardly stop with a two-world theory that is at times reminiscent of [Schelling's] ontology of strata, a chiliastic antithesis of immanent utopia and revealed transcendence. But here is Bloch's comment on an anecdote about a young worker whom a benefactor temporarily treats to the good life and then sends back into the mines, at which point the worker murders him: "Is life, which plays with us, any different than the rich man, the good man? He himself, it is true, must be superseded, and the worker shot him; the social fate that the wealthy class imposes on the poor class must be superseded. But the rich man is still there, like the idol of a different fate, our natural fate, with death at its end, a fate whose crudeness the wealthy devil copies and makes palpable until it becomes his own fate" (5off.). Or, in a variation, "In death, which is not and by definition cannot be anyone's 'own' death (for our space is always life or something more than life, but not something less than it)—in death too there is something of the wealthy cat that lets the mouse run free before it devours it. No one could blame the 'saint' for shooting this god down the way the worker shot the millionaire" (5 1ff.). Bloch constructs an *analogia entis,* an analogy of being, between social oppression and life's mythical bondage to death, but this Platonic *chorismos* continues to gape wide, and the creation of a rational order on earth would be like a drop of water falling on the hot stone of fate and death. Bloch's hardboiled naiveté refuses to be talked out of this. It encourages cheap advice from both sides, both from dialectical materialism and from Being as the meaning of what exists. Just as everything progressive always also lags behind the things it leaves behind, so it is an element of earthiness that distinguishes Bloch from the polish of official philosophy, and something jungle-like that distinguishes him from the administrative sterility of Eastern-bloc philosophy. He thereby sabotages his reception as a cultural commodity, although he also facilitates an apocryphal, sectarian reception of his thought.

This architectonic schema shapes even Bloch's thought itself. While his philosophy overflows with materials and colors, it does not escape abstractness. What is colorful and particular in it serves largely to exemplify the single idea of utopia and breakthrough, which it nurses and cherishes the way Schopenhauer cherished his: "For in the final analysis everything a person encounters, everything a person thinks of, is one and the same thing" (16). Bloch's philosophy has to distill utopia into a general concept that subsumes the concreteness that utopia actually is. The "form of the unconstruable question" becomes a system, dazzled by a grandiosity that ill suits Bloch's revolt against power and glory. The general concept, which washes away the trace and cannot plausibly genuinely sublate it, nevertheless by its very intention has to speak as though the trace were present within it. It condemns itself to a lifetime of overwork. This drowns out the Expressionist scream: the power of the will, without which no trace would be discovered, works against what is willed. For the trace itself is involuntary, spontaneous, inconspicuous, intentionless. To reduce it to an intention is to violate it, just as examples violate the dialectic, as Hegel said in the *Phenomenology*. The color Bloch is after becomes gray when it becomes total. Hope is not a principle. But philosophy cannot fall silent in the face of color. Philosophy cannot move within the medium of thought, of abstraction, and then practice asceticism when it comes to the interpretation in which such movement terminates. If it does, its ideas become enigmas. This was the path Benjamin took in his *One-Way Street,* a work which has many affinities with Bloch's *Spuren.* Like *One-Way Street,* Bloch's traces—even in their title—sympathize with what is small. In contrast to Benjamin, however, Bloch does not give himself over to the miniature but instead uses it expressly as a category (see p. 66ff.). Even the microscopic remains abstract, too big for itself. Bloch declines the fragmentary. Dynamically, he, like Hegel, goes farther, beyond what forms the basis of his experience; in this respect he is an idealist *malgré lui.* To use an old-fashioned expression, his speculative thought wants to take root in the air, to be *ultima philosophia,* and yet its structure is that of *prima philosophia* and its ambition is the grand totality. His philosophy conceives the end of the world as its ground, that which moves what exists, which, as its *telos,* it already inhabits. It makes the last first. That is Bloch's innermost antinomy, one which cannot be resolved. This too he shares with Schelling.

Bloch's conception of something suppressed forcing its way up from below, something which will put an end to the outrage, is political.

About this too he tells stories, as if he were speaking about something predecided, virtually assuming the transformation of the world, unconcerned about what has become of the Revolution in the thirty years since the first edition of the *Spuren* and what has happened to the concept and possibility of revolution under altered technological and social conditions. The absurdity of the status quo suffices for his verdict; he does not enter into calculations about what ought to happen. "A drunken woman was lying in the rue Blondel. A policeman seizes hold of her. Je suis pauvre, says the woman. That's no excuse for filling the street with vomit, growls the policeman. Que voulez vous, monsieur, la pauvreté, c'est déjà à moitié la saleté, says the woman and takes a drink. In this way she describes, explains, and cancels herself out in one stroke. Whom or what is the policeman to arrest?" (17). The strength to refrain from sophistry about what is rational is accompanied by the shadow of a political *petitio principii*, which has at times been exploited in regions where world history is declared *causa judicata*, a matter that has been settled. But Bloch does not allow himself to be constrained by what is authoritarian and repressive. He is one of the very few philosophers who does not recoil in fear from the idea of a world without domination and hierarchy; it would be inconceivable for him to disparage the abolition of evil, sin, and death from the perspective of some profound official wisdom. He does not infer from the fact that these things have not yet been abolished the perfidious maxim that they could not and should not be abolished. Despite all else, this gives what he promises, the transfiguration of the "happy end," the ring of something that is not in vain. There is not a trace of mustiness in the *Spuren*. A heretic when it comes to the dialectic, Bloch is not to be bought off with the materialist thesis that a classless society should not be depicted. With unwavering sensuousness he delights in the image of that society, without stretching it deceptively thin. In the French worker eating lobster, or the celebration of the 14th of July there shimmers "a certain Later when money will no longer yap for goods or wag its tail through them" (19). Nor does he repeat the litany of the unmediated unity of theory and practice. To the question, Should one act or think? he responds, "Philosophy, they say, leaves people cold. But as Hegel remarked, that is not its job. And philosophy could exist without this job, but not even this job could exist without philosophy. For it is thought that creates a world in which things can be changed and not merely bungled" (261). There could not be a blunter way to tell vulgar materialism about genuine humanness [*Hu-*

manität], which gives thought its due at a time when it is everywhere being reduced to a mere appendage to action. This kind of humanness makes possible, even today, what Benjamin once said of Bloch: he can warm himself at his thoughts. They are like the great green tile stove that is heated from outside and suffices for the whole flat, powerful and consoling, without a chimney-corner in the room and without filling the place with smoke. The person who tells fairy tales saves them from the fate of having outlived their time. The expectation that something will come is paired with a profound skepticism. The two are combined in a joke from a Jewish legend in which someone reports a miracle and then, at the climactic moment, denies it: " 'What does God do? The whole story is untrue' " (253). Bloch omits an interpretation but adds, "Not a bad statement for a liar, not a bad motto if it came from better people" (253). What does God do?—The casual question masks an unallayed doubt about God's existence, because "the whole story is untrue," because, Hegel and dialectics to the contrary, the history of the world is not yet the history of truth. Through the joke, philosophy understands itself as deception, and it too thereby becomes more than it is: "One must be witty as well as transcendent" (253). The joke opens up the same vast perspective contained in the lines by Karl Kraus: "Nothing is true, and it is possible that something else will happen," and that the semblance it destroys will not have the last word after all. Philosophy should not let itself be talked out of what it has not succeeded in doing simply because humankind has not yet succeeded in doing it.

Extorted Reconciliation: On Georg Lukács' Realism in Our Time

*T*he aura that continues to grace the name of Georg Lukács, even outside the Soviet bloc, he owes to the writings of his youth—to the volume of essays *Soul and Form*, to *The Theory of the Novel*, and to the studies collected as *History and Class Consciousness*, where, writing as a dialectical materialist, he first systematically applied the category of reification to philosophical problematics. Originally inspired by figures like Simmel and Kassner and then trained under the southwest-German school, he soon opposed psychological subjectivism with an objectivist philosophy of history that exercised significant influence. Through the depth and élan of its conception as well as the density and intensity of its presentation, extraordinary for its time, *The Theory of the Novel* in particular established a standard for philosophical aesthetics that still holds today. In the early 1920s, when Lukács' objectivism yielded, not without initial conflicts, to official communist doctrine, he followed the Eastern custom and repudiated those writings. Misusing Hegelian motifs, he accepted the party hierarchy's servile criticisms of him and for decades tried in his books and essays to accommodate his obviously indestructible intellectual powers to the dismal level of Soviet pseudo-intellectual production, which had in the meantime degraded the philosophy it mouthed to a mere means to the ends of domination. It is only on account of his early works, however, repudiated and condemned by his party, that anyone outside the Eastern bloc has paid attention to the things Lukács has published during the last thirty years, which include a thick book on the young Hegel, even though one still sensed the old talent in some of the individual works on nineteenth-century German realism, as for instance in his writings on Keller and Raabe. It was probably in his *The Destruction of Reason* that the destruction of Lukács' own reason manifested itself most crassly. In that work the certified dialectician lumped together, most undialectically, all the irrationalist tendencies in recent philosophy under the category of reaction and fascism, without pausing to consider that in those tendencies—in contrast to academic idealism—thought was combating the very same reification of existence and thinking that Lukács was in the business of criticizing. For him, Nietzsche and Freud became fascists pure and simple, and he even managed to speak of Nietzsche's "more than ordinary ability" in the tone of a provincial Wilhelminian schoolmaster. Under the guise of an ostensibly radical critique of society he smuggled back the most pitiful clichés of the conformism to which that critique had once been directed.

But the book *Wider den missverstandenen Realismus* * [literally, *Against Misunderstood Realism*], which came out in the West with Claassen Verlag in 1958, shows signs of a different attitude on the part of the seventy-five-year-old Lukács. The change is probably connected with the conflict in which Lukács became involved through his participation in the Nagy regime. Not only is there reference to the crimes of the Stalin era, but there is positive talk about a "general advocacy of the freedom to write," a formulation that would previously have been unthinkable. Lukács discovers posthumous merit in his perennial opponent Brecht, and praises the latter's "Ballade vom toten Soldaten" ["Ballad of the Dead Soldier"], which must be a cultural-bolshevist abomination in the eyes of the East German powers-that-be, as a work of genius. Like Brecht, Lukács would like to broaden the concept of socialist realism, which for decades has been used to strangle every unruly impulse, everything the apparatchiks find unintelligible and suspect, to make room in it for more than the most miserable trash. He ventures a timid opposition, crippled from the outset by a consciousness of his own impotence. His timidity is no mere tactic. Lukács as a person is above suspicion. But the conceptual structure to which he sacrificed his intellect is so constricted that it suffocates anything that would like to breathe more freely in it; the *sacrifizio dell'intelletto* does not leave the intellect

---

*Published in the United States as *Realism in Our Time: Literature and the Class Struggle*, translated by John and Necke Mander (New York: Harper and Row, 1964; first published in English as *The Meaning of Contemporary Realism*, by Merlin Press in 1962). Page numbers here refer to this edition, although translations have often been altered.

unscathed. This puts Lukács' obvious nostalgia for his early writings in a melancholy perspective. The "Lebensimmanenz des Sinnes" ["life-immanence of meaning"], from the *Theory of the Novel,* is back, but reduced to the dictum that life under the construction of socialism simply is meaningful—a dogma just right for a philosophical-sounding justification of the rosy positiveness required of art in the people's republics. The book offers a sherbet—something between the so-called thaw and a renewed freeze. Despite emphatic protestations to the contrary, Lukács continues to share with the commissars of culture a subsumptive modus operandi which operates from above with labels like critical and socialist realism. Hegel's critique of Kantian formalism in aesthetics is reduced to the oversimplified assertion that in modern art style, form, and technique are vastly overrated (see especially p. 19)—as if Lukács did not know that it is through these moments that art as knowledge is distinguished from scientific knowledge, that works of art which were indifferent to their mode of presentation would negate their own concept. What looks like formalism to Lukács aims, through the structuring of the elements in accordance with the work's own formal law, at the same "immanence of meaning" that Lukács is pursuing, instead of forcing the meaning into the work from the outside by fiat, something he himself considers impossible and yet objectively defends. He willfully misinterprets the form-constitutive moments of modern art as *accidentia,* contingent additions to an inflated subject, instead of recognizing their objective function in the aesthetic substance. The objectivity he misses in modern art and which he expects from the material and its "perspectivist" treatment devolves upon the methods and techniques he would like to eliminate, which dissolve the purely material aspect and only thereby put it into perspective. He takes a neutral stance on the philosophical question whether the concrete substance of a work of art is in fact identical to the pure "reflection of objective reality" (101), an idol to which he clings with stubborn vulgar materialism. His own text certainly shows no respect for the norms of responsible presentation that his early writings helped to establish. No bearded privy councillor could pontificate about art in a manner more alien to it. He writes in the tone of one who is accustomed to the podium and permits no interruptions, one who does not shrink from lengthy digressions and has obviously renounced the sensitivity he criticizes as aestheticist, decadent, and formalistic, the very sensitivity that permits a relationship to art in the first place. While the Hegelian concept of the concrete rates high with Lukács, as it always did, especially when it is a question of holding literature to the depiction of empirical reality, his argumentation itself is largely abstract. His text is hardly ever subjected to the discipline of a specific work of art and its immanent problems. Instead, he issues decrees. The pedantry of his manner is matched by sloppiness in the details. Lukács does not shrink from such worn-out bits of wisdom as "Speaking is not the same thing as writing." He repeatedly uses the expression *Spitzenleistung* [peak performance], which derives from the sphere of commerce and sports records, he calls the elimination of the distinction between abstract and concrete possibility "appalling" [*verheerend*], and he points out that "from Giotto on a new secularity . . . triumph[s] more and more over the allegorizing of an earlier period" (40). We whom Lukács would call decadent may seriously overvalue form and style, but so far that has preserved us from expressions like "from Giotto on," just as it has preserved us from praising Kafka for being a "marvelous observer" (45). Nor will members of the avant-garde have spoken very often of the "series of extraordinarily numerous emotions which together combine to structure the inner life of man." In the face of these peak performances, which follow one another as in the Olympics, one might well ask whether someone who writes like this, ignorant of the métier of the literature he treats so cavalierly, has any right to particpate in serious discussion of literary matters. But in the case of Lukács, who at one time could write well, one senses the method of *justament*—malice aforethought—at work in his mixture of pedantry and irresponsibility, the resentful will to write badly, which he believes will have the magical sacrificial force of demonstrating polemically that anyone who does otherwise and takes pains with his writing is a good-for-nothing. In any case, stylistic indifference is almost always a symptom of dogmatic rigidification of the content. The exaggerated lack of vanity in a presentation that thinks of itself as objective when in fact it is only failing to engage in self-reflection, only disguises the fact that the objectivity has been removed from the dialectical process along with the subject. The dialectic is paid lip service, but for this kind of thought the dialectic has been determined in advance. Thought becomes undialectical.

The core of the theory remains dogmatic. The whole of modern literature, except where it fits the formula of critical or socialist realism, is rejected and immediately stigmatized as decadent, a word of abuse that covers all the atrocities of persecution and extermination, and not only in Russia. The use of that conservative term is incompatible with the theory whose authority Lukács, like his superiors, would like to appropriate for his national community through it. Talk about decadence cannot be separated from its positive counterimage of a nature bursting with strength; natural categories are projected onto things that are socially mediated. The tenor of Marx and Engels' critique of ideology, however, is directed against precisely that. Even associations with Feurbach's notion of healthy sensuality would hardly have procured this social Darwinist term access to their texts. Even in the rough draft of the *Grundrisse of the Critique of Political Economy* dating from 1857–58, that is, during the phase in which *Capital* was being written, we find the following:

> As much, then, as the whole of this movement appears as a social process, and as much as the individual moments of this movement arise from the conscious will and particular purposes of individuals, so much does the totality of the process appear as an objective interrelation, which arises spontaneously from nature; arising, it is true, from the mutual influence of conscious individuals on one another, but neither located in their consciousness, nor subsumed under them as a whole. Their own collisions with one another produce an *alien* social power standing above them, produce their mutual interaction as a process and power independent of them. . . . The social relation of individuals to one another as a power over the individuals which has become autonomous, whether conceived as a natural force, as chance or in whatever other form, is a necessary result of the fact that the point of departure is not the free social individual.[1]

This kind of critique does not stop at the sphere in which the affectively charged illusion of naturalness on the part of what is social dies the hardest, the sphere in which all the indignation about degeneracy arises: that of relations between the sexes. Somewhat earlier, Marx had reviewed G. F. Daumer's *Religion des neuen Weltalters* [*Religion of the New Age*] and skewered the following passage: "Nature and women are what is truly divine, in contrast to humanity and man. . . . The devotion of the human to the natural, of the masculine to the feminine is the genuine and the only true humility and self-sacrifice, the highest and in fact the only virtue and piety there is." To which Marx adds the following commentary: "We see here how the insipid ignorance of this speculative founder of a religion is transformed into a very pronounced cowardice. In the face of the historical tragedy that approaches him menacingly, Herr Daumer flees to what is allegedly nature, that is, into a stupid idyll of rural life, and preaches the cult of woman in order to disguise his own womanish resignation."[2] Wherever there is blustering about decadence this flight is being repeated. Lukács is forced into it by a situation in which social injustice continues after it has been officially declared to have been eliminated. The responsibility is shifted from a situation for which human beings are responsible to nature or a degeneracy conceived as its opposite in terms of the same model. Granted, Lukács tried to weasel out of the contradiction between Marxist theory and official Marxism by forcibly turning the concepts of healthy and sick art back into social concepts:

> Men's relationships are subject to historical change, and intellectual and emotional evaluations of these relationships change accordingly. Recognition of this fact, however, does not imply an acceptance of relativism. In a particular time, a certain human relationship is progressive, another is reactionary. Thus we find that the conception of what is socially healthy is equally and simultaneously the basis of all really great art, for what is socially healthy becomes a component of man's historical self-awareness.[3]

The weakness of this attempt is obvious: If it is a question of historical relationships, words like sick and healthy should be avoided altogether. They have nothing to do with the progress/reaction dimension; they are brought in purely for the sake of their demagogic appeal. The dichotomy between healthy and sick, moreover, is as undialectical as that between a rising and a declining bourgeoisie, which itself derives its norms from a bourgeois consciousness that did not keep pace with its own development. I will not deign to stress the fact that Lukács groups completely disparate figures under the concepts of decadence and avantgardism (for him they are the same thing)—not only Proust, Kafka, Joyce, and Beckett but also Benn, Jünger, and perhaps Heidegger; and as theoreticians, Benjamin and myself. It is all too easy to resort to the currently fashionable ploy of pointing out that something under attack does not really exist but it actually several divergent things, in order to soften the concept in question and evade the argument being advanced with a gesture that says "that doesn't apply to me." At the risk, then, of simplifying by my opposition to simplification, I will stay with the central thread of Lukács' argument and not differentiate among those he attacks any more than he does, except where he makes gross distortions.

Lukács' attempt to provide the Soviet verdict on modern literature— that is, literature that shocks the naive-realistic normal consciousness— with a good philosophical conscience uses a restricted set of instruments, all of Hegelian origin. For his attack on avant-garde literature as deviation from reality, Lukács works over the distinction between "abstract" and "real" possibility:

> These two categories, their interrelation and opposition, are rooted in life itself. *Potentiality*—seen abstractly or subjectively—is richer than actual life. Innumerable possibilities for man's development are imaginable, only a small percentage of which will be realized. Modern subjectivism, taking these imagined possibilities for actual complexity of life, oscillates between melancholy and fascination. When the world declines to realize these possibilities, this melancholy becomes tinged with contempt. (21–22)

The percentage notwithstanding, one cannot simply shrug off this objection. When Brecht, for instance, tried, using an infantile simplification, to crystallize out the pure archetypes, so to speak, of fascism as gangsterdom by portraying the resistible dictator Arturo Ui as the representative of an imaginary and apocryphal cauliflower trust rather than the representative of the groups with the greatest economic power, the unrealistic device did not work to the advantage of his play. As the enterprise of a criminal group that is to a certain extent socially extraterritorial and thereby easily "stoppable," "resistible" at will, fascism loses its horror, which is the horror of its large-scale social significance. The caricature thereby loses its force and becomes silly by its own criterion: the political rise of the petty criminal loses its plausibility even within the play itself. Satire that does not characterize its object adequately loses its bite, even as satire. But the requirement of pragmatic fidelity can apply only to the basic experience of reality and to the *membra disjecta* of the motifs from which the writer constructs his conception—in the case of Brecht, then, to his knowledge of the empirical relationships between economics and politics and the accuracy of the initial social facts, but not to what becomes of them within the work. Proust, in whose work the most precise "realistic" observation is so intimately connected with the formal aesthetic law of involuntary memory, provides the most striking example of the unity of pragmatic fidelity and—in terms of Lukács' categories—unrealistic method. If the intensity of this fusion is diminished; if "concrete possibility" is interpreted in the sense of an unreflected overall realism that rigidly contemplates the object from the outside, while the aspect that is antithetical to the material is tolerated only as "perspective," that is, only as something that lets meaning shine through, without being able to force its way into the center of the portrayal, into the elements of reality, the result of a misuse of Hegelian distinctions in the service of a traditionalism whose aesthetic backwardness is the index of its historical untruth.

The central charge Lukács raises, however, is that of ontologism, a charge through which he tries to link all of avant-garde literature to Heidegger's archaistic existential categories. Granted, Lukács himself, in line with current fashion, accepts the notion that one must ask "What is man?" (19), without being put off by the direction the question implies, but at least he modifies the question by referring to Aristotle's familiar definition of man as a social animal. From that definition he derives the hardly debatable assertion that the "human significance," the "specific individuality" of the characters in great literature "cannot be separated from the context in which they were created" (19). "The ontological view governing the image of man in the work of leading modernist writers," he continues, "is the exact opposite of this. Man, for these writers, is by nature solitary, asocial, unable to enter into relationships with other human beings" (20). He supports this with a rather silly statement by Thomas Wolfe, one which is in any case not definitive for his literary work, about man's solitude as an inescapable fact of his existence. But certainly Lukács, who claims to think in radically historical terms, ought to see that in an individualistic society that solitude is socially mediated and essentially historical in substance. In Baudelaire— and all categories like decadence, formalism, and aestheticism ultimately date back to him—it was not a question of an invariant human essence, of man's solitude or "thrownness" [*Geworfenheit*] but of the essence of modernity. In Baudelaire's poetry essence is not some abstract thing in itself but something social. The idea that is objectively dominant in his work aims at what is historically most advanced, what is newest, as the Ur-phenomenon it wants to conjures up; it is, to use Benjamin's term, a "dialectical image," not an archaic image. Hence the *Tableaux Parisiens*. Even in Joyce, the foundation of the work is not the timeless man-as-such that Lukács would like to assume it is but a most historical man. All the Irish folklore that appears in it notwithstanding, Joyce does not create a fictional mythology beyond the world he represents but rather tries to conjure up that world's essence, or its essential horror, by mythifying it, as it were, through the stylistic principle the Lukács of today holds in contempt. One is almost tempted to judge the stature of avant-garde writing by the criterion of whether historical moments become essential in them as historical moments rather than being flattened out into timelessness. Presumably Lukács would dismiss the use of concepts like essence and image in aesthetics as idealistic. But their status in the realm of art is fundamentally different from their status in philosophies of essence or archetypes, from any refurbished Platonism. The most fundamental weakness of Lukács' position may be that he cannot maintain this distinction and applies categories that refer to the relationship between consciousness and reality to art as though they simply meant the same thing there. Art exists within reality, has its function in it, and is also inherently mediated with reality in many ways. But nevertheless, as art, by its very concept it stands in an antithetical relationship to the status quo. Philosophy reflected this in the term "aesthetic semblance." Even Lukács will hardly be able to get around the fact that the content of works of art is not real in the same sense as social reality. If this distinction were eliminated all work in aesthetics would lose its foundation. But art's illusory character, the fact that it became qualitatively distinct from the immediate reality from which it sprang in the form of magic, is neither its ideological fall from grace nor an index imposed upon it from the outside, as though it were merely reproducing the world without claiming to be immediately real itself. This kind of subtractive conception would be a mockery of dialectics. Rather, the difference between empirical existence and art concerns the intrinsic structure of the latter. If art offers essences, "images," that is not an idealistic sin; the fact that some artists were adherents of idealist philosophies says nothing about the substance of their works. Rather, vis à vis what merely exists, art itself—where it does not betray its own nature by merely duplicating it—has to become essence, essence and image. Only thereby is the aesthetic constituted; only thereby and not by gazing at mere immediacy, does art become knowledge, does it, that is, do justice to a reality that conceals its own essence and suppresses what the essence expresses for the sake of a merely classificatory order of things. Only in the crystallization of its own formal law and not in a passive acceptance of objects does art converge with what is real. In art knowledge is aesthetically mediated through and through. In art even what Lukács considers to be solipsism and a regression to the illusionary immediacy of the subject does not signify a denial of the object, as it does in bad epistemologies, but rather aims dialectically at reconciliation with the object. The object is taken into the subject in the form of an image rather than turning to stone in front of it like an object under the spell of the alienated world. Through the contradiction between this object that has been reconciled within an image, that is, spontaneously assimilated into the subject, and the real, unreconciled object out there in the world, the work of art criticizes reality. It represents negative knowledge of reality. In analogy to a current philosophical expression, we might speak of "aesthetic difference" from existence: only by virtue of this difference, and not by denying it, does the work of art become both work of art and correct consciousness. A theory of art that refuses to acknowledge this is philistine and ideological at the same time.

Lukács contents himself with Schopenhauer's insight that the principle of solipsism is "only really viable in philosophical abstraction," and even then "only with a measure of sophistry" (21). But his argument defeats itself: if solipsism cannot be maintained, if what it initially "bracketed out," to use the phenomenological expression, is reproduced within it, then there is no need to fear it as a stylistic principle either. For objectively, in their works, the avant-garde writers moved beyond the position Lukács ascribes to them. Proust decomposes the unity of the subject by means of the subject's introspection: the subject is ultimately transformed into an arena in which objective entities manifest themselves. Proust's individualistic work becomes the opposite of what Lukács criticizes it as being: it becomes anti-individualistic. The *monologue intérieur*, the worldlessness of modern art that Lukács is so indignant about, is both the truth and the illusion of a free-floating subjectivity. The truth, because in a world that is everywhere atomistic, alienation rules human beings and because—as we may concede to Lukács—they thereby become shadows. But the free-floating subject is an illusion, because the social totality is objectively prior to the individual; that totality becomes consolidated and reproduces itself in and through alienation, the social contradiction. The great avant-garde works of art cut through this illusion of subjectivity both by throwing the frailty of the individual into relief and by grasping the totality in the individual, who is a moment in the totality and yet can know nothing about it. In Joyce, Lukács thinks, Dublin, and in Kafka and Musil, the Hapsburg Monarchy, can be felt —*hors programme*, so to speak—as an atmospheric "backcloth" to the action (21), but that, he says, is a mere by-product; for the sake of his *thema probandum*, he turns the negative epic abundance that accumulates, the substantial, into a secondary issue. The concept of atmosphere is completely inappropriate for Kafka. It is derived from an impressionism that Kafka supersedes precisely through his objective tendency, which aims at historical essence. Even in Beckett—perhaps in Beckett most of all—where all concrete historical elements seem to have been eliminated and only primitive situations and modes of behavior are tolerated, the ahistorical facade is the provocative antithesis of the Being-as-such idolized by reactionary philosophy. The primitivism which is the abrupt point of departure for his works reveals itself to be the final phase of a regression; this is only too clear in *Endgame*, where a terrestrial catastrophe is presupposed, as from the far reaches of the self-evident. Beckett's Ur-humans are the last humans. He makes thematic something that Horkheimer and I, in the *Dialectic of Enlightenment*, called the convergence between a society totally in the grips of the culture industry and the reactions of an amphibian. The substantive content of a work of art can consist in the accurate and tacitly polemical representation of emerging meaninglessness, and that content can be lost when it is stated positively and hypostatized as existing, even if this occurs only indirectly, through a "perspective," as in the didactic antithesis between the right and the wrong way to live in Tolstoy's work after *Anna Karenina*. Lukács' old pet idea of an "immanence of meaning" refers to the same dubious preoccupation with the status quo that his own theory says ought to be destroyed. Conceptions like Beckett's, however, are objectively polemical. Lukács falsifies them in describing them as the "adoption of perversity and idiocy as types of the *condition humaine*" (32)—following the practice of the film censor who blames the presentation for what it presents. Lukács' conflation of Beckett with the cult of Being in particular, or even with Montherlant's inferior version of vitalism (32), demonstrates his blindness to the phenomenon under consideration. It derives from the fact that he stubbornly refuses to accord literary technique its rightful central place. Instead, he sticks indefatigably to what is narrated. But it is only through "technique" that the intention of what is presented —to which Lukács assigns the concept, itself disreputable, of "perspective"—can be realized in literature at all. One would like to know what would become of Greek tragedy, which Lukács, like Hegel, canonizes, if one made its plots, which were available to everyone, the criterion of its success. Composition and style are no less constitutive of the traditional and—in terms of Lukács' schema—"realistic" novel: Flaubert. Now that mere reliance on empirical reality has degenerated to superficial reportage, the relevance of technique has increased tremendously. Constructive technique can hope for immanent mastery of the contingency of what is merely individual, the contingency Lukács rails against. Lukács does not draw the full consequences from the insight that emerges in the last chapter of his book: that to resolutely take a presumably more objective standpoint is of no help against chance. Lukács ought to be genuinely familiar with the idea of the crucial significance of the development of the technical forces of production. Of course this idea was developed with reference to material and not intellectual production. But can Lukács seriously oppose the idea that artistic technique too develops according to a logic of its own? Can he talk himself into believing that to affirm abstractly that different aesthetic criteria would hold automatically and en bloc in a different society is enough to cancel out the development of technical forces of production and restore other forces to validity, older forces that the inherent logic of the matter has made outmoded? Under the dictates of socialist realism does he not become the advocate of a doctrine of invariance that differs from the one he rightly rejects only in being cruder?

Although Lukács, following the tradition of classical philosophy, rightly conceives art as a form of knowledge and does not contrast it to science and scholarship as something purely irrational, in doing so he becomes trapped in the same mere immediacy that he shortsightedly accuses avant-garde production of: the immediacy of the established fact. Art does not come to know reality by depicting it photographically or "perspectivally" but by expressing, through its autonomous constitution, what is concealed by the empirical form reality takes. Even the assertion that the world is unknowable, which Lukács never tires of faulting in authors like Eliot or Joyce, can become a moment of knowledge, knowledge of the gulf between the overwhelming and unassimilatable world of objects, on the one hand, and experience, which glances helplessly off that world, on the other. Lukács simplifies the dialectical unity of art and science so that it becomes a pure identity, as though works of art merely anticipated something perspectivally which the social sciences then diligently confirmed. What essentially distinguishes the work of art as knowledge *sui generis* from scientific or scholarly knowledge is that nothing empirical remains unaltered, that the contents become objectively meaningful only when fused with subjective intention. Although Lukács differentiates his realism from naturalism, he fails to take into account that if the distinction is intended seriously, realism will necessarily be amalgamated with the subjective intentions he would like to banish from it. The opposition between realistic and "formalistic" approaches which he inquisitorially elevates to a criterion is simply unsalvageable. On the one hand, the formal principles that are anathema to Lukács as being unrealistic and idealistic prove to have an objective aesthetic function; conversely, the early nineteenth-century novels he unhesitatingly advances as paradigmatic, Dickens and Balzac, are not so realistic after all. Marx and Engels may have considered them realistic in their polemic against the commercial romanticism flourishing at their time. Today not only have archaic pre-bourgeois features become evident in both novelists, but Balzac's whole *Comédie humaine* proves to be an imaginative reconstruction of an alienated reality, that is, a reality that can no longer be experienced by the subject.[4] In this regard it is not so very different from the avant-garde victims of Lukács' class justice, except that Balzac, in accordance with the sense of form in his works, considered his monologues to represent the fullness of the world, whereas the great novelists of the twentieth century enclose the fullness of their worlds within the monologue. Accordingly, Lukács' approach collapses. His idea of "perspective" inevitably degenerates to the very thing he so desperately tries to distinguish it from in the last chapter of his book, to an engrafted politics or, in his words, "agitation." His conception is aporetic. He cannot rid himself of his awareness that, aesthetically, social truth lives only in autonomously formed works of art. But today, in the concrete work of art, this autonomy necessarily brings with it everything that he can no more tolerate now than he could before, given the dictates of the prevailing communist doctrine. The hope that regressive artistic techniques which are inadequate in immanent aesthetic terms would legitimate themselves by assuming a different position in a different social system, that is, legitimate themselves from outside their immanent logic, is pure superstition. The fact that what under socialist realism has been declared an advanced state of consciousness serves up only the crumbling and insipid remnants of bourgeois art forms cannot simply be dismissed as an epiphenomenon the way Lukács dismisses it; it requires an objective explanation. Socialist realism originated not in a socially sound and healthy world, as the communist clerics would like to think, but in the backwardness of consciousness and of the social forces of production in their provinces. They use the thesis of a qualitative break between socialism and bourgeois society only to misrepresent that backwardness, which has long since become unmentionable, as something more progressive.

Lukács combines the charge of ontologism with the charge of individualism, that is, a standpoint of unreflected solitude, on the model of Heidegger's theory of "thrownness" from *Being and Time*. He criticizes the notion that the literary work proceeds from the subject in its contingency, on the same grounds on which Hegel once—stringently enough—criticized the notion that philosophy proceeds from the sense certainty of the individual. But precisely because this immediacy is already internally mediated, when given coherent form in the work of art it contains the moments Lukács claims are lacking, while on the other hand the literary subject must proceed from what is closest to it for the sake of the anticipated reconciliation of the material world with consciousness. Lukács extends his denunciation of individualism to Dostoevski. His *Notes from the Underground*, Lukács says, is "perhaps the first authentic description of the [decadent] isolation of modern bourgeois man" (62). But by coupling "decadent" and "isolation," Lukács reevaluates the atomization that springs from the very principle of bourgeois society, making it a mere manifestation of decline. Furthermore, the word "decadent" suggests biological degeneration in individuals: a parody of the fact that this solitude presumably reaches back far beyond bourgeois society, for animals that live in herds are also, as Rudolf Borchardt said, a "lonely community"; the *zoon politikon* is something that has to be developed. Something that is a historical a priori of all modern art—and is transcended only where art acknowledges it in its full force—appears in Lukács as an error that could be avoided, or even a bourgeois delusion. Once Lukács turns to contemporary Russian literature, however, he discovers that the structural transformation he assumes did not take place. Except that that does not teach him to do without concepts like decadent solitude. In terms of the debate between conflicting positions, the position taken by the avant-garde writers he criticizes—in his earlier terminology, their "transcendental locus"—is historically mediated solitude, not ontological solitude. The ontologists of today all too readily accept ties that though ascribed to Being as such in fact endow all manner of heteronomous authorities with the semblance of eternity. In this regard they would get along quite well with Lukács. We must concede Lukács the point that, as an a priori of form, solitude is a mere illusion, that it is socially produced; it transcends itself once it reflects upon itself.[5] But it is precisely here that the aesthetic dialectic turns against him. It is not up to the individual subject to go beyond a collectively determined solitude through his own choice and decision. That comes through clearly enough where Lukács settles accounts with the tendentiousness of the standardized Soviet novels. In general, reading his book, and especially the impassioned section on Kafka (49f.), one cannot escape the impression that he reacts to the literature he condemns as decadent the same way the legendary cab horse reacts to the sound of military music before it goes back to pulling its cart. To defend himself against its attractions, Lukács chimes in with the chorus of censors who have been hacking at what is "interesting" since Kierkegaard, whom Lukács himself classed with the avant-garde writers, if not since the uproar about Friedrich Schlegel and early Romanticism. That verdict should be reviewed. The fact that an idea or a depiction is "interesting" in character cannot simply be reduced to a matter of sensationalism and the intellectual marketplace, although of course they promoted the category. While not a guarantee of truth, that category has now become a necessary precondition of truth. It is what *mea interest*, what concerns the subject, as opposed to the subject being pieced off with the superior power of the powers that be, that is, with commodities.

It would be impossible for Lukács to praise what attracts him in Kafka and still put him on his index if he did not, like the skeptics of late Scholasticism, have a doctrine of two kinds of truth up his sleeve:

> All this argues the superiority—historically speaking—of socialist realism (I cannot sufficiently emphasize that this superiority does not confer automatic success on each individual work of socialist realism). The reason for this superiority is the insights which socialist ideology, socialist perspective, make available to the writer: they enable him to give a more comprehensive and deeper account of man as a social being than any traditional ideology. (115)

In other words, artistic quality and the artistic superiority of social realism are two different things. What is valid in literary terms is distinguished from what is valid in terms of Soviet literature, which is to be *dans le vrai* through an act of grace, so to speak, on the part of the *Weltgeist*. This kind of double standard ill becomes a thinker who pathetically defends the unity of reason. But once he explains that that solitude is inevitable—and he almost acknowledges that it is prescribed by social negativity, by universal reification—and at the same time, in Hegelian fashion, becomes aware of its objective illusory character, then the inference is compelling that that solitude, taken to its logical conclusion, turns into its own negation, that when the solitary consciousness reveals itself in the literary work to be the hidden consciousness of all human beings, it has, potentially, to sublate itself. This is precisely what we see in works that are genuinely avant-garde. They become objectified through unqualified monadological immersion in their own formal laws, that is, aesthetically, and thereby mediated in their social basis as well. This alone gives Kafka, Joyce, Beckett, and the great works of modern music their power. The world's hour has struck, and it resounds in their monologues: this is why they are so much more provocative than literature that simply depicts the world in communicative form. The fact that this kind of transition to objectivity remains contemplative and does not turn into action has its basis in a state of society in which the monadological condition continues on everywhere, concrete and ubiquitous, despite all assurances to the contrary. Moreover, the classicistically inclined Lukács could hardly expect works of art here and now to break through this contemplation. His proclamation of artistic quality is incompatible with a pragmatism that, when faced with advanced and responsible artistic production, contents itself with the summary verdict "bourgeois, bourgeois, bourgeois."

Lukács cites, and states his agreement with, my work on the aging of the new music in order to then use my dialectical reflections, which are paradoxically similar to Sedlmayr,* against modern art and against my own intentions. This much we should grant him: "Only those thoughts are true which fail to understand themselves,"[6] and no author owns the title to them. But Lukács' argumentation does not in fact take the title away from me after all. The idea that art cannot establish itself as pure expression, which is directly equivalent to anxiety, was expressed in the *Philosophy of Modern Music*,[7] even though I do not share Lukács' official optimism with its view that historically speaking there is less cause for anxiety today, that the "decadent intelligentsia" has less to be afraid of. But going beyond the pure ostensive "this" of expression can mean neither instituting a thinglike style devoid of tension, something I accused the aging new music of, nor making a leap into a positivity that in the Hegelian sense is not substantial and not authentic and does not constitute form prior to any reflection.[8] The implication of the aging of the new music is not a return to the already aged old music but the emphatic self-critique of the new. From the outset, however, the unvarnished depiction of anxiety was also more than that; it meant resistance through expression, through the power of an undeviating act of naming: the opposite of all the associations the abusive term "decadent" evokes.

---

*Adorno is referring to Hans Sedlmayr, *Verlust der Mitte* (Salzburg: Müller, 1951) (translated as *Art in Crisis*, Chicago: Regnery, 1958). —Translator's note.

Lukács does credit the art he disparages with responding negatively to a negative reality, to the domination of the "abominable." "But since," he continues, "modernism portrays the distortion without critical detachment, indeed it devises stylistic techniques which emphasize the necessity of distortion in any kind of society, it may be said to distort distortion further. By attributing distortion to reality itself, modernism dismisses as ontologically irrelevant the counter-forces at work in reality" (75f.). The official optimism of countervailing forces and tendencies forces Lukács to suppress the Hegelian thesis that the negation of the negation —the "distortion of the distortion"—is the positive. It is only this thesis that can illuminate the truth of the fatally irrationalistic term "Vielschichtigkeit" [multi-layeredness] in art: in authentic modern works of art, the expression of suffering and pleasure in dissonance, a pleasure that Lukács disparages as sensationalism, "a delight in novelty for novelty's sake" (105), are indissolubly linked. This must be understood in connection with the dialectic of the relationship between the aesthetic sphere and reality, something Lukács avoids. Since the work of art does not have something immediately real as its subject matter, it never says, as knowledge usually does: "this is so" ["es ist so"]. Instead, it says, "this is how it is" ["so ist es"]. Its logicity is not that of a statement with subject and predicate but that of immanent coherence: only in and through that coherence, through the relationship in which it places its elements, does it take a stance. Its antithetical relationship to empirical reality, which falls within it and into which it itself falls, consists precisely of the fact that, unlike intellectual forms that deal directly with reality, it never defines reality unequivocally as being one thing or another. It passes no judgments; it becomes a judgment when taken as a whole. The moment of untruth contained, as Hegel showed, in every individual judgment, because nothing is completely what the individual judgment says it to be, is corrected by art in that the work of art synthesizes its elements without any one of those elements being stated by any other: the notion of *Aussage* [message] currently in vogue has no relation to art. What art, as synthesis without judgment, loses in specificity regarding detail it regains through its greater justice to what judgment usually eliminates. The work of art becomes knowledge only as a totality, only in and through all its mediations, not in its individual intentions. Individual intentions cannot be abstracted from it, nor can it be judged by them. But this is precisely the principle on which Lukács proceeds, despite his protests against the certified novelists who proceed this way in their writing.

While he is well aware of what is inadequate in their standardized products, his own philosophy of art has no defense against the same short circuit, the effects of which—an idiocy decreed from above—then horrify him.

Faced with the essential complexity of the work of art, which cannot be sloughed off as an accidental individual case, Lukács shuts his eyes. When he does look at specific literary works, he emphasizes what is right in front of him and thereby misses the import of the whole. He laments about an admittedly modest poem by Gottfried Benn which reads:

> O daß wir unsere Ururahnen wären.
> Ein Klümpchen Schleim in einem warmen Moor.
> Leben und Tod, Befruchtung und Gebären
> glitte aus unseren stummen Säften vor.
>
> Ein Algenblatt oder ein Dünenhügel,
> vom Wind geformtes und nach unten schwer.
> Schon ein Libellenkopf, ein Mövenflügel
> wäre zu weit und litte schon zu sehr.
>
> [Oh, that we were our Ur-Ur-ancestors.
> A glob of slime in a warm bog.
> Life and death, fecundation and parturition
> would slide forth from our mute juices.
> A strand of seaweed or a dune,
> formed by the wind and heavy at the bottom.
> Even the head of a dragonfly or the wing of a gull
> would be going too far and would suffer too much.]

Lukács sees in this poem "the opposition of man as animal, as a primeval reality, to man as social being"—à la Heidegger, Klages, and Rosenberg—and ultimately a "glorification of the abnormal and . . . an undisguised anti-humanism" (32), whereas even if one identified the poem with its content completely, the last line indicts the higher level of individuation as suffering in Schopenhauerian fashion, and the yearning for the prehistoric era merely reflects the intolerable pressure of the present. The moralistic coloration of Lukács' critical concepts is the same as that of his lamentations about subjectivistic "worldlessness," as though the avant-garde writers had literally practiced what in Husserl's phenomenology is called, grotesquely enough, the methodological annihilation of the world. Thus Lukács denounces Robert Musil: "Ulrich, the hero of his novel *The Man Without Qualities*, when asked what he would do if he were in God's place, replies: 'I would be compelled to abolish reality.' The abolition of outward reality is the complement of a subjective existence 'without qualities' "(25). Yet the sentence Lukács incriminates is obviously intended to convey despair, runaway *Weltschmerz*, love in its negative form. Lukács says nothing about all that and instead operates with a truly "unmediated," completely unreflected concept of the normal and its complement, the notion of pathological distortion. Only a mental state blissfully purged of every trace of psychoanalysis can fail to recognize the connection between that normality and the social repression that proscribed the partial instincts. A critique of society that continues to talk unabashedly about the "normal" and the "perverse" is itself still under the spell of what it portrays as having been overcome. Lukács' Hegelian and manly chest-beatings about the primacy of the substantive universal over the illusory and untenable "bad existence" of mere individuation call to mind those of district attorneys who demand the extermination of deviants and those unfit to live. Their comprehension of lyric poetry is to be doubted. The first line of Benn's poem, "O daß wir unsere Ururahnen waren," has a completely different value in the context of the poem than it would if it expressed a literal wish. There is a grin built into the word "Ururahnen." Through the stylization, the impulse of the poetic subject—which, incidentally, is more old-fashioned than modern —presents itself as humorously inauthentic, as a melancholy game. The repulsive quality of what the poet pretends to wish himself back to and what one cannot in fact wish oneself back to lends emphasis to his protest against a suffering that is socially produced. All that, along with the montage-like "alienation effect" produced by Benn's use of scientific words and themes, is intended to be felt in the Benn poem. Through exaggeration, he suspends the regression that Lukács immediately ascribes to him. The person who fails to hear these overtones is like the junior writer who assiduously and expertly imitated Thomas Mann's mode of writing and of whom Mann once said, laughing: "He writes exactly like I do, but he means it." Simplifications like the one Lukács makes in his excursus on Benn not merely fail to recognize the nuances; rather, along with the nuances they fail to recognize the work of art itself, which becomes a work of art only by virtue of the nuances. Such simplifications are symptomatic of the stultification that befalls even the most intelligent when they fall in line with directives like those ordaining socialist realism. Even earlier, in an attempt to convict modern literature of fascism, Lukács triumphantly sought out a bad poem by Rilke and rampaged around in it like a bull in a china shop. It remains an open question whether the regression one senses in Lukács, the regression of a consciousness that was once one of the most advanced, is an objective expression of the shadow of a regression threatening the European mind —the shadow that the underdeveloped nations throw across the more developed ones, which are already beginning to align themselves with the former; or whether it reveals something of the fate of theory itself— a theory that is not only wasting away in terms of its anthropological presuppositions, that is, in terms of the intellectual capacities of the theoreticians, but whose substance is also objectively shriveling up in a state of existence in which less depends on theory than on a practice whose task is identical to the prevention of catastrophe.

Even the much-praised Thomas Mann is not proof against Lukács' neo-naiveté; Lukács plays him off against Joyce with a philistinism that would have horrified Mann, the chronicler of disintegration and decline. The controversy about time started by Bergson is treated like the Gordian knot. Since Lukács is a good objectivist, objective time must always be in the right, and subjective time must be a mere distortion caused by decadence. It was the unbearableness of the reified, alienated, meaning-less time the young Lukács described so forcefully in Flaubert's *Éduca-tion sentimentale* that led Bergson to his theory of lived time and not a spirit of subjective disintegration, as pious stupidity of all forms may imagine. In his *Magic Mountain*, Thomas Mann also paid his tribute to Bergson's *temps durée*. In order to salvage Mann for his thesis of critical realism, Lukács gives many of the characters in the novel good grades because even subjectively, their "experience of time is normal and objec-tive" (51). Then he writes, and I quote word for word: "Indeed, Ziemssen is aware that the modern experience of time may be simply a result of the abnormal mode of life in the sanatorium, hermetically sealed off from everyday life" (51). The irony governing the figure of Ziemssen escapes the aesthetician; socialist realism has blunted his sensitivity to the critical realism he praises. For Lukács, Ziemssen, the narrow-minded officer, a kind of post-Goethean Valentin who dies bravely and like a soldier, if in bed, is the direct spokesman of an authentic mode of life, much as Tolstoy's Levin was planned to be but failed. In actuality, Thomas Mann represented the relationship between the two concepts of time—without reflection but with the utmost sensitivity—as conflicting and ambiguous, in a manner consistent with his approach as a whole and his dialectical relationship to everything bourgeois. Right and wrong are distributed between the reified consciousness of the philistine who escapes in vain from the sanatorium into his profession, and the phantasmagorical time of those who remain in the sanatorium, an allegory of Bohemianism and romantic subjectivism. Wisely, Mann neither reconciled the two kinds of time nor took a stand for one or the other in the construction of his work.

The fact that Lukács can philosophize right past the aesthetic import of even his favorite text so drastically has its cause in his pre-aesthetic *parti pris* is favor of the material and the communicated content of literary works, which he confuses with their artistic objectivity. He fails to concern himself with stylistic devices like irony, which is by no means so hidden, to say nothing of the more obvious ones, and is not rewarded for this abstention with the truth content of the works, purged of subjective illusion. Instead he is put off with the works' meager leavings, their material content [*Sachgehalt*], which is of course necessary to reach the truth content. As much as Lukács would like to prevent the novel from regressing, he parrots articles of the catechism like socialist realism, the ideologically sanctioned copy theory of knowledge, and the dogma of a mechanistic progress on the part of humankind, that is, one independent of a spontaneity that has been stifled in the meantime—even though this "belief in the world's rationality and in man's ability to penetrate its secrets" (43) is expecting a lot, in view of the irrevocable past. Lukács thereby involuntarily comes close to the infantile conceptions of art that embarrass him in bureaucrats less well-versed than he. His attempts to break out are futile. The extent of the damage to his own aesthetic consciousness can be seen in a passage on allegorical interpretation in Byzantine mosaics: in literature, he says, works of art of this quality could only be "exceptional cases" (40). As though there were such a thing as a distinction between the rule and the exception in art, except in academies and conservatories; as though everything aesthetic, being something individuated, were not always an exception by virtue of following its own principle and its own universality, whereas everything that corresponds directly to universal rules thereby disqualifies itself as having aesthetic form. The term "exceptional cases" is derived from the same vocabulary as "peak performances." The late Franz Borkenau once said, following his break with the Communist Party, that he could no longer stand hearing people talk about municipal regulations in the categories of Hegelian logic and Hegelian logic in the spirit of the city council. Such contaminations, which admittedly date back to Hegel himself, tie Lukács to the level he would like to raise to his own. In Lukács' hands, Hegel's critique of the "unhappy consciousness," speculative philosophy's impulse to rise above the illusory ethos of isolated subjectivity, becomes an ideology for narrow-minded party officials who have not yet reached the level of subjectivity. He dignifies their aggressive ignorance, a residue of the nineteenth-century petit bourgeoisie, as the limitedness of adaptation to reality that has had all mere individuality removed from it. But the dialectical leap is not a leap out of the dialectic that would transform the unhappy consciousness into happy complicity through sheer conviction and at the expense of the objective social and technical moments of artistic production. In accordance with a Hegelian doctrine that Lukács would scarcely question, the allegedly higher standpoint must necessarily remain abstract. Nor does the desperate profundity that Lukács offers to oppose the idiocy of "boy meets tractor" literature preserve him from declamations that are both abstract and childish: "The more the content dealt with is common to them, the more writers from different sides probe the same conditions of development and the same developmental tendencies in the same reality, and the more reality, and with it all the distinctions depicted, is transformed into a largely or purely socialist reality, the closer critical realism will have to come to socialist realism, and the more its negative (non-rejecting) perspective will be transformed, through many transitions, into a positive (affirmative), a socialist perspective" (114). The jesuitical distinction between the negative, that is, not rejecting, and the positive, that is, affirming, perspective shifts questions of literary quality directly into the sphere of regulated convictions from which Lukács would like to escape.

There can, however, be no doubt that he wants to escape it. To do justice to his book one must bear in mind that in countries where the crucial things cannot be called by name, the marks of official terror have been branded onto everything said in their place. But conversely, because of this even ideas that are weak and deflected, half-ideas, acquire a force in that constellation that their literal content does not have. The whole third chapter of the book must be read in this light, despite the disproportion between intellectual expenditure and the questions dealt with. There are numerous formulations where the line of thought need only be extended to reach open space. The following, for example:

> A study of Marxism (not to speak of other activity in the Socialist movement, even Party membership) is not of itself sufficient. A writer may acquire useful experience in this way, and become aware of certain

intellectual and moral problems. But it is no easier to translate "true consciousness" of reality into adequate aesthetic form than it is bourgeois "false consciousness." (96–97)

Or, attacking the sterile empiricism of the reportage novel which flourishes everywhere these days: "In critical realism, as Zola's example shows, the ideal of a documentary totality, more suitable to the scientific monograph, was the product of certain inherent problems. I shall show that similar, and perhaps even greater, problems are inherent in socialist realism" (100). In this context Lukács, using the terminology of his youth, pleads for the primacy of intensive over extensive totality. He would need only to take his demand farther, into the literary work itself, to assert the very thing he reproaches avant-garde writers with in his *ex cathedra* pontifications; it is grotesque that despite this he still wants to "vanquish" the "anti-realism of the decadent movement." At one point he even comes close to seeing that the Russian Revolution by no means brought about conditions that would require and support a "positive" literature: "We must bear in mind that, however violent the political break, people (including writers) will not be automatically transformed" (104–5). Then, although in muted form, as though he were discussing a mere aberration, he lets slip what is really going on with socialist realism: "The result will be a diluted, inferior version of bourgeois realism, lacking the virtues of that tradition" (116). In such literature, he says, the "real nature of the artist's perspective" is misunderstood. In other words, "many writers identify tendencies that point toward the future but exist only in that form—and precisely because of that could provide a decisive standpoint for evaluating the current period, if correctly understood—with reality itself; they represent tendencies present only in embryonic form as fully developed realities; in other words, they mechanically equate perspective and reality" (116). Once the terminological husk is removed, this means simply that the procedures of socialist realism and the socialist romanticism that Lukács recognizes as its complement are ideological transfigurations of a bad status quo. For Lukács, the official optimism of the totalitarian view of literature proves to be merely subjective in its own right. He contrasts it with a more humane notion of aesthetic objectivity: "Art too is governed by objective laws. An infringement of these laws may not have such practical consequences as do the infringement of economic laws; but it will result in work of inferior quality" (117). Here, where thought has the courage of its own convictions, Lukács' judgments are far more accurate than his philistine evaluations of modern art: "The break-up of these mediating elements leads—in theory and in practice—to a false polarization. On the one hand, theory, from being a guide to practice, becomes a dogma, while, on the other hand, the element of a contradiction between the two is eliminated" (118). He states the central issue succinctly: In such works, "literature ceased to reflect the dynamic contradictions of social life; it became the illustration of an abstract 'truth' " (119). Responsible for this, he says, is "agitation" as the "point of departure," as a model for art and thought, which then shrivel up, turn rigid, and become schematic and ideologically fixated on practice. "Instead of a dialectical structure we . . . get a static schematism" (121). No avant-garde writer could add anything to that.

In all this we are left with the feeling of a person who rattles his chains hopelessly, imagining that their clanking is the march of the *Weltgeist*. He is blinded not only by the powers that be, which will scarcely take Lukács' insubordinate ideas to heart in their cultural politics, if indeed they tolerate them at all. In addition, Lukács' critique is caught up in the delusion that contemporary Russian society, which is in fact oppressed and bled dry, is contradictory but not antagonistic, to use a distinction worked out in China. All the symptoms Lukács is protesting are themselves the product of the need on the part of dictators and their adherents to hammer into the masses a thesis that Lukács implicitly endorses in his notion of socialist realism, and to banish from awareness anything that might cause them to stray from it. The authority of a doctrine that fulfills real functions of this kind cannot be destroyed simply by demonstrating that it is false. Lukács quotes a cynical sentence from Hegel which expresses the social meaning of the process described in the classical bourgeois *Bildungsroman:* "For the end of such apprenticeship consists in this, that the subject sows his wild oats, builds himself with his wishes and opinions into harmony with subsisting relationships and their rationality, enters the concatenation of the world and acquires for himself an appropriate attitude to it" (112). Lukács adds this comment:

> In one sense, many of the great bourgeois novels contradict Hegel; in another, they confirm him. They contradict him inasmuch as the educational process does not always culminate in acceptance of, and adaptation to, bourgeois society. The realization of youthful convictions and dreams is obstructed by the pressures of society; the rebellious hero is broken, and

driven into isolation, but the reconciliation with society of which Hegel speaks is not always extracted. On the other hand, since the individual's conflict with society often ends in resignation, the end-effect is not so different from what Hegel suggests. (112)

The postulate of a reality that must be represented without a breach between subject and object and which must be "reflected"—the term Lukács stubbornly adheres to—for the sake of that lack of a breach: that postulate, which is the supreme criterion of his aesthetics, implies that that reconciliation has been achieved, that society has been set right, that the subject has come into its own and is at home in its world. This much Lukács admits in an anti-ascetic digression. Only then would there disappear from art the moment of resignation that Lukács perceives in Hegel and that he would certainly have to acknowledge in Goethe, the prototype of his concept of realism, who preached renunciation. But the division, the antagonism, continues, and to say that it has been overcome in the nations of the Eastern bloc, as they call it, is simply a lie. The spell that holds Lukács in its power and bars his longed-for return to the utopia of his youth reenacts the extorted reconciliation he himself detected in absolute idealism.

⦚⦚⦚⦚

Trying to Understand Endgame

To S. B., in memory of Paris, Fall 1958

*B*eckett's oeuvre has many things in common with Parisian existentialism. It is shot through with reminiscences of the categories of absurdity, situation, and decision or the failure to decide, the way medieval ruins permeate Kafka's monstrous house in the suburbs. Now and then the windows fly open and one sees the black, starless sky of something like philosophical anthropology. But whereas in Sartre the form—that of the *pièce à thèse*—is somewhat traditional, by no means daring, and aimed at effect, in Beckett the form overtakes what is expressed and changes it. The impulses are raised to the level of the most advanced artistic techniques, those of Joyce and Kafka. For Beckett absurdity is no longer an "existential situation" diluted to an idea and then illustrated. In him literary method surrenders to absurdity without preconceived intentions. Absurdity is relieved of the doctrinal universality which in existentialism, the creed of the irreducibility of individual existence, linked it to the Western pathos of the universal and lasting. Beckett thereby dismisses existentialist conformity, the notion that one ought to be what one is, and with it easy comprehensibility of presentation. What philosophy Beckett provides, he himself reduces to cultural trash, like the innumerable allusions and cultural tidbits he employs, following the tradition of the Anglo-Saxon avant-garde and especially of Joyce and Eliot. For Beckett, culture swarms and crawls, the way the intestinal convolutions of *Jugendstil* ornamentation swarmed and crawled for the avant-garde before him: modernism as what is obsolete in modernity. Language, regressing, demolishes that obsolete material. In Beckett, this kind of objectivity annihilates the meaning that culture once was, along with its rudiments. And so culture begins to fluoresce. In this Beckett is carrying to its conclusion a tendency present in the modern novel. Reflection, which the cultural criterion of aesthetic immanence proscribed as abstract, is juxtaposed with pure presentation; the Flaubertian principle of a completely self-contained subject matter is undermined. The less events can be presumed to be inherently meaningful, the more the idea of aesthetic substance as the unity of what appears and what was intended becomes an illusion. Beckett rids himself of this illusion by coupling the two moments in their disparity. Thought becomes both a means to produce meaning in the work, a meaning which cannot be rendered directly in tangible form, and a means to express the absence of meaning. Applied to drama, the word "meaning" is ambiguous It covers the metaphysical content that is represented objectively in the complexion of the artifact; the intention of the whole as a complex of meaning that is the inherent meaning of the drama; and finally the meaning of the words and sentences spoken by the characters and their meaning in sequence, the dialogic meaning. But these equivocations point to something shared. In Beckett's *Endgame* that common ground becomes a continuum. Historically, this continuum is supported by a change in the a priori of drama: the fact that there is no longer any substantive, affirmative metaphysical meaning that could provide dramatic form with its law and its epiphany. That, however, disrupts the dramatic form down to its linguistic infrastructure. Drama cannot simply take negative meaning, or the absence of meaning, as its content without everything peculiar to it being affected to the point of turning into its opposite. The essence of drama was constituted by that meaning. Were drama to try to survive meaning aesthetically, it would become inadequate to its substance and be degraded to a clattering machinery for the demonstration of worldviews, as if often the case with existentialist plays. The explosion of the metaphysical meaning, which was the only thing guaranteeing the unity of the aesthetic structure, causes the latter to crumble with a necessity and stringency in no way unequal to that of the traditional canon of dramatic form. Unequivocal aesthetic meaning and its subjectivization in concrete, tangible intention was a surrogate for the transcendent meaningfulness whose very denial constitutes aesthetic content. Through its own organized meaninglessness, dramatic action must model itself on what has transpired with the truth content of drama in general. Nor does this kind of construction of the meaningless stop at the linguistic molecules; if they, and the connections between them, were rationally meaningful, they would necessarily be synthesized into the overall coherence of meaning that the drama as a whole negates. Hence interpretation of *Endgame* cannot pursue the chimerical aim of expressing the play's meaning in a form mediated by philosophy. Understanding it can mean only understanding its unintelligibility, concretely reconstructing the meaning of the fact that it has no meaning. Split off, thought no longer presumes, as the Idea once did, to be the meaning of the work, a transcendence produced and vouched for by the work's immanence. Instead, thought transforms itself into a kind of second-order material, the way the philosophical ideas expounded in Thomas Mann's *Magic Mountain* and *Doctor Faustus* have their fate as material does, a fate that takes the place of the sensuous immediacy that dwindles in the self-reflective work of art. Until now this transformation of thought into material has been largely involuntary, the plight of works that compulsively mistook themselves for the Idea they could not attain; Beckett accepts the challenge and uses thoughts *sans phrase* as clichés, fragmentary materials in the *monologue intérieur* that spirit has become, the reified residues of culture. Pre-Beckettian existentialism exploited philosophy as a literary subject as though it were Schiller in the flesh. Now Beckett, more cultured than any of them, hands it the bill: philosophy, spirit itself, declares itself to be dead inventory, the dreamlike leavings of the world of experience, and the poetic process declares itself to be a process of wastage. *Dégoût*, a productive artistic force since Baudelaire, becomes insatiable in Beckett's historically mediated impulses. Anything that no longer works becomes canonical, thus rescuing from the shadowlands of methodology a motif from the preistory of existentialism, Husserl's universal world-annihilation. Adherents of totalitarianism like Lukács, who wax indignant about the decadence of this truly *terrible simplificateur*, are not ill-advised by the interest of their bosses. What they hate in Beckett is what they betrayed. Only the nausea of satiety, the *taedium* of the spirit, wants something completely different; ordained health has to be satisfied with the nourishment offered, homely fare. Beckett's *dégoût* refuses to be coerced. Exhorted to play along, he responds with parody, parody both of philosophy, which spits out his dialogues, and of forms. Existentialism itself is parodied; nothing remains of its invariant categories but bare existence. The play's opposition to ontology, which outlines something somehow First and Eternal, is unmistakable in the following piece of dialogue, which involuntarily caricatures Goethe's dictum about *das alte*

Wahre, what is old and true, a notion that deteriorates to bourgeois sentiment:

> *HAMM:* Do you remember your father.
> *CLOV* (wearily): Same answer. (Pause.) You've asked me these questions millions of times.
> *HAMM:* I love the old questions. (With fervor.) Ah, the old questions, the old answers, there's nothing like them![1]

Thoughts are dragged along and distorted, like the residues of waking life in dreams, *homo homini sapienti sat.* This is why interpreting Beckett, something he declines to concern himself with, is so awkward. Beckett shrugs his shoulders at the possibility of philosophy today, at the very possibility of theory. The irrationality of bourgeois society in its late phase rebels at letting itself be understood; those were the good old days, when a critique of the political economy of this society could be written that judged it in terms of its own *ratio.* For since then the society has thrown its *ratio* on the scrap heap and replaced it with virtually unmediated control. Hence interpretation inevitably lags behind Beckett. His dramatic work, precisely by virtue of its restriction to an exploded facticity, surges out beyond facticity and in its enigmatic character calls for interpretation. One could almost say that the criterion of a philosophy whose hour has struck is that it prove equal to this challenge.

French existentialism had tackled the problem of history. In Beckett, history swallows up existentialism. In *Endgame,* a historical moment unfolds, namely the experience captured in the title of one of the culture industry's cheap novels, *Kaputt.* After the Second World War, everything, including a resurrected culture, has been destroyed without realizing it; humankind continues to vegetate, creeping along after events that even the survivors cannot really survive, on a rubbish heap that has made even reflection on one's own damaged state useless. The word *kaputt,* the pragmatic presupposition of the play, is snatched back from the marketplace:

> *CLOV:* (He gets up on ladder, turns the telescope on the without.) Let's see. (He looks, moving the telescope.) Zero . . . (he looks) . . . zero . . . (he looks) . . . and zero.
> *HAMM:* Nothing stirs. All is—
> *CLOV:* Zer—

> *HAMM:* (violently) Wait till you're spoken to. (Normal voice.) All is
> . . . all is . . . all is what? (Violently.) All is what?
> *CLOV:* What all is? In a word. Is that what you want to know? Just a
> moment. (He turns the telescope on the without, looks, lowers the
> telescope, turns toward Hamm.) Corpsed. [In the German transla-
> tion quoted by Adorno, "Kaputt!"] (29–30)

The fact that all human beings are dead is smuggled in on the sly. An
earlier passage gives the reason why the catastrophe may not be men-
tioned. Hamm himself is vaguely responsible for it:

> *HAMM:* That old doctor, he's dead naturally?
> *CLOV:* He wasn't old.
> *HAMM:* But he's dead?
> *CLOV:* Naturally. (Pause.) *You* ask *me* that? (24–25)

The situation in the play, however, is none other than that in which
"there's no more nature" (11). The phase of complete reification of the
world, where there is nothing left that has not been made by human
beings, is indistinguishable from an additional catastrophic event caused
by human beings, in which nature has been wiped out and after which
nothing grows any more:

> *HAMM:* Did your seeds come up?
> *CLOV:* No.
> *HAMM:* Did you scratch round them to see if they had sprouted?
> *CLOV:* They haven't sprouted.
> *HAMM:* Perhaps it's still too early.
> *CLOV:* If they were going to sprout they would have sprouted. (Vio-
> lently.) They'll never sprout! (13)

The dramatis personae resemble those who dream their own death, in a
"shelter" in which "it's time it ended" (3). The end of the world is
discounted, as though it could be taken for granted. Any alleged drama
of the atomic age would be a mockery of itself, solely because its plot
would comfortingly falsify the historical horror of anonymity by displac-
ing it onto human characters and actions and by gaping at the "important
people" who are in charge of whether or not the button gets pushed. The
violence of the unspeakable is mirrored in the fear of mentioning it.
Beckett keeps it nebulous. About what is incommensurable with experience as such one can speak only in euphemisms, the way one speaks in

Germany of the murder of the Jews. It has become a total a priori, so that bombed-out consciousness no longer has a place from which to reflect on it. With gruesome irony, the desperate state of things provides a stylistic technique that protects that pragmatic presupposition from contamination by childish science fiction. If Clov had really exaggerated, as his companion, nagging him with common sense, accuses him of doing, that would not change much. The partial end of the world which the catastrophe would then amount to would be a bad joke. Nature, from which the prisoners are cut off, would be as good as no longer there at all; what is left of it would merely prolong the agony.

But at the same time, this historical nota bene, a parody of Kierkegaard's point of contact between time and eternity, places a taboo on history. What existentialist jargon considers the *condition humaine* is the image of the last human being, which devours that of the earlier ones, humanity. Existentialist ontology asserts that there is something universally valid in this process of abstraction that is not aware of itself. It follows the old phenomenological thesis of the *Wesensschau*, eidetic intuition, and acts as though it were aware of its compelling specifications in the particular—and as though it thereby combined apriority and concreteness in a single, magical stroke. But it distills out the element it considers supratemporal by negating precisely the particularity, individuation in time and space, that makes existence existence and not the mere concept of existence. It courts those who are sick of philosophical formalism and yet cling to something accessible only in formal terms. To this kind of unacknowledged process of abstraction, Beckett poses the decisive antithesis: an avowed process of subtraction. Instead of omitting what is temporal in existence—which can be existence only in time—he subtracts from existence what time, the historical tendency, is in reality preparing to get rid of. He extends the line taken by the liquidation of the subject to the point where it contracts into a "here and now," a "whatchamacallit," whose abstractness, the loss of all qualities, literally reduces ontological abstractness *ad absurdum*, the absurdity into which mere existence is transformed when it is absorbed into naked self-identity. Childish silliness emerges as the content of philosophy, which degenerates into tautology, into conceptual duplication of the existence it had set out to comprehend. Modern ontology lives off the unfulfilled promise of the concreteness of its abstractions, whereas in Beckett the concreteness of an existence that is shut up in itself like a mollusk, no longer capable of universality, an existence that exhausts itself in pure self-positing, is revealed to be identical to the abstractness that is no longer capable of experience. Ontology comes into its own as the pathogenesis of the false life. It is presented as a state of negative eternity. Dostoevski's messianic Prince Mishkin once forgot his watch because no earthly time was valid for him; for Beckett's characters, Mishkin's antitheses, time can be lost because time would contain hope. Bored, the characters affirm with yawns that the weather is "as usual" (27); this affirmation opens the jaws of Hell:

> *HAMM:* But that's always the way at the end of the day, isn't it, Clov?
> *CLOV:* Always.
> *HAMM:* It's the end of the day like any other day, isn't it, Clov?
> *CLOV:* Looks like it. (13)

Like time, the temporal has been incapacitated; even to say that it didn't exist any more would be too comforting. It is and it isn't, the way the world is for the solipsist, who doubts the world's existence but has to concede it with every sentence. A passage of dialogue equivocates in this way:

> *HAMM:* And the horizon? Nothing on the horizon?
> *CLOV* (lowering the telescope, turning towards Hamm, exasperated): What in God's name would there be on the horizon? (Pause.)
> *HAMM:* The waves, how are the waves?
> *CLOV:* The waves? (He turns the telescope on the waves.) Lead.
> *HAMM:* And the sun?
> *CLOV* (looking): Zero.
> *HAMM:* But it should be sinking. Look again.
> *CLOV* (looking): Damn the sun.
> *HAMM:* Is it night already then?
> *CLOV* (looking): No.
> *HAMM:* Then what is it?
> *CLOV* (looking): Gray. (Lowering the telescope, turning towards Hamm, louder.) Gray! (Pause. Still louder.) GRRAY! (31)

History is kept outside because it has dried up consciousness' power to conceive it, the power to remember. Drama becomes mute gesture, freezes in the middle of dialogue. The only part of history that is still apparent is its outcome—decline. What in the existentialists was inflated into the be-all and end-all of existence here contracts to the tip of the historical and breaks off. True to official optimism, Lukács complains that in Beckett human beings are reduced to their animal qualities.[2] His complaint tries to ignore the fact that the philosophies of the remainder, that is, those which subtract the temporal and contingent element of life in order to retain only what is true and eternal, have turned into the remains of life, the sum total of the damages. Just as it is ridiculous to impute an abstract subjectivist ontology to Beckett and then put that ontology on some index of degenerate art, as Lukács does, on the basis of its worldlessness and infantilism, so it would be ridiculous to put Beckett on the stand as a star political witness. A work which sees the potential for nuclear catastrophe even in the oldest struggle of all will scarcely arouse us to do battle against nuclear catastrophe. Unlike Brecht, this simplifier of horror resists simplification. Beckett, however, is not so dissimilar to Brecht. His differentiatedness becomes an allergy to subjective differences that have degenerated into the conspicuous consumption of those who can afford individuation. There is a social truth in that. Differentiatedness cannot absolutely and without reflection be entered on the positive side of the ledger. The simplification of the social process which is underway relegates it to the *faux frais*, the "extras," in much the same way that the social formalities by means of which the capacity for differentiation was developed are disappearing. Differentiatedness, once the precondition of humanness [*Humanität*], is gradually becoming ideology. But an unsentimental awareness of this is not regressive. In the act of omission, what is left out survives as something that is avoided, the way consonance survives in atonal harmony. An unprotesting depiction of ubiquitous regression is a protest against a state of the world that so accommodates the law of regression that it no longer has anything to hold up against it. There is a constant monitoring to see that things are one way and not another; an alarm system with a sensitive bell indicates what fits in with the play's topography and what does not. Out of delicacy, Beckett keeps quiet about the delicate things as well as the brutal. The vanity of the individual who accuses society while his "rights" add to the accumulation of injustices is manifested in embarrassing declamations like Karl Wolfskehl's *Deutschlandsgedicht* [*Poem on Germany*]. There is nothing like that in Beckett. Even the notion that he depicts the negativity of the age in negative form would fit in with the idea that people in the Eastern satellite states, where the revolution was carried out in the form of an administrative act, must now devote themselves cheerfully to reflecting a cheerful era. Playing with elements of reality without any mirroring, taking no stand and finding pleasure in this freedom from prescribed activity, exposes more than would taking a stand with the intent to expose. The name of the catastrophe is to be spoken only in silence. The catastrophe that has befallen the whole is illuminated in the horrors of the last catastrophe; but only in those horrors, not when one looks at its origins. For Beckett, the human being —the name of the species would not fit well in Beckett's linguistic landscape—is only what he has become. As in utopia, it is its last day that decides on the species. But mourning over this must reflect—in the spirit—the fact that mourning itself is no longer possible. No weeping melts the armor; the only face left is the one whose tears have dried up. This lies at the basis of an artistic method that is denounced as inhuman by those whose humanness has already become an advertisement for the inhuman, even if they are not aware of it. Of the motives for Beckett's reductions of his characters to bestialized human beings, that is probably the most essential. Part of what is absurd in his writing is that it hides its face.

The catastrophes that inspire *Endgame* have shattered the individual whose substantiality and absoluteness was the common thread in Kierkegaard, Jaspers, and Sartre's version of existentialism. Sartre even affirmed the freedom of victims of the concentration camps to inwardly accept or reject the tortures inflicted upon them. *Endgame* destroys such illusions. The individual himself is revealed to be a historical category, both the outcome of the capitalist process of alienation and a defiant protest against it, something transient himself. The individualistic position constitutes the opposite pole to the ontological approach of every kind of existentialism, including that of *Being and Time*, and as such belongs with it. Beckett's drama abandons that position like an outmoded bunker. If individual experience in its narrowness and contingency has interpreted itself as a figure of Being, it has received the authority to do so only by asserting itself to be the fundamental characteristic of Being. But that is precisely what is false. The immediacy of individuation was deceptive; the carrier of individual experience is mediated, conditioned. *Endgame* assumes that the individual's claim to autonomy and being has lost its credibility. But although the prison of individuation is seen to be both prison and illusion—the stage set is the *imago* of this kind of insight —art cannot break the spell of a detached subjectivity; it can only give concrete form to solipsism. Here Beckett runs up against the antinomy of contemporary art. Once the position of the absolute subject has been exposed as the manifestation of an overarching whole that produces it, it cannot hold up; expressionism becomes obsolete. Art is denied the transition to a binding universality of material reality which would call a halt to the illusion of individuation. For unlike discursive knowledge of reality, something from which art is not distinguished by degrees but categorically distinct, in art only what has been rendered subjective, what is commensurable with subjectivity, is valid. Art can conceive reconciliation, which is its idea, only as the reconciliation of what has been estranged. Were it to simulate the state of reconciliation by joining the world of mere objects, it would negate itself. What is presented as socialist realism is not, as is claimed, something beyond subjectivism but rather something that lags behind it, and at the same time the pre-artistic complement of subjectivism. The expressionist invocation "O Mensch" ["Oh Man"] is the perfect complement to a social reportage seasoned with ideology. An unreconciled reality tolerates no reconciliation with the object in art. Realism, which does not grasp subjective experience, to say nothing of going beyond it, only mimics reconciliation. Today the dignity of art is measured not according to whether or not it evades this antinomy through luck or skill, but in terms of how it bears it. In this, *Endgame* is exemplary. It yields both to the impossibility of continuing to represent things in works of art, continuing to work with materials in the manner of the nineteenth century, and to the insight that the subjective modes of response that have replaced representation as mediators of form are not original and absolute but rather a resultant, something objective. The whole content of subjectivity, which is inevitably self-hypostatizing, is a trace and a shadow of the world from which subjectivity withdraws in order to avoid serving the illusion and adaptation the world demands. Beckett responds to this not with a stock of eternal truths but with what the antagonistic tendencies will still—precariously, and subject to revocation—permit. His drama is "fun" the way it might have been fun to hang around the border markers between Baden and Bavaria in old Germany as though they encompassed the realm of freedom. *Endgame* takes place in a neutral zone between the inner and the outer, between the materials without which no subjectivity could express itself or even exist and an animation which causes the materials to dissolve and blend as though it had breathed on the mirror in which they are seen. So paltry are the materials that aesthetic formalism is, ironically, rescued from its opponents on either side: the materials vendors of Diamat, dialectical materialism, on the one hand, and the cultural spokespersons of authentic expression on the other. The concretism of lemurs, who have lost their horizon in more than one sense, passes directly into the most extreme abstraction. The material stratum itself gives rise to a procedure through which the materials, touched tangentially in passing, come to approximate geometric forms; what is most limited becomes most general. The localization of *Endgame* in that zone mocks the spectator with the suggestion of something symbolic, something which, like Kafka, it then withholds. Because no subject matter is simply what it is, all subject matter appears to be the sign of an inner sphere, but the inner sphere of which it would be a sign no longer exists, and the signs do not point to anything else. The strict ration of reality and characters which the drama is allotted and with which it makes do, is identical to what remains of subject, spirit, and soul in view of the permanent catastrophe. What is left of spirit, which originated in mimesis, is pitiful imitation; what is left of the soul, which dramatizes itself, is an inhumane sentimentality; and what is left of the subject is its most abstract characteristic: merely existing, and thereby already committing an outrage. Beckett's characters behave in precisely the primitive, behavioristic manner appropriate to the state of affairs after the catastrophe, after it has mutilated them so that they cannot react any differently; flies twitching after the fly swatter has half-squashed them. The aesthetic *principium stilisationis* turns human beings into the same thing. Subjects thrown completely back upon their own resources, worldlessness become flesh, they consist of nothing but the wretched realities of their world, which has shriveled to bare necessity. They are empty *personae*, truly mere masks through whom sound merely passes. Their phoniness is the result of the disenchantment of spirit as mythology. In order to underbid history and thereby perhaps survive it, *Endgame* takes up a position at the nadir of what the construction of the subject-object laid claim to at the zenith of philosophy: pure identity becomes the identity of what has been annihilated, the identity of subject and object in a state of complete alienation. In Kafka, meanings were decapitated or disheveled; Beckett simply puts a stop to the infinity, in the bad sense, of intentions: their meaning, according to him, is meaninglessness. This is his objective and non-polemical judgment on existential philosophy, which by means of the equivocations in the concept of meaning transfigures meaninglessness itself to meaning under the name of "thrownness," *Geworfenheit*, and, later, absurdity. Beckett does not oppose this with a *Weltanschauung*; instead, he takes it literally. What becomes of the absurd once the characteristic of the meaning of existence have been demolished is not something universal—if it were, the absurd would turn back into an idea. Instead, the absurd turns into forlorn particulars that mock the conceptual, a layer composed of minimal utensils, refrigerators, lameness, blindness, and the distasteful bodily functions. Everything waits to be carted off to the dump. This stratum is not a symbolic one but rather the stratum characteristic of a post-psychological condition such as one finds in old people and in those who have been tortured.

Dragged out of the sphere of inwardness, Heidegger's *Befindlichkeiten* [states-of-being] and Jaspers' situations become materialist. The hypostasis of the individual and that of the situation were in harmony in them. "Situation" was temporal existence as such and the totality of the living individual as the primary certainty. It presupposed the identity of the person. Beckett proves himself to be Proust's student and Joyce's friend by returning to the concept of situation its actual content, what the philosophy that exploits it avoids—the dissociation of the unity of consciousness into disparate elements, into non-identity. But once the subject is no longer unquestionably identical with itself, no longer a self-contained complex of meaning, its boundary with what is outside it becomes blurred, and the situations of inwardness become those of *physis*, of physical reality. The verdict on individuality, which existentialism retained as an idealist core, condemns idealism. Nonidentity is both the historical disintegration of the unity of the subject and the emergence of something that is not itself subject. That changes what the term "situation" can be used to mean. Jaspers defines it as "a reality for an existing subject who has a stake in it."[3] He subordinates the concept of situation to the subject, which is conceived as stable and identical, just as he assumes that the situation acquires meaning through its relationship to this subject. Immediately afterwards he also calls it "not just a reality governed by natural laws. It is a sense-related reality," which, moreover, remarkably, is for him already conceived as "neither psychological nor physical, but both in one."[4] But when, in Beckett's view, the situation actually becomes both, it loses its existential-ontological constituents: personal identity and meaning. This becomes striking in the concept of the "boundary situation" [*Grenzsituation*]. That concept too originates with Jaspers:

Situations like the following: that I am always in situations; that I cannot live without struggling and suffering; that I cannot avoid guilt; that I must die—these are what I call boundary situations. They never change, except in appearance; [with regard to our existence, they are final].[5]

The construction of *Endgame* takes that up with a sardonic "I beg your pardon?" Platitudes like "I cannot live without struggling and suffering; . . . I cannot avoid guilt; . . . I must die" lose their blandness when they are retrieved from the a priori and returned to the sphere of phenomena. The qualities of nobility and affirmation disintegrate; these are the qualities with which philosophy—by subsuming the aconceptual under a concept that causes what ontology pompously calls "difference" to magically disappear—adorns an existence Hegel already called "foul." Beckett picks up existential philosophy, which has been standing on its head, and puts it back on its feet. His play responds to the comedy and ideological distortion in sentences like "Courage in the boundary situation is an attitude that lets me view death as an indefinite opportunity to be myself,"[6] whether Beckett is familiar with them or not. The poverty of the participants in *Endgame* is the poverty of philosophy.

The Beckettian situations of which his drama is composed are the photographic negative of a reality referred to meaning. They have as their model the situations of empirical existence, situations which, once isolated and deprived of their instrumental and psychological context through the loss of personal unity, spontaneously assume a specific and compelling expression—that of horror. Such situations were already to be found in the praxis of Expressionism. The horror aroused by Leonhard Frank's schoolteacher Mager, a horror that occasions his murder, is evident in the description of the elaborate manner in which Herr Mager peels an apple in front of his class. His deliberateness, which looks so innocent, is a figure of sadism: the image of the person who takes his time is like the person who keeps people waiting for a grisly punishment. But Beckett's treatment of these situations, the frightening and artificial derivatives of the perennial simple-minded situation comedy, helps to articulate something that was already evident in Proust. In a posthumous work, *Unmittelbarkeit und Sinndeutung* [*Immediacy and the Interpretation of Meaning*], Heinrich Rickert speculates on the possibility of an objective physiognomy of the spirit, a "soul" in a landscape or a work of art that would not be a mere projection.[7] Rickert cites a passage from Ernst Robert Curtius, who considers it "only partially correct . . . to see in Proust merely or primarily a great psychologist. A Stendhal is accurately characterized by this term. It . . . places him in the Cartesian tradition of the French spirit. But Proust does not acknowledge the distinction between thinking substance and extended substance. He does not divide the world into the psychic and the physical. To view his work from the perspective of the 'psychological novel' is to misunderstand its meaning. In Proust's books the world of sense objects occupies the same space as that of the psychic." Or: "If Proust is a psychologist, then he is one in a completely new sense of the word: he is a psychologist in that he immerses everything real, including sense perception, in a psychic fluid." To show that "the customary notion of the psychic does not fit here," Rickert cites Curtius again: "But the concept of the psychological has thereby lost its opposite—and because of this it can no longer be used for characterization." [8] The physiognomy of objective expression retains its enigmatic character nonetheless. The situations say something—but what? In this regard art itself, the quinessence of situations, converges with that physiognomy. It combines the most extreme specificity with its radical opposite. In Beckett this contradiction is turned inside-out. What normally hides behind a communicative facade is sentenced to appear. Working within a subterranean mystical tradition, Proust continues to cling affirmatively to that physiognomy, as though involuntary memory revealed the secret language of things. In Beckett that becomes the physiognomy of what is no longer human. His situations are the counter-images of the inextinguishable substance conjured up in Proust's, wrested from the tide of schizophrenia, which a terrified healthiness defends itself against by crying bloody murder. In the realm of schizophrenia, Beckett's drama retains its self-control. It subjects even schizophrenia to reflection:

> *HAMM:* I once knew a madman who thought the end of the world had come. He was a painter—and engraver. I had a great fondness for him. I used to go and see him, in the asylum. I'd take him by the hand and drag him to the window. Look! There! All that rising corn! And there! Look! The sails of the herring fleet! All that loveliness! (Pause.) He'd snatch away his hand and go back into his corner. Appalled. All he had seen was ashes. (Pause.) He alone had been spared. (Pause.) Forgotten. (Pause.) It appears the case is . . . was not so . . . so unusual. (44)

The madman's perception coincides with that of Clov, who peers out the window on command. *Endgame* moves away from the nadir only by calling its own name, as one does with a sleepwalker: the negation of negativity. Sticking in Beckett's memory is something like an apoplectic middle-aged man taking his midday nap with a cloth over his eyes to protect them from light or flies. The cloth makes him unrecognizable.

This run-of-the-mill image, hardly unfamiliar even optically, becomes a sign only for the gaze that is aware of the face's loss of identity, of the possibility that its shrouded state is that of a dead man, of how repulsive the physical suffering is that already places the living man among the corpses by reducing him to his body.[9] Beckett stares at such things until the everyday family life from which they are drawn pales into irrelevance: at the beginning is the tableau of Hamm covered with an old sheet; at the end he brings the handkerchief, his last possession, up to his face:

> *HAMM:* Old Stancher! (Pause.) You . . . remain. (84)

Such situations, emancipated from their context and from the character's personality, are structured into a second, autonomous context, the way music assembles the intentions and expressive features that become submerged in it until their sequence forms a structure in its own right. A key passage in the play,

> If I can hold my peace, and sit quiet, it will be all over with sound, and
>   motion, all over and done with—(69)

reveals the principle, perhaps in a reminiscence of the way Shakespeare handled his in the players' scene in *Hamlet.*

> *HAMM:* Then babble, babble, words, like the solitary child who turns
>   himself into children, two, three, so as to be together, and whisper
>   together, in the dark. (Pause.) Moment upon moment, pattering
>   down, like the millet grains of . . . (he hesitates) that old Greek,
>   and all life long you wait for that to mount up to a life. (70)

In the horror of not being in a hurry, such situations allude to the irrelevance and superfluousness of anything the subject is still able to do. Hamm considers riveting down the covers of the garbage cans in which his parents live, but he revokes that decision in the same words he uses to change his mind about urinating, which requires the torment of the catheter:

> *HAMM:* Time enough. (24)

A slight aversion to medicine bottles, dating back to the moment when one became aware that one's parents were physically weak, mortal, falling apart, is reflected in the question:

HAMM: Is it not time for my pain-killer? (7)

Speaking to one another has been consistently transformed into Strindbergian nagging:

HAMM: You feel normal?
CLOV (irritably): I tell you I don't complain. (4)

and at another point:

HAMM: I feel a little too far to the left. (Clove moves chair slightly.)
  Now I feel a little too far to the right. (Clov moves chair slightly.)
  Now I feel a little too far forward. (Clov moves chair slightly.)
  Now I feel a little too far back. (Clov moves chair slightly.) Don't
  stay there [i.e. behind the chair], you give me the shivers. (Clov
  returns to his place beside the chair.)
CLOV: If I could kill him I'd die happy. (27)

But the waning of a marriage is the situation in which one scratches onself:

NELL: I am going to leave you.
NAGG: Could you give me a scratch before you go?
NELL: No. (Pause.) Where?
NAGG: In the back.
NELL: No. (Pause.) Rub yourself against the rim.
NAGG: It's lower down. In the hollow.
NELL: What hollow?
NAGG: The hollow! (Pause.) Could you not? (Pause.) Yesterday you
  scratched me there.
NELL (elegaic): Ah yesterday!
NAGG: Could you not? (Pause.) Would you like me to scratch you?
  (Pause.) Are you crying again?
NELL: I was trying. (19–20)

After the former father and preceptor of his parents has told the allegedly metaphysical Jewish joke about the trousers and the world, he himself bursts out laughing over it. The embarrassment that comes over us when someone laughs about his own words becomes existential; life is still a quintessence only as the quintessence of everything one has to be ashamed of. Subjectivity dismays us as domination in a situation where one person whistles and the other comes running.[10] But what shame protests against has its social value: in the moments when the bourgeois act like true bourgeois, they sully the notion of humanity that is the basis for their own pretensions. Beckett's prototypes are also historical in that they hold up as typical of human beings only the deformations inflicted upon them by the form of their society. There is no room left for others. The bad habits and ticks of the normal personality, which *Endgame* intensifies unimaginably, are the universal form—which has long since put its stamp on all classes and individuals—of a totality that reproduces itself only in and through particularity in the bad sense, the antagonistic interests of individuals. But because there has been no life other than the false life, the catalog of its defects becomes the counterpart of ontology.

In a play that does not forgo the traditional cast of characters, however, this fragmentation into disconnected and non-identical elements is nevertheless tied up with identity. It is only in opposition to identity, and thus falling within its concept, that dissociation as such is possible; otherwise it would be pure, unpolemical, innocent multiplicity. For now, the historical crisis of the individual finds its limit in the individual biological entity which is its arena. Thus the sequence of situations in Beckett, which flows on without opposition from the individuals, ends in the stubborn bodies to which they regress. Judged in terms of this unity, the schizoid situations are comical, like hallucinations. Hence the clowning which one sees immediately in the behavior and the constellations of Beckett's figures.[11] Psychoanalysis explains the clown's humor as a regression to an extremely early ontogenetic stage, and Beckett's drama of regression descends to that level. But the laughter it arouses ought to suffocate the ones who laugh. This is what has become of humor now that it has become obsolete as an aesthetic medium and repulsive, without a canon for what should be laughed about, without a place of reconciliation from which one could laugh, and without anything harmless on the face of the earth that would allow itself to be laughed at. An intentionally idiotic double entendre about the weather reads:

> CLOV: Things are livening up. (He gets up on ladder, raises the telescope, lets it fall.) It did it on purpose. (He gets down, picks up the telescope, turns it on auditorium.) I see . . . a multitude . . . in transports . . . of joy. (Pause.) That's what I call a magnifier. (He lowers the telescope, turns toward Hamm.) Well? Don't we laugh? (29)

Humor itself has become silly, ridiculous—who could still laugh at basic comic texts like *Don Quixote* or *Gargantua?*—and Beckett carries out the sentence on it. Even the jokes of those who have been damaged are damaged. They no longer reach anyone; the pun, the degenerate form of which there is a bit in every joke, covers them like a rash. When Clov, the one who looks through the telescope, is asked about the color and frightens Hamm with the word "gray," he corrects himself with the formulation "light black." That botches a line from Molière's *Miser*, who describes the allegedly stolen cashbox as "grayish red." Jokes, like colors, have had the marrow sucked out of them. At one point the two non-heroes, one blind and one crippled, the stronger already both and the weaker in the process of becoming both, plot a "trick," an escape, "some kind of plan" à la *The Threepenny Opera*, not knowing whether it will only prolong life and agony or put an end to both of them in absolute annihilation:

> *CLOV:* Ah good. (He starts pacing to and fro, his eyes fixed on the ground, his hands behind his back. He halts.) The pains in my legs! It's unbelievable! Soon I won't be able to think any more.
> *HAMM:* You won't be able to leave me. (Clov resumes his pacing.) What are you doing?
> *CLOV:* Having an idea. (He paces.) Ah. (He halts.)
> *HAMM:* What a brain! (Pause.) Well?
> *CLOV:* Wait! (He meditates. Not very convinced.) Yes . . . (Pause. More convinced.) Yes! (He raises his head.) I have it! I set the alarm! (46–47)

This is probably an association to the (probably also originally Jewish) joke about the Busch Circus in which stupid August, who catches his wife with his friend on the sofa, cannot decide whether to throw out his wife or his friend, because he cares too much about both of them, and hits on the solution of selling the sofa. But even the last trace of silly sophistic rationality is erased. The only thing that is still funny is the fact that humor itself evaporates along with the meaning of the punchline. This is the way someone starts when, having climbed to the top step of a flight of stairs, he keeps going and steps off into empty space. Extreme crudeness carries out the sentence on laughter, which has long been its accomplice. Hamm lets the torsos of his parents, who have turned into babies in the garbage cans, starve to death, the triumph of the son as father. Chatter accompanies this:

> *NAGG:* Me pap!
> *HAMM:* Accursed progenitor!

NAGG: Me pap!

HAMM: The old folks at home! No decency left! Guzzle, guzzle, that's all they think of. (He whistles. Enter Clov. He halts beside the chair.) Well! I thought you were leaving me.

CLOV: Oh not just yet, not just yet.

NAGG: Me pap!

HAMM: Give him his pap.

CLOV: There's no more pap.

HAMM (to Nagg): Do you hear that? There's no more pap. You'll never get any more pap. (9)

To the irreparable harm the non-hero adds insult, his indignation at the old people who no longer have any decency, the way old people usually wax indignant about immoral youth. In this ambience, what remains of humanity—the fact that the two old people share their last zwieback with one another—becomes repulsive through the contrast with transcendental bestiality, and what remains of love becomes lip-smacking intimacy. To the extent to which they are still human beings, human things still go on:

NELL: What is it, my pet? (Pause.) Time for love?

NAGG: Were you asleep?

NELL: Oh no!

NAGG: Kiss me.

NELL: We can't.

NAGG: Try. (Their heads strain towards each other, fail to meet, fall apart again.) (14)

Like humor, dramatic categories as a whole are shifted around. All are parodied. But not derided. In its emphatic sense, parody means the use of forms in the era of their impossibility. It demonstrates this impossibility and by doing so alters the forms. The three Aristotelian unities are preserved, but drama itself has to fight for its life. *Endgame* is the epilogue to subjectivity, and the play loses the hero along with subjectivity. The only aspect of freedom still known to it is the powerless and pitiful reflex action of trivial decisions.[12] In this too Beckett's play isheir to Kafka's novels. His relationship to Kafka is analogous to that of the serial composers to Schönberg: he provides Kafka with a further self-reflection and turns him upside down by totalizing his principle. Beckett's critique of the older writer, which points irrefutably the divergence between what is happening and an objectively pure epic language, contains the same difficulty as the relationship between contemporary integral composition and the inherently antagonistic music of Schönberg: what is the raison d'être of forms when the tension between them and something that is not homogeneous to them has been abolished, without that slowing down progress in the artistic mastery of materials? *Endgame* handles the matter by adopting that question as its own, by making it thematic. The same thing that militates against the dramatization of Kafka's novels becomes Beckett's subject matter. The dramatic constituents put in a posthumous appearance. Exposition, complication, plot, peripetia and catastrophe return in decomposed form as participants in an examination of the dramaturgical corpse. Representing the catastrophe, for instance, is the announcement that there are no more painkillers (14). Those constituents have collapsed, along with meaning, to which drama once served as an invitation. *Endgame* performs a test-tube study on the drama of the age, a drama that no longer tolerates any of its constituents. For example: at the climax of the plot, tragedy had at its disposal as the quintessence of antithesis the technique of stichomythia, an extreme tightening of the dramatic fabric—a dialogue in which a trimeter of one character is followed by a trimeter of another. Dramatic form had relinquished this technique as being too remote from secular society in its stylization and its unconcealed pretentiousness. Beckett makes use of it, as though the detonation had provided access to things that were buried under drama. *Endgame* contains rapid-fire monosyllabic dialogues like the play of question and answer that once took place between the deluded king and the messenger of fate. But whereas in *Oedipus* that served as a medium for a rising curve of tension, here it is a medium in which the interlocutors slacken. Short of breath to the point of being mute, they can no longer manage to synthesize linguistic periods, and they stammer in protocol sentences—whether of the positivist or the expressionist variety one does not know. The asymptote toward which Beckett's drama tends is silence, which was already defined as a rest in the Shakespearian origins of modern tragedy. The fact that *Endgame* is followed by an *Acte sans paroles* [act without words], as a kind of epilogue, is *Endgame*'s own *terminus ad quem*. The words in *Endgame* sound like stopgap measures because that state of muteness has not yet been satisfactorily achieved; they are like an accompaniment to the silence they disturb.

What has become of form in *Endgame* can almost be traced in literary

history. In Ibsen's *Wild Duck*, Hjalmar Ekdal, a photographer who has
gone to seed and is already a potential non-hero, forgets to bring the
adolescent Hedwig the promised menu from a sumptuous dinner at old
Werle's house to which, wisely, he has been invited without his family.
Psychologically, this is motivated in terms of his careless, egotistical
character, but it is also symbolic of Hjalmar, of the course of the action,
and of the meaning of the whole: the fruitless sacrifice of the young
woman. This anticipates the later Freudian theory of parapraxis, which
interprets the "slip" in terms of its relationship both to the person's past
experiences and to his wishes, hence to the unity of the person. Freud's
hypothesis that all our experiences "have a sense"[13] translates the traditional dramatic idea into a psychological realism in which Ibsen's tragi-
comedy about the wild duck rekindles the spark of form. When symbolism is emancipated from its psychological determinants it becomes reified
and turns into something that exists in itself; the symbol becomes symbolist, as in Ibsen's late work—when, for example, the bookkeeper
Foldal in *John Gabriel Borkmann* is run down by "Youth." The contradiction between this kind of consistent symbolism and a conservative
realism is responsible for the inadequacy of Ibsen's last plays. But by the
same token it becomes a leavening agent for the expressionist Strindberg.
his symbols tear themselves free of empirical human beings and are
woven into a tapestry in which everything and nothing is symbolic
because everything can mean everything. Drama has only to recognize
the inevitable ridiculousness of this kind of pan-symbolism, which abolishes itself, and make use of it, and Beckettian absurdity has been reached
through the immanent dialectic of form. Meaning nothing becomes the
only meaning. The deadliest fear of the characters in the drama, if not of
the parodied drama itself, is the fear, disguised as humor, that they
might mean something.

> *HAMM:* We're not beginning to . . . to . . . mean something?
> *CLOV:* Mean something! You and I, mean something! (Brief laugh.) Ah
>   that's a good one! (32–33)

With the disappearance of this possibility, which has long since been
suppressed by the superior power of an apparatus in which individuals
are interchangeable or superfluous, the meaning of language disappears
as well. Irritated by the degenerate clumsiness of the impulse of life in
his parents' trashcan conversation and nervous because "it doesn't end,"
Hamm asks, "What do they have to talk about? What does anyone still

have to talk about?" (23). The play lives up to that question. It is built on the foundation of a prohibition of language, and it expresses that taboo in its own structure. But it does not escape the aporia of expressionist drama: that even where language tends to reduce itself to pure sound, it cannot divest itself of its semantic element, cannot become purely mimetic[14] or gestural, just as forms of painting that are emancipated from objective representation cannot completely free themselves of resemblance to material objects. Once definitively separated from the values of signification, mimetic values become arbitrary and accidental and ultimately turn into a second-order convention. The way *Endgame* deals with this distinguishes it from *Finnegans Wake*. Instead of trying to liquidate the discursive element in language through pure sound, Beckett transforms it into an instrument of its own absurdity, following the ritual of the clown, whose babbling becomes nonsense by being presented as sense. The objective decay of language, that bilge of self-alienation, at once stereotyped and defective, which human beings' words and sentences have swollen up into within their own mouths, penetrates the aesthetic arcanum. The second language of those who have fallen silent, an agglomeration of insolent phrases, pseudo-logical connections, and words galvanized into trademarks, the desolate echo of the world of the advertisement, is revamped to become the language of a literary work that negates language.[15] Here Beckett's work converges with the drama of Eugène Ionesco. If one of Beckett's later plays revolves around the *imago* of the tape recorder, the language of *Endgame* is reminiscent of the abominable party game in which the nonsense talked at a party is secretly taped and then played back to the guests to humiliate them. The shock, which people scurry away from in embarrassed giggles, is developed in full in Beckett's work. Just as after an intensive reading of Kafka alert experience thinks it sees situations from his novels everywhere, so Beckett's language effects a healing disease in the sick person: the person who listens to himself talk starts to worry that he sounds the same way. For a long time now, people leaving the movie theater seem to see the film's planned contingency continuing in chance events on the street. Gaps open up between the mechanically assembled phrases of everyday speech. When one of Beckett's two characters asks, with the routine gesture of someone jaded by the inviolable boredom of existence, "What in God's name could there be on the horizon?" (31), this linguistic shrugging of the shoulders becomes apocalyptic precisely by virtue of its utter familiarity. The slick and aggressive impulse of healthy common sense, "What in God's name could there be?," is blackmailed into confessing its own nihilism. Somewhat later, Hamm, the master, orders Clov, the *soi-disant* servant, to fetch the "gaff" for a circus trick, the vain attempt to push the chair back and forth. A short dialogue follows:

> *CLOV:* Do this, do that, and I do it. I never refuse. Why?
> *HAMM:* You're not able to.
> *CLOV:* Soon I won't do it any more.
> *HAMM:* You won't be able to any more. (Exit Clov.) Ah the creatures, the creatures, everything has to be explained to them. (43)

Every day millions of bosses beat the fact that "everything has to be explained to them" into their subordinates. Through the nonsense it is supposed to justify in that passage, however—Hamm's explanation negates his own command—the line not only casts a harsh light on the craziness of the cliché, which habit obscures, but also expresses what is deceptive about dialogue: the fact that those who are hopelessly estranged from one another can no more reach one another by conversing than the two old cripples in the trashcans. Communication, the universal law of the cliché, proclaims that there is no communication any more. The absurdity of talk does not unfold in opposition to realism but rather develops out of it. For by its very syntactic form—its logicity, its deductive relationships, its fixed concepts—communicative language postulates the law of sufficient cause. But this requirement is scarcely ever satisfied any more: when human beings converse with one another they are motivated in part by their psychology, the prelogical unconscious, and in part they pursue ends which, as ends of mere self-preservation, deviate from the objectivity whose illusory image is reflected in logical form. Nowadays, certainly, one can prove this to them with their tape recorders. As both Freud and Pareto understood it, the *ratio* of verbal communication is always rationalization as well. But *ratio* itself sprang from the interest of self-preservation, and hence its compulsive rationalizations demonstrate its own irrationality. The contradiction between rational facade and unalterable irrationality is itself already the absurd. Beckett has only to mark it as such, to use it as a principle of selection, and realism, divested of the semblance of rational stringency, comes to its senses.

Even the syntactic form of question and answer is undermined. It presupposes an openness about what is to be said that, as Huxley had already recognized, no longer exists. The predesignated answer can be heard in the question, and this turns the play of question and answer into empty delusion, a futile effort to conceal the unfreedom of informative language under the linguistic gestures of freedom. Beckett strips away this veil, and the philosophical veil as well. The philosophy that calls everything radically into question by confronting it with the void stops itself from the outset—by means of a pathos derived from theology— from reaching the frightening conclusion whose possibility it suggests. Through the form of the question it infiltrates the answer with precisely the same meaning the question calls into doubt; it is no accident that in fascism and pre-fascism these *destructeurs* were able to condemn the destructive intellect so heartily. Beckett, however, spells out the lie implicit in the question mark: the question has become a rhetorical one. If the Hell of existentialist philosophy is like a tunnel midway through which one can already see the light from the other end shining, Beckett's dialogue rips up the tracks of conversation; the train no longer reaches the point where it starts to get light. Wedekind's old technique of misunderstanding becomes total. The course of the dialogue itself approaches the aleatory principle of the literary production process. The dialogue sounds as though the law of its progression were not the rationality of statement and rejoinder, nor even their psychological interconnection, but rather a process of hearing something out, akin to the process of listening to music that is emancipated from preexisting forms. The drama listens in order to hear what kind of statement will follow the one before. It is only in relation to the initial spontaneity of these questions that the absurdity of the content becomes clear. This too has its infantile prototype in visitors to the zoo who wait to see what the hippopotamus or the chimpanzee will do next.

In its disintegration, language becomes polarized. On the one hand it becomes the Basic English, or French, or German of individual words, commands sputtered out archaically in the jargon of a universal disrespect, the familiarity of irreconcilable antagonists; on the other, it becomes the ensemble of its empty forms, a grammar that has abandoned all relationship to its content and with it its synthetic function. The interjections are accompanied by practice sentences, God knows what for. This too Beckett broadcasts: one of the rules of *Endgame* is that the asocial partners, and the spectators along with them, are always peeking at one another's cards. Hamm considers himself an artist. He has chosen Nero's *qualis artifex pereo* as the motto for his life. But the stories he projects run aground on syntax:

HAMM: Where was I? (Pause. Gloomily.) It's finished, we're finished. (Pause.) Nearly finished. (50)

Logic staggers around among the paradigms. Hamm and Clov are talking in their authoritarian, cutting manner:

HAMM: Open the window.
CLOV: What for?
HAMM: I want to hear the sea.
CLOV: You wouldn't hear it.
HAMM: Even if you opened the window?
CLOV: No.
HAMM: Then it's not worthwhile opening it?
CLOV: No.
HAMM (violently): Then open it! (Clove gets up on the ladder, opens the window. Pause.) Have you opened it?
CLOV: Yes. (64–65)

One is almost tempted to see in Hamm's last "then" the key to the play. Because it is not worthwhile to open the window, because Hamm cannot hear the sea—perhaps it has dried up, perhaps it is no longer moving— he insists that Clov open it: the senselessness of an action becomes the reason for doing it, a belated legitimation of Fichte's free activity for its own sake. This is how contemporary actions seem, and they arouse the suspicion that it was never much different. The logical figure of the absurd, which presents as stringent the contradictory opposite of stringency, negates all the meaningfulness logic seems to provide in order to convict logic of its own absurdity: to convict it of using subject, predicate, and copula to lay out the non-identical as though it were identical, as though it could be accommodated with forms. It is not as a *Weltanschauung* that the absurd replaces the worldview of rationality; rather, in the absurd that worldview comes into its own.

The preestablished harmony of despair governs the relationship between the forms and the residual content of the play. The ensemble, melted down, consists of only four characters. Two of them are excessively red, as though their vitality were a skin disease; the old people, in contrast, are excessively white, like potatoes sprouting in the cellar. None of them have properly functioning bodies any more. The old people consist only of torsos—they lost their legs, incidentally, not in the catastrophe but apparently in a private accident with the tandem in the

Ardennes, "on the road to Sedan" (16), where one army regularly destroys another; one should not imagine that all that much has changed. But even the memory of their particular misfortune becomes enviable in view of the vagueness of the general disaster, and they laugh as they remember it. In contrast to the Expressionists' Fathers and Sons, they all have proper names, but all four are one-syllable names, "four letter words" like obscenities. The practical and intimate short forms popular in Anglo-Saxon countries are exposed as mere stumps of names. Only the name of the old mother, Nell, is somewhat familiar, if obsolete; Dickens uses it for the touching figure of the child in *The Old Curiosity Shop*. The three others are invented, as though for billboards. The old man is called Nagg, by association with nagging, and perhaps also through a German association: the married couple is a couple by virtue of its *Nagen*, gnawing. They discuss whether the sawdust in their trashcans has been changed, but it is now sand instead of sawdust. Nagg confirms that it was once sawdust, and Nell responds wearily, "Once!" (17), the way a wife scornfully exposes the expressions her husband frozenly repeats. However petty the debate about sawdust or sand may be, the difference between them is crucial for what is left of the plot, the transition from the minimum to nothing at all. Beckett too could claim what Benjamin praised in Baudelaire, the ability to say the most extreme things with the utmost discretion;[16] the consoling platitude that things could always be worse becomes a condemnation. In the realm between life and death, where it is no longer possible even to suffer, everything rides on the distinction between sawdust and sand; sawdust, wretched byproduct of the object-world, becomes a scarce commodity, and being deprived of it means an intensification of one's life-long death penalty. The two make their home in trash cans (an analogous motif appears, incidentally, in Tennessee Williams' *Camino Real*, although surely neither of the plays drew on the other): as in Kafka, the colloquial phrase is taken literally. "Today the old people are thrown on the garbage heap," and it happens. *Endgame* is true gerontology. By the criterion of socially useful labor, which they are no longer capable of, the old people are superfluous and should be tossed aside; this notion is distilled from the scientific fussing of a welfare system that underlines the very thing it denies. *Endgame* prepares us for a state of affairs in which everyone who lifts the lid of the nearest trashcan can expect to find his own parents in it. The natural connection between the living has now become organic garbage. The Nazis have irrevocably overthrown the taboo on old age. Beckett's trashcans are emblems of the culture rebuilt after Auschwitz. This subplot, however, goes farther than too far; it extends all the way to the demise of the two old people. They are refused their baby food, their pap, which is replaced by a biscuit that the toothless old people can no longer chew, and they choke to death because the last human being is too squeamish to spare the lives of the next to last. This is linked to the main plot in that the deaths of the two old people move it forward to that exit from life whose possibility constitutes the dramatic tension. This is a variation on *Hamlet:* to croak or to croak, that is the question.

Grimly, the name of Beckett's hero abbreviates Shakespeare's; the name of the now liquidated dramatic subject, that of the first dramatic subject. There is also an association to one of Noah's sons and hence to the Flood: the father of the black race, who, in a Freudian negation, stands for the white master-race. Finally, in English, "ham actor" means a hack comedian. Beckett's Hamm, keeper of the keys and impotent at the same time, plays what he no longer is, as though he had read the recent sociological literature that defines the *zoon politikon* as a role. Being a "personality" would mean putting on airs as expertly as the impotent Hamm does. Personality may even have been a role from the start, nature behaving like something more than nature. Changing situations in the play provide the occasion for one of Hamm's roles. From time to time a stage direction makes the drastic recommendation that he speak with the "voice of a rational being" (33). In his long-winded tale he affects the "narrative tone" (50). The remembrance of something that cannot be brought back becomes a fraud. The disintegration retrospectively condemns as fictitious the continuity of life, which makes life what it is. The difference in tone between people who are telling stories and people who are speaking directly passes judgment on the identity principle. The two tones alternate in Hamm's long speech, which is a sort of interpolated aria without music. He stops at the breaks, with the artificial pauses of a leading man past his prime. *Endgame* presents the antithesis to existential philosophy's norm that human beings should be what they are because there is nothing else they can be — the idea that this very self is not the self but a slavish imitation of something that does not exist. Hamm's duplicity points up the lie involved in saying "I" and thereby ascribing to oneself the substantiality whose opposite is the contents that the ego synthesizes. The enduring, as the quintessence of the ephemeral, is its ideology. But of thought, which used to be the truth content of the subject, only the gestural shell is retained. The two figures act as though they were thinking something over, without in fact thinking anything over:

> *HAMM:* The whole thing is comical, I grant you that. What about having a good guffaw the two of us together?
> *CLOV* (after reflection): I couldn't guffaw again today.
> *HAMM (after reflection):* Nor I. (60)

Hamm's foil is what he is even in his name: a twice-mutilated clown the last letter of whose name has been amputated. His name sounds the same as an obsolete expression for the devil's "cloven" hoof and is like the current word "glove." He is his master's devil, who threatens him with the worst possible thing—leaving him—and also his master's glove, which Hamm uses to makes contact with the world of objects to which he no longer has direct access. Not only the figure of Clov but also Clov's relationship to Hamm is constructed from such associations. On the old piano edition of Stravinsky's *Ragtime for Eleven Instruments,* one of the most important pieces in his surrealist phase, was a drawing by Picasso, probably inspired by the "Rag" in the title, which shows two seedy figures, precursors of Vladimir and Estragon, the vagabonds who are waiting for Godot. This virtuoso piece of graphic art consists of a single tortuous line. *Endgame*'s double sketch is in the same spirit, as are the battered repetitions that Beckett's whole oeuvre irresistibly drags in. In those repetitions history is annulled. The repetition compulsion is learned by watching the regressive behavior of the prisoner, who tries again and again. Not the least of the ways in which Beckett converges with the most contemporary trends in music is that he, a Western man, amalgamates features of Stravinsky's radical past, the oppressive stasis of a continuity that has disintegrated, with advanced expressive and constructive techniques from the Schönberg school. The outlines of Hamm and Clov are also drawn with a single line; the process of individuation into properly autonomous monads is denied them. They cannot live without one another. Hamm's power over Clov seems to rest on the fact that he is the only one who knows how to open the larder, much as only the head of the firm knows the combination of the safe. He would be prepared to tell him the secret if Clov would promise to "finish" him— or "us." In a phrase thoroughly characteristic of the texture of the play, Clov responds, "I couldn't finish you," and as though the play were making fun of anyone who assumes rationality, Hamm says, "Then you won't finish me" (36). He is dependent on Clov because only Clov can still do the things necessary to keep them both alive. That, however, is of questionable value, because like the captain of the ghost ship both must fear that they will not be able to die. The little thing on which everything hangs is the possibility that something might change. This movement, or its absence, constitutes the plot. To be sure, it is never made more explicit that the reiterated leitmotif "Something is taking its course" (13; cf. 32), as abstract as the pure form of time. The Hegelian dialectic of master and servant, which Günther Anders discussed in relation to *Godot,* is not "given form" in accordance with the tenets of traditional aesthetics so much as ridiculed. The servant is no longer capable of taking charge and doing away with domination. The mutilated Clov would scarcely be capable of it, and in any case, according to the historico-philosophical sundial of the play it is too late for spontaneous action. There is nothing left for Clov to do but wander off into a world that does not exist for these recluses and take the chance that he will die in the process. For he cannot even rely on his freedom to die. He does manage to decide to leave and comes in as though to say goodbye: "Panama hat, tweed coat, raincoat over his arm, umbrella, bag" (82), with the emphatic effect of a musical finale. But we do not see his exit; he "halts by the door and stands there, impassive and motionless, his eyes fixed on Hamm, till the end." (82) This is an allegory whose intention has fizzled out. Aside from differences which may be decisive but may also be completely irrelevant, it is identical with the beginning. No spectator, and no philosopher, would be capable of saying for sure whether or not the play is starting all over again. The pendulum of the dialectic has come to a standstill.

The action of the play as a whole is composed on two themes, in musical fashion, as double fugues used to be. The first theme is that things should come to an end, a homely version of Schopenhauer's negation of the will to life. Hamm sets the tone: the characters, who are no longer characters, become the instruments of their situation, as though they had to play chamber music. "Of all Beckett's bizarre instruments, Hamm, in *Endgame,* who sits in his wheelchair, blind and immobile, is the one with the most tones, the most surprising sound." [17] Hamm's non-identity with himself motivates the course of the action. While he desires the end, as the end of the agony of an existence that is unending in the bad sense, he is as concerned about his life as a man in the fateful "best years of his life." The minor paraphernalia of health are of excessive importance to him. But he fears not death but rather that death could miscarry—an echo of Kafka's motif in "The Hunter Gracchus."[18] Just as important to him as his own bodily necessities is the fact that Clov, appointed lookout, sees no sail and no column of smoke, that there is no rat or insect stirring from which the disaster could begin all over again, not even the child who may have survived, who would represent hope, and for whom he lies in wait like Herod the butcher stalking the *agnus dei*. Insecticide, which pointed toward the death camps from the very beginning, becomes the end-product of the domination of nature, which now abolishes itself. Life's sole remaining content is that there shall be nothing living. Everything that exists is to be made identical to a life that is itself death, abstract domination. The second theme is assigned to Clov, the servant. According to an admittedly very obscure story, he came to Hamm looking for a refuge, but he also has much of the son of the enraged, impotent patriarch in him. To put an end to one's obedience to the powerless is the most difficult thing there is; everything insignificant and outmoded is irresistibly opposed to its own abolition. The counterpoint between the two plots is provided by the fact that Hamm's will to death is the same as his life principle, whereas Clov's will to life could well bring about the death of them both; Clov [in the English version, Hamm] says, "Outside of here, it's death" (9). Nor is the antithesis formed by the two heroes a fixed one. Their impulses intermingle; it is Clov who first speaks of the end. The schema the course of the action follows is that of the endgame in chess, a typical and to some extent norm-governed situation separated by a caesura from the midgame with its combinations. The latter are absent in the play as well. Intrigue and plot are tacitly suspended. Only technical errors or accidents, such as the existence of a living thing somewhere, could give rise to something unforeseen, not the spirit of invention. The field is almost empty, and what happened before can be inferred only with great difficulty from the positions of the few characters. Hamm is the king around whom everything revolves and who can do nothing himself. On the stage, the disproportion between chess as a pastime and the inordinate effort it involves takes the form of the disproportion between the athletic actions of the actors and the insignificance of their actions. Whether the game ends in a stalemate or in an eternal check, or whether Clov wins, is not made clear, as though too much certainty about this would provide too much meaning. And in any case it is probably not so important: everything comes to a standstill in a draw just as it does in a mate. The only other thing that stands out is the fleeting image of the child (78), a very weak reminiscence of Fortinbras or the Child King. It might even be Clov's own abandoned child. But the oblique light that falls from it into the room is as weak as the impotent helping arms that reach out the window at the end of Kafka's *Trial*.

The final history of the subject is made the theme of an intermezzo that can allow itself its symbolism because it reveals its own inadequacy and thereby the inadequacy of its meaning. The hybris of idealism, the enthronement of human meaning as the creator at the center of his creation, has entrenched itself in that "bare interior" like a tyrant in his last days. There, with an imagination reduced to the smallest proportions, Hamm recapitulates what men once wanted to be, a vision of which they were deprived as much by the course of society as by the new cosmology, and which they nevertheless cannot let go of. Clov is his male nurse. Hamm has him push him in his wheelchair to the middle of the room, the room which the world has become and which is at the same time the interior of his own subjectivity:

> *HAMM:* Take me for a little turn. (Clov goes behind the chair and pushes it forward.) Not too fast! (Clov pushes chair.) Right round the world! (Clov pushes chair.) Hug the walls, then back to the center again. (Clov pushes chair.) I was right in the center, wasn't I? (25)

The loss of a center which that parodies, because that center was already a lie, becomes the pitiful object of a nagging and impotent pedantry:

> *CLOV:* We haven't done the round.
> *HAMM:* Back to my place. (Clov pushes chair back to center.) Is that my place?
> *CLOV:* I'll measure it.
> *HAMM:* More or less! More or less!
> *CLOV* (moving chair slightly): There!
> *HAMM:* I'm more or less in the center?
> *CLOV:* I'd say so.
> *HAMM:* You'd say so! Put me right in the center!
> *CLOV:* I'll go and get the tape.
> *HAMM:* Roughly! Roughly! (Clov moves chair slightly.) Bang in the center! (26–27)

But what is being requited in this stupid ritual is not something the subject has done. Subjectivity itself is at fault; the fact that one exists at all. Heretically, original sin is fused with creation. Being, which existential philosophy trumpets as the meaning of being, becomes its antithesis. Panic fear of the reflex movements of the living not only serves as an incitement to indefatigable domination of nature; it is directed to life itself, as the cause of the catastrophe life has become.

> *HAMM:* All those I might have helped. (Pause.) Helped! (Pause.) Saved. (Pause.) Saved! (Pause.) The place was crawling with them! (Pause. Violently.) Use your head, can't you, use your head, you're on earth, there's no cure for that! (68)

From which he draws the conclusion: "The end is in the beginning and yet you go on" (69). The autonomous moral law reverses itself antinomically; pure domination of nature becomes the duty to exterminate, which was always lurking behind it.

> *HAMM:* More complications! (Clov gets down.) Not an underplot, I trust. (Clov moves ladder nearer window, gets up on it, turns telescope on the without.)

[In the German edition to which Adorno refers, the dialogue continues as follows:

> *CLOV:* Oi, oi, oi, oi!
> *HAMM:* A leaf? A flower? A toma . . . (he yawns) . . . to?
> *CLOV* (looking): You'll get your tomatoes right away! Someone! There's someone there!
> *HAMM* (stops yawning): Well, go wipe him out. (Clov gets down from the ladder. Softly.) Someone! (with trembling voice.) Do your duty! (78)]

A question addressed by Clov, the frustrated rebel, to his frustrated master passes judgment on the idealism from which this totalitarian concept of duty is derived:

> *CLOV:* Any particular sector you fancy? Or merely the whole thing? (73)

That sounds like a test of Benjamin's idea that a single cell of reality, truly contemplated, counterbalances the whole rest of the world. The totality, a pure positing by the subject, is the void. No statement sounds more absurd than this most rational of statements, which reduces "everything" to an "only," the mirage of a world that can be dominated anthropocentrically. As rational as this utmost *Absurdum* may be, however, it is not possible to argue away the absurd aspect of Beckett's play solely because hasty apologetics and a desire for labels have appropriated it. *Ratio*, which has become completely instrumental, devoid of self-reflection and reflection on what it has disqualified, must inquire after the meaning that it itself has expunged. But in the state that makes this question necessary there is no answer left but the void that the question, as pure form, already is. The historical inevitability of this absurdity makes it seem ontological: that is the delusoriness of history itself. Beckett's drama demolishes it. The immanent contradiction of the absurd, the nonsense in which reason terminates, opens up the emphatic possibility of something true that cannot even be conceived of anymore. It undermines the absolute claim of the status quo, that which simply is the way it is. Negative ontology is the negation of ontology: it was history alone that produced what the mythical power of the timeless and eternal has appropriated. The historical fiber of situation and language in Beckett does not concretize, *more philosophico*, something ahistorical—precisely this practice on the part of existentialist dramatists is as alien to art as it is philosophically backward. Rather, what is eternal and enduring for Beckett is the infinite catastrophe; it is only the fact that "the earth is extinguished, though I never saw it lit" (81) that justifies Clov's answer to Hamm's question, "Do you not think this has gone on long enough?": "I've always thought so" (45). Prehistory lives on; the phantasm of eternity is only its curse. After Clov has told Hamm, who is completely paralyzed, what he has seen of the earth, which the latter ordered him to look at (72), Hamm confides to him, as though confiding his secret:

CLOV (absorbed): Mmm.
HAMM: Do you know what it is?
CLOV (as before): Mmm.
HAMM: I was never there. (74)

No one has ever set foot on the earth; the subject is not yet a subject. Determinate negation takes dramatic form through its consistent inversion. The two partners qualify their understanding that there is no nature anymore with the bourgeois phrase "you exaggerate" (11). Presence of mind is the proven means of sabotaging reflection. It occasions the melancholy reflection:

CLOV (sadly): No one that ever lived ever thought so crooked as we. (11)

Where they come closest to the truth, they sense, with double comedy, that their consciousness is false; this is how a situation that can no longer be reached by reflection is reflected. But the whole play is constructed by means of this technique of reversal. It transfigures the empirical world into what it had already been called in the late Strindberg and Expressionism. "The whole house stinks of corpses. . . . The whole universe" (46). Hamm, who responds, "To hell with the universe," is just as much a descendant of Fichte, who despises the world because it is nothing but raw materials and products, as he is the one who has no hope but the cosmic night, which he supplicates with poetic quotations. Absolute, the world becomes hell: nothing exists but it. Beckett uses typography to emphasize Hamm's statement: "Beyond is the . . . [OTHER] hell" (26; capitals omitted in the English version). He lets a twisted secular metaphysics shine through, with a Brechtian commentary:

> CLOV: Do you believe in the life to come?
> HAMM: Mine was always that. (Exit Clov.) Got him that time! (49)

In this conception Benjamin's notion of dialectics at a standstill comes into its own:

> HAMM: It will be the end and there I'll be, wondering what can have
> brought it on and wondering what can have . . . (he hesitates) . . .
> why it was so long coming. (Pause.) There I'll be, in the old refuge,
> alone against the silence and . . . (he hesitates) . . . the stillness. If
> I can hold my peace, and sit quiet, it will be all over, with sound,
> and motion, all over and done with. (69)

That stillness is the order that Clov allegedly loves and that he defines as the goal of his activities:

> CLOV: A world where all would be silent and still and each thing in its
> last place, under the last dust. (57)

The Old Testament "dust thou shalt become" is translated into: filth. Excretions become the substance of a life that is death. But the imageless image of death is an image of indifference, that is, a state prior to differentiation. In that image the distinction between absolute domination —the hell in which time is completely confined within space, in which absolutely nothing changes any more—and the messianic state in which everything would be in its right place, disappears. The last absurdity is that the peacefulness of the void and the peacefulness of reconciliation cannot be distinguished from one another. Hope skulks out of the world, which cannot conserve it any more than it can pap and bon-bons, and back to where it came from, death. From it the play draws its only consolation, a stoic one:

> *CLOV:* There are so many terrible things now.
> *HAMM:* No, no, there are not so many now. (44)

Consciousness gets ready to look its own end in the eye, as though it wanted to survive it the way these two have survived the destruction of their world. Proust, about whom Beckett wrote an essay in his youth, is said to have tried to record his own death throes; the notes were to be inserted into the description of Bergotte's death. *Endgame* carries out this intention as though it were a mandate bequeathed it in a will.

NOTES

THE ESSAY AS FORM

1. Georg Lukács, "On the Nature and Form of the Essay," in *Soul and Form*, translated by Anna Bostock (Cambridge, Mass.: MIT Press, 1974), p. 13. (First published as *Die Seele und die Formen*, Berlin, E. Fleischel, 1911).

2. Ibid., p. 10: "The essay is always concerned with something already formed, or at best, with something that has been; it is part of its essence that it does not draw something new out of an empty vacuum, but only gives a new order to such things as once lived. And because he only newly orders them, not forming something new out of the formless, he is bound to them; he must always speak 'the truth' about them, find, that is, the expression for their essence."

3. Cf. ibid., pp. 1–18.

4. Ibid., pp. 9–10.

5. René Descartes, *A Discourse On Method*, translated by John Veitch (New York: E. P. Dutton, 1951), p. 15.

6. Max Bense, "Über den Essay und seine Prosa," *Merkur* 1:3 (1947), p. 418.

7. Ibid., p. 420.

8. Friedrich Nietzsche, *The Will to Power*, translated by W. Kaufmann and R. J. Hollingdale (London: Weidenfeld and Nicolson, 1968), pp. 532–33.

ON EPIC NAIVETÉ

1. *The Odyssey of Homer*, translated by Richmond Lattimore (New York: Harper & Row, 1965), Book XXIII, 11. 233ff. Adorno quotes Voss' eighteenth-century translation.

2. Cf. Gilbert Murray, *Five Stages of Greek Religion*, New York: Columbia, 1925, p. 16; U. von Wilamowitz-Möllendorf, *Der Glaube der Hellenen*, I, p. 9.

3. *Odyssey*, Book XXIV, 11. 152ff.

4. Schröder translates: "und wahrlich Odysseus blieb zuruck" [and truly Odysseus remained behind]. The literal translation of the $\mathring{\eta}$ as a particle of affirmation rather than explication does not alter the enigmatic character of the passage.

5. Friedrich Hölderlin, *Gesamtausgabe*, edited by Zinkernagel (Leipzig: Insel, n.d.), p. 139; *Hölderlin, his poems*, translated by Michael Hamburger (New York: Pantheon, 1952), p. 129. There are literary-historical links between Voss and Hölderlin.

6. "No one would deny that . . . true similes have been in constant use from the beginnings of human speech. . . . But besides these, there are others which, as we have seen, are formally similes, but in reality are disguised identifications or transformations." (J. A. K. Thomson, *Studies in the Odyssey*, Oxford: Clarendon, 1914, p. 7). Similes, accordingly, are traces of the historical process.

7. Cf. Friedrich Schelling, *Werke*, vol. 2 (Leipzig: F. Eckardt, 1907), p. 302 *(System des transzendental Idealismus)*. Later, in his *Philosophy of Art*, Schelling expressly rejected the allegorical interpretation of Homer.

8. Cf. Friedrich Neitzsche, "Homer's Contest," in the *Complete Works*, edited by Oscar Levy, vol. 2, translated by Maximilian Mügge (London: George Allen & Unwin, 1911), pp. 51–62. (Original German title "Homers Wettkampf.")

IN MEMORY OF EICHENDORFF

1. Walter Benjamin, *One-Way Street*, in *Reflections*, translated by Edmund Jephcott (New York: Harcourt Brace Jovanovich, 1978), p. 69.

2. Theodor A. Meyer, *Das Stilgesetz der Poesie* (Leipzig: S. Hirzel, 1901), p. 2. (Now reprinted Darmstadt: Wissenschaftliche Buchgesellschaft, 1968.)

LOOKING BACK ON SURREALISM

1. G. W. F. Hegel, *Phenomenology of Spirit*, translated by A. V. Miller (Oxford: Clarendon Press, 1977), p. 360.

THE ARTIST AS DEPUTY

1. The English translation of this work appears as "Degas Dance Drawing," in volume 12 of the *Collected Works of Paul Valéry: Degas, Manet, Moriscot*, edited by Jackson Matthews, translated by David Paul (New York: Bollingen/Pantheon, 1960). Page numbers in parentheses hereon refer to this edition.

READING BALZAC

1. Cf. Georg Lukács, *Balzac und der französische Realismus* (Berlin: Aufbau, 1953), p. 59.

2. Bertolt Brecht, *Brechts Dreigroschenbuch* (Frankfurt am Main: Suhrkamp, 1960), p. 93 f.

3. Karl Marx, *Capital*, translated by Samuel Moore and Edward Aveling (New York: International, 1967; translation first published 1887), 1:589.

4. Ibid., vol. 3.

5. Friedrich Engels to Margaret Harkness, London, April 1888, in Lee Baxandall and Stefan Morowski, editors, *Marx & Engels on Literature & Art* (St. Louis: Telos Press, 1973), pp. 114–16.

6. Engels to Laura Lafargue, Dec. 12, 1883, in ibid., p. 112.

7. Cf. Georg Lukács, *Karl Marx und Friedrich Engels als Literaturhistoriker* (Berlin: Aufbau, 1952), p. 65; and "Marx and Engels on Aesthetics," in Lukács,

Writer and Critic and Other Essays (New York: Grosset & Dunlap, 1971), pp. 61–88.

8. Marquis de Sade, *Histoire de Justine*, (Holland, 1797), 1:13.

VALÉRY'S DEVIATIONS

1. Adorno quotes from Paul Valéry, *Windstriche. Aufzeichnungen und Aphorismen* (Wiesbaden: Insel, 1959) and Paul Valéry, *Über Kunst. Essays* (Frankfurt am Main: Suhrkamp, 1959). Here the passages are given in the English translations from the *Collected Works of Paul Valéry*, edited by Jackson Mathews, Bollingen Series XLV. In this English edition the specific works to which Adorno refers are scattered through a number of volumes, as follows: the *Rhumbs* are included in volume 14, *Analects*, translated by Stuart Gilbert (Princeton, N.J.: Princeton University Press, 1970). The *Pièces sur l'art* are distributed among volume 7, *The Art of Poetry*, translated by Denise Folliot (New York: Pantheon, 1958); volume 12, *Degas Manet Morisot*, translated by David Paul (New York: Pantheon, 1960); and volume 13, *Aesthetics*, translated by Ralph Manheim (New York: Pantheon, 1964), with "Histoire d'Amphion" in volume 3, *Plays*, translated by David Paul and Robert Fitzgerald (New York: Pantheon, 1960) and the "Propos sur le progrès" in volume 10, *History and Politics*, translated by Denise Foliot and Jackson Mathews (New York: Pantheon, 1962). In the text, the volume and page numbers provided in parentheses following a quotation refer to this edition. For a few passages I was unable to locate in the English edition I have provided my own translations and have given page references to the French original in the Pléiade edition: Paul Valéry, *Oeuvres*, vol. 2 (Paris: Gallimard, 1977), along with the title of the work from which the passage was taken.

2. Cf. Theodor W. Adorno, "Musik, Sprache und ihr Verhältnis im gegenwärtigen Komponieren," in *Jahresring 56/57. Ein Querschnitt durch die deutsche Literatur und Kunst der Gegenwart*, Stuttgart 1956, p. 99. Reprinted in Adorno, *Gesammelte Schriften* 16 (Frankfurt am Main: Suhrkamp, 1978), pp. 649ff.

3. Cf. Theodor W. Adorno, *Klangfiguren* (Berlin & Frankfurt am Main, 1959), p. 182ff. Reprinted in Adorno, *Gesammelte Schriften* 16, p. 126ff.

EXTORTED RECONCILIATION

1. Karl Marx, *Grundrisse*, translated by Martin Nicolaus (New York: Vintage, 1973), pp. 196–97.

2. Karl Marx, review of G. F. Daumer, *Die Religion des neuen Weltalters* (Hamburg, 1850), in *Neue Rheinische Zeitung*. Reprinted Berlin, 1955, p. 107.

3. Georg Lukács, "Healthy or Sick Art?," in Lukács, *Writer & Critic and Other Essays*, translated by Arthur Kahn (New York: Grosset & Dunlap, 1971; first published Merlin Press, 1970), p. 103.

4. Cf. Theodor W. Adorno, "Reading Balzac," this volume pp. 121–36.

5. Cf. Theodor W. Adorno, *Philosophy of Modern Music*, translated by Anne Mitchell and Wesley Blomster (New York: Seabury, 1973), pp. 46–48.

6. Cf. Theodor W. Adorno, *Minima Moralia*, translated by E. F. N. Jephcott (London: NLB, 1974).

7. Adorno, *Philosophy of Modern Music*, pp. 48–51.

8. G. W. F. Hegel, *Aesthetics*, translated by T. M. Knox (Oxford: Oxford University Press, 1975), I:593.

TRYING TO UNDERSTAND ENDGAME

1. Samuel Beckett, *Endgame* (New York: Grove Press, 1958), p. 38. Page numbers in parentheses hereon refer to this edition.

2. Cf. Theodor W. Adorno, "Extorted Reconciliation," in this volume, p. 226f., and Georg Lukács, *Realism in Our Time* (New York: Harper & Row, 1964).

3. Karl Jaspers, *Philosophy*, translated by E. G. Ashton (Chicago: University of Chicago Press, 1970), vol. II, p. 177.

4. Ibid.

5. Ibid., p. 178; bracketed material omitted in the English translation.

6. Ibid., p. 197.

7. Cf. Heinrich Rickert, *Unmittelbarkeit und Sinndeutung* (Tübingen: Mohr, 1939), pp. 133f.

8. Ernst Robert Curtius, *Französischer Geist im neuen Europa* (1925); reprinted in his *Französischer Geist im zwanzigsten Jarhhundert* (Bern: Francke, 1952), pp. 312–13; quoted in Rickert, p. 133f.

9. Max Horkheimer and Theodor W. Adorno, *Dialectic of Enlightenment*, translated by John Cumming (New York: Seabury, 1972), p. 234.

10. Cf. *Endgame*, p. 45.

11. Cf. Günther Anders, *Die Antiquiertheit des Menschen* (Munich: Beck, 1956), p. 217.

12. Theodor W. Adorno, "Notes on Kafka," in *Prisms*, translated by Samuel and Shierry Weber (London: Spearman, 1967; reprinted Cambridge, Mass.: MIT Press, 1981), pp. 262–63n.

13. Sigmund Freud, *Introductory Lectures on Psychoanalysis*, translated by James Strachey (New York: Norton, 1966), p. 40.

14. Theodor W. Adorno, "Voraussetzungen," in *Noten zur Literatur* III (Frankfurt am Main: Suhrkamp, 1965), pp. 136f, and Horkheimer and Adorno, *Dialectic of Enlightenment*, p. 24f.

15. Cf. Theodor W. Adorno, *Dissonanzen*, 2d ed. (Gottingen: Vandenhoeck & Ruprecht, 1958), pp. 34 and 44; reprinted *Gesammelte Schriften*, v. 14, (Frankfurt am Main: Suhrkamp, 1973), pp. 39f. and 49 f.

16. Walter Benjamin, "On Some Motifs in Baudelaire," in *Illuminations*, translated by Harry Zohn (New York: Schocken, 1969), pp. 183–84.

17. Marie Luise Kaschnitz, *Zwischen Immer und Nie. Gestalten und Themen der Dichtung* (Frankfurt am Main: Insel, 1971), p. 207.

18. Cf. Adorno, "Notes on Kafka," *Prisms*, p. 260.

INDEX

Adorno, Theodor W.: *Dialectic of En-lightenment*, 226; *Philosophy of Modern Music*, 231
Alcaeus, 40
Anders, Günther, 269
Aristotle, 15, 206, 223

Bach, J. S., 77, 212; *Well-Tempered Clavier*, 78
Bacon, Francis, 20
Balzac, Honoré de, 6, 121–36, 178, 228; *Contes drolatiques (Droll Stories)*, 134; *Sarrasine*, 124
Baudelaire, Charles, 20, 37, 44, 50, 58, 82, 83, 107, 142, 144, 145, 158, 162, 171, 223, 243; *Les Fleurs du mal*, 138; "Petites vieilles," 45; *Les Tableaux Parisiens*, 45, 223
Beckett, Samuel, 221, 225–26, 231; *Endgame*, 226, 241–75
Beethoven, Ludwig van, 124, 204
Benjamin, Walter, 3, 13, 98, 147, 158, 162, 178, 186, 206, 208, 221, 223, 272, 274; *One-Way Street*, 61, 213
Benn, Gottfried, 190, 221, 233, 234
Berg, Alban, 74, 174
Bergson, Henri, 140, 148, 177, 235; *Introduction to Metaphysics*, 175
Bloch, Ernst, 111; *The Spirit of Utopia*, 205; *Spuren*, 200–15
Borkenau, Franz, 236
Bott, Alan: *Our Fathers*, 88
Brahms, Johannes, 57, 76, 77
Brecht, Bertolt, 46, 65, 69, 143, 191, 200–1, 222, 248; "Ballade vom to-ten Soldaten" ("Ballad of the Dead Soldier"), 217; *The Threepenny Opera*, 258; "Vom armen B. B.," 202
Brentano, Clemens, 72
Breton, André, 86
Broch, Hermann, 32
Büchner, Georg, 65

Calmette, Gaston, 181
Cervantes, Miguel de: *Don Quixote*, 30, 257
Cézanne, Paul, 100
Claudel, Paul, 50
Cocteau, Jean, 86, 168

Dali, Salvador, 87, 178
Dante, 53
Daudet, Léon, 181
Daumer, G. F.: *Religion des neuen Weltalters (Religion of the New Age)*, 220
Daumier, Honoré, 123
Debussy, Claude, 168, 169
De Coster, Charles: *A Merry Book Despite Death and Tears*, 134
Degas, Edgar, 100, ,101, 102, 104, 106, 107
Delacroix, Eugène, 162
Descartes, René, 20, 140; *Discourse on Method*, 14–15; *Meditations*, 152
Dickens, Charles, 228; *The Old Curiosity Shop*, 266
Doré, Gustav, 42
Dostoevski, Fyodor, 31–32, 35, 247; *Notes from the Underground*, 229

Eichendorff, Joseph von, 56–79, *Ahnung und Gegenwart (Intimation and Presence)*, 62, 65; "Frühlingsnacht" ("Spring Night"), 74; *Geistliche Gedichte (Spiritual Poems)*, 59–60; *Das Marmorbild (The Marble Statue)*, 69; "Nachtigallen" ("Nightingales"), 64; "Schöne Fremde" ("Beautiful Foreigner"), 66–67, 74; "Sehnsucht" ("Longing"), 70–71; "Übern Garten durch die Lüfte" ("Over the garden through the breezes"), 63–64; "Zwielicht" ("Twilight"), 65
Eliot, T. S., 227
Engels, Friedrich, 94, 131, 132, 220, 228
Ernst, Max, 88
Eulenberg, Herbert, 5

Fielding, Joseph: *Tom Jones*, 32
Flaubert, Gustave, 27, 33, 103, 226; *Education sentimentale*, 235
Frank, Leonhard, 201, 253
Freud, Sigmund, 31, 86, 87, 125, 217, 263

García Lorca, Federico, 46
García Lorca, Federico, 46
George, Stefan, 53–54, 98; and George Circle, 91, 94; *Seventh Ring*, 50–53
Gide, André, 99, 179; *Faux-Monnayeurs*, 34
Girardi, Alexander, 203
Goethe, Johann W., 3, 25, 26, 46, 65, 66, 76, 80, 81, 129, 146, 201, 240, 243–44; *Elective Affinities*, 28, 101, 162; *Faust*, 111–120, 207; *Herrmann und Dorothea*, 48; "Kennst du das Land," 71; *Maxims and Reflections*, 39; *Pandora*, 113; "Selige Sehnsucht" ("Blessed Longing"), 72; "Wanderers Nachtlied" ("Wanderer's Night-Song"), 41, 42, 120; *Wilhelm Meister's Wander* *Years*, 28, 136; "Willkommen und Abschied" ("Welcome and Farewell"), 69
Grimm, Baron, 61

Haecker, Theodor, 95
Harkness, Margaret, 131
Hauff, Wilhelm, 202
Hauptmann, Gerhart, 65
Hebbel, Friedrich, 188
Hegel, G. W. F., 12, 18, 19, 20, 21, 42, 43, 49, 100, 101, 116, 118, 122, 132, 133, 140, 142, 167, 202, 206, 207, 211, 212, 216, 218, 226, 229, 232, 236–37, 239–40; *Logic*, 174; *Phenomenology*, 88–89, 141, 213; *Philosophy of Right*, 61, 126, 141
Heidegger, Martin, 205, 221, 233, 253; *Being and Time*, 228, 249
Heimpel, Hermann, 55
Heine, Heinrich, 76, 80–85; *Book of Songs*, 80; *Der Heimkehr (The Return Home)*, 84–85; "Die Loreley," 80
Heym, Georg, 211
Hoffmann, E. T. A., 169
Hofmansthal, Hugo von, 179
Hölderlin, Friedrich, 27, 28
Homer, 25, 27, 28; *Odyssey*, 24, 27
Honegger, Arthur, 145, 169
Horkheimer, Max: *Dialectic of Enlightenment*, 226
Hume, Thomas, 177
Husserl, Edmund, 233, 243
Huxley, Aldous, 263; *Brave New World*, 157

Ibsen, Henrik: *John Gabriel Borkmann*, 261; *Wild Duck*, 261

Jacobsen, Jens P.: *Niels Lyhne*, 32
Jaspers, Karl, 249, 252
Jochmann, Carl Gustav, 104

Jouve, Pierre Jean, 138
Joyce, James, 31, 35, 178, 221, 223, 224, 227, 231, 241, 252; *Finnegans Wake*, 262
Jung, Carl, 86
Jünger, Ernst, 221

Kafka, Franz, 34–35, 157, 176, 181, 183, 219, 221, 224, 229, 230, 231, 241, 251, 259–60, 262, 266, 270; "In the Penal Colony," 203; *The Trial*, 271
Kant, Immanuel, 12, 14, 15, 21, 72, 100, 107, 197, 206, 207, 218
Keller, Gottfried: *Der grüne Heinrich*, 91; *Martin Salander*, 26
Kempner, Friederike, 113
Kierkegaard, Søren, 73, 135, 145, 230, 246, 249
Klee, Paul, 156
Kraus, Karl, 36, 80, 91, 94, 139, 153, 188, 215

Leonardo da Vinci, 101, 105, 107
Lessing, Gotthold, 65; *Laocoon*, 68
Loos, Adolf, 89
Lukács, Georg, 3, 5, 18, 132, 181, 210–11, 216–240, 247–48; *The Destruction of Reason*, 217; *History and Class Consciousness*, 216; *Realism in Our Time*, 216–40; *Soul and Form*, 5, 216; *The Theory of the Novel*, 35, 216, 218; *Wider den missverstandenen Realismus* (published in U.S. as *Realism in Our Time: Literature and the Class Struggle;* first published in English as *The Meaning of Contemporary Realism*), 216–40

Mach, Ernst, 177
Mahler, Gustav, 83, 168, 204
Mallarmé, Stéphane, 52, 68, 98, 102, 103, 138, 143, 148
Manet, Édouard, 107, 138, 142, 145
Mann, Heinrich, 133
Mann, Thomas, 65, 234; *Black Swan*,
34; *Doctor Faustus*, 243; *Holy Sinner*, 34; *Magic Mountain*, 235, 243; *Reflections of a Non-Political Man*, 139
Marx, Karl, 81, 94, 122, 129, 150, 181, 220, 228; *Capital*, 220; *Grundrisse of the Critique of Political Economy*, 220
Maupassant, Guy de, 121
Maurois, André, 179
Meyer, Theodor: *Das Stilgesetz der Poesie (The Stylistic Law of Poetry)*, 68
Molière: *The Miser*, 258
Mörike, Eduard, 49, 51, 66, 171; "Auf einer Wanderung" ("On a Walking Tour"), 47–50
Murray, Gilbert, 25
Musil, Robert, 224; *The Man Without Qualities*, 233

Nadler, Joseph, 56
Nietzsche, Friedrich, 12, 23, 29, 37, 80, 107, 139, 150, 151, 158, 164, 165, 186, 207, 217

Paul, Jean, 124
Perutz, Leo, 202
Pindar, 40
Platen, August von, 81
Plato: *Symposium*, 23
Popper, Leo, 5
Preuss, Karl Theodor, 25
Proust, Marcel, 8, 32, 33, 34, 35, 69, 96, 123, 137, 144, 174–84, 185, 193–96, 197, 208, 221, 222, 224, 252, 253, 254, 275; *Cities of the Plain*, 178; *The Captive*, 182–84; *The Guermantes' Way*, 177–81; *Swann's Way*, 175–78; *Within a Budding Grove*, 181–82

Racine, Jean, 50, 145, 157
Rasch, Wolfdietrich, 66
Rickert, Heinrich: *Unmittelbarkeit und Sinndeutung (Immediacy and the Interpretation of Meaning)*, 253

Rilke, Rainer Maria, 58, 98, 234; *Dinggedichte*, 40; *Malte Laurids Brigge*, 32

Rimbaud, Arthur, 139

Sack, Gustav: *Ein verbummelter Student (A Student Vagabond)*, 33

Sade, Marquis de, 133

Saint-Beuve, 5

Sappho, 40

Sartre, Jean-Paul, 249

Scheffel, J. V. von: *The Trumpeter of Säckingen*, 203–4

Schelling, Friedrich, 28, 64, 107, 211, 212

Schlabrendorf, Count, 61

Schlegel, Friedrich, 72, 230

Schönberg, Arnold, 56, 124; *George-lieder*, 73; *Style and Idea*, 105

Schopenhauer, Arthur, 207, 212, 224

Schubert, Franz, 57; *Schöne Müllerin*, 73; *Winterreise*, 73

Schumann, Robert, 58, 64, 124; "Auf einer Burg" ("In a Castle"), 77; "Dein Bildnis wunderselig" ("Your Divinely Lovely Likeness"), 76; "Frühlingsnacht" ("Spring Night"), 75; "Ich hör die Bächlein rauschen" ("I hear the little brooks rushing"), 77; "Im Walde" ("In the Forest"), 75, 78; "In der Fremde" ("Abroad"), 75; "In der Heimat hinter den Blitzen rot" ("In the Homeland behind the Red Lightning Flashes"), 76; *Kinderszenen (Scenes from Childhood)*, 74; *Liederkreis (Song Cycle)* opus 39, 73–79; "Mondnacht" ("Moonnight"), 75, 76, 78; "Schöne Fremde" ("Beautiful Foreigner"), 75, 77; "Sehnsucht" ("Longing"), 77; "Die Stille" ("Silence"), 75; "Waldesgespräch" ("Forest Dialogue"), 75, 76; "Wehmut" ("Melancholy"), 75; "Zwielicht" ("Twilight"), 75, 77

Scott, Walter, 134

Sedlmayr, Hans: *Verlust der Mitte (Art in Crisis)*, 231

Shakespeare, William, 65; *Hamlet*, 255, 267; *Macbeth*, 115

Simmel, Georg, 3, 17, 216

Smith, Adam, 126

Spinoza, Baruch, 81

Stendhal, 253

Sternheim, Carl, 180

Stifter, Adalbert, 25, 26, 30, 66, 129

Storm, Theodor, 93

Strauss, Richard, 76, 105

Stravinsky, Igor, 166–67; *Ragtime for Eleven Instruments*, 268

Strindberg, August, 274

Swinburne, Algernon, 98

Thomson, J. A. K., 28

Tolstoy, Leo, 235; *Anna Karenina*, 226

Trakl, Georg, 28

Valéry, Paul, 52, 98–108, 137–73; *Amphion*, 169; *Degas Dance Drawing*, 97–108; *Epaulinos*, 99; *Monsieur Treste*, 99; "Les Pas," 99; *Pièces sur l'art*, 137–73; *Rhumbs*, 137–173; "The Triumph of Manet," 138

Verlaine, Paul, 52, 55, 146

Vogelweide, Walther von der, 40

Voltaire, 184

Wagner, Richard, 76, 105, 107, 124, 139, 142, 162, 168; *Tristan and Isolde*, 183

Waugh, Evelyn, 122

Webern, Anton von, 50, 147

Wedekind, Frank, 65, 264

Williams, Tennessee: *Camino Real*, 266

Wolfe, Thomas, 223

Wolfskehl, Karl: *Deutschlandsgedicht*, 248

Zola, Émile, 132, 133, 138, 238; *Ventre de Paris*, 129

Zweig, Stefan, 56

European Perspectives
A Series in Social Thought and Cultural Criticism
Lawrence D. Kritzman, Editor

Julia Kristeva	*Strangers to Ourselves*
Theodor W. Adorno	*Notes to Literature*, vols. 1 and 2
Richard Wolin, editor	*The Heidegger Controversy*
Antonio Gramsci	*Prison Notebooks*, vols. 1 and 2
Jacques LeGoff	*History and Memory*
Alain Finkielkraut	*Remembering in Vain: The Klaus Barbie Trial and Crimes Against Humanity*
Julia Kristeva	*Nations Without Nationalism*
Pierre Bourdieu	*The Field of Cultural Production*
Pierre Vidal-Naquet	*Assassins of Memory: Essays on the Denial of the Holocaust*
Hugo Ball	*Critique of the German Intelligentsia*
Gilles Deleuze and Félix Guattari	*What Is Philosophy?*
Karl Heinz Bohrer	*Suddenness: On the Moment of Aesthetic Appearance*
Julia Kristeva	*Time and Sense*
Alain Finkielkraut	*The Defeat of the Mind*
Julia Kristeva	*New Maladies of the Soul*
Elisabeth Badinter	*XY: On Masculine Identity*
Karl Löwith	*Martin Heidegger and European Nihilism*
Gilles Deleuze	*Negotiations, 1972–1990*
Pierre Vidal-Naquet	*The Jews: History, Memory, and the Present*
Norbert Elias	*The Germans*
Louis Althusser	*Writings on Psychoanalysis: Freud and Lacan*
Elisabeth Roudinesco	*Jacques Lacan: His Life and Work*
Ross Guberman	*Julia Kristeva Interviews*
Kelly Oliver	*The Portable Kristeva*
Pierra Nora	*Realms of Memory: The Construction of the French Past*
	vol. 1: *Conflicts and Divisions*
	vol. 2: *Traditions*
	vol. 3: *Symbols*
Claudine Fabre-Vassas	*The Singular Beast: Jews, Christians, and the Pig*
Paul Ricoeur	*Critique and Conviction: Conversations with Francois Azouvi and Marc de Launav*
Theodor W. Adorno	*Critical Models: Interventions and Catchwords*

Alain Corbin	*Village Bells: Sound and Meaning in the Nineteenth-Century French Countryside*
Zygmunt Bauman	*Globalization: The Human Consequences*
Emmanuel Levinas	*Entre Nous*
Jean-Louis Flandrin and Massimo Momanari	*Food: A Culinary History*
Alain Finkielkraut	*In the Name of Humanity: Reflections on the Twentieth Century*
Julia Kristeva	*The Sense and Non-Sense of Revolt: The Powers and Limits of Psychoanalysis*
Régis Debray	*Transmitting Culture*
Sylviane Agacinski	*The Politics of the Sexes*
Alain Corbin	*The Life of an Unknown: The Rediscovered World of a Clog Maker in Nineteenth-Century France*
Michel Pastoureau	*The Devil's Cloth: A History of Stripes and Striped Fabric*
Julia Kristeva	*Hannah Arendt*
Carlo Ginzburg	*Wooden Eyes: Nine Reflections on Distance*
Elisabeth Roudinesco	*Why Psychoanalysis?*
Alain Cabantous	*Blasphemy: Impious Speech in the West from the Seventeenth to the Nineteenth Century*
Julia Kristeva	*Melanie Klein*
Julia Kristeva	*Intimate Revolt and The Future of Revolt: The Powers and Limits of Psychoanalysis*, vol. 2
Claudia Benthien	*Skin: On the Cultural Border Between Self and the World*
Emmanuel Todd	*After the Empire: The Breakdown of the American Order*
Gianni Vattimo	*Nihilism and Emancipation: Ethics, Politics, and Law*
Julia Kristeva	*Colette*
Steve Redhead, ed.	*The Paul Virilio Reader*
Roland Barthes	*The Neutral*
Gianni Vattimo	*Dialogue with Nietzsche*
Gilles Deleuze	*Nietzsche and Philosophy*